PERSONALITY GAMES

Pino Gilioli

PERSONALITY GAMES

Get to know the *real* you

Drawings by Aldo Ripamonti

GUILD PUBLISHING LONDON

A Macdonald BOOK

Translated by Simon Pleasance

This edition published in 1986 by
Book Club Associates
by arrangement with
Macdonald & Co (Publishers) Ltd

A member of BPCC plc

Filmset by Tradespools Ltd, Frome, Somerset

Printed and bound in Italy
by Officine Grafiche A. Mondadori Editore, Verona

Macdonald & Co (Publishers) Ltd
Greater London House
Hampstead Road
London NW1 7QX

Jacket by Don Macpherson based on an original design by CDE Gruppo Mondadori

Contents

Preface

This book is the distillation of original "games-tests" I have prepared for a wide variety of publications over a period of ten years.

I have organized the various tests here into six sections, after a brief look at the historical background to psychological tests in general. Chapter one aims to test the reader's imagination by the use of situation drawings, and reveals character traits through a series of questions. Chapter two is made up of what I choose to call "Psycho-tales," original stories in the form of children's fairy tales, to which the reader is asked to respond in kind, bringing to his reading the receptive simplicity of a child, then answering questions about the characters and situations in each story. The third chapter concentrates on professional aptitudes, a subject of obvious importance to us all, through which we can discover how suited we would be for certain careers. Chapter four reveals the relationship between personality and verbal expression. In chapter five, 12 different versions of a short suspense thriller are given. The reader is asked to select the version he has most enjoyed reading, and in the process discover some interesting aspects of his own character. A selection of 16 photographs, interposed at intervals throughout the book, make up an interesting and innovative test to find out about the nature of your sexuality.

All the games in this book, based on psychological techniques, aim to give you an insight into your character and behaviour, and to help you discover hidden aspects of your inner self. The reader makes his choices on the basis of visual, logical, or emotional stimuli, which might otherwise have lain dormant.

In completing the various tests, you may well come across what appear to be contrasting findings; after all, the human personality consists of many diverse characteristics that, together, make up an integrated whole. You may also come across a few unexpected home truths! The emphasis, however, must be on the concept of "games," for it goes without saying that the comparatively lighthearted manner in which the subjects of personality, behaviour, natural aptitudes etc. are treated cannot altogether be said to bow to the strict disciplines of scientific psychology.

These games aim to go no further than to indicate certain aspects of the personality, as revealed by basic patterns. The various assessments should therefore be seen as pointers rather than strictly scientific analyses of character and behaviour. At the end of the day, for those readers who have gone all the way with us in these games-tests, there remains the anticipatory pleasure, having added up the points obtained in the individual tests, of having perhaps discovered new aspects of themselves or their friends. After all, we are none of us what we seem: appearances can be deceptive. And it is these concealed areas of the human personality that are, in my view, the most intriguing.

Introduction

Man alone feels the need to know himself, to derive the fullest advantage from outward experiences. It was in answer to such a quest for self-knowledge that the "test" was introduced in the nineteenth century, as a psycho-diagnostic tool in the analysis of the human personality.

The word "test" was used and popularized through the work of James McKoon Cattell, a student of experimental psychology in the United States at the turn of the century. The word is derived from the Latin *testum*, meaning a vase of the type used by alchemists of old. Test therefore passes for a kind of vase, as it were, ready to be filled with our psychic revelations.

Personality tests date from the second half of the nineteenth century, when the first attempts to measure intelligence were made. Methods of measuring intelligence, devised by the Frenchman Binet around 1905, purely for teaching purposes, were taken up and applied on a large scale in many countries, being subject to modification and refinement as their use became more widespread. In the United States, during the First World War, scientific tests carried out in the selection of recruits for the Army, proved highly successful. Today it would be rare indeed to find practical psychological examinations carried out without the use of tests.

In 1904, the celebrated psychoanalyst, Carl Gustav Jung, pupil and later rival of Freud, developed a most interesting word association test – given a word, the examinee has to counter with the first associated

Illustrated below is an example of Rosenzweig's "picture frustration test" (see page 11). You are to try to visualize yourself as the figure on the right. The person on the left has addressed a remark to you (written in the balloon), to which you have to reply. We suggest three possible replies you could make – select the one you probably would have made. 1) It's your fault. You've always wanted to show it off. 2) Sorry, it was an accident. 3) What can I do to make you forgive me?

(explanations on page 12)

Below are 15 visual concepts, with accompanying word-concepts which you have to match up. Here are the 15 word-concepts to accompany the designs.

noise sex ocean doubt fear tenderness dance space

anger thirst adoration repose heat scream affectation

(explanations on page 12)

word that comes into his mind. Equally well known is the test devised by the Swiss neuropsychiatrist, Rorschach in 1921, a year before he died at the age of 37, which made use of black and coloured ink stains. In the T.A.T. (Thematic Apperception Test), invented by the American psychologist Murray in 1949, the subject is presented with 20 sheets, 19 of which carry pictures, around which the subject has to invent a series of stories. The last sheet is blank, leaving the subject to fill in his own picture story.

A more complicated test is the M.A.P.S. (Make a Picture Story) created by Shneidman in 1952, which aims to evaluate an individual's imagination, as well as his creative ability and aptitude for interpersonal relationships. The test consists of 22 scenes from everyday life, such as a room, a forest, or just a blank, with 67 figures, including 19 male figures, 11 female, and two of indefinite sex, together with 12 babies, ten individuals of different race, six charactes from history or legend, a dog, a serpent, and five faceless profiles. The subject has to choose a scene, some characters, and then construct a story around them.

The "Blacky Pictures" test was thought up by Blum in 1950; in practice it consisted of a series of designs in the form of comic strips for children, the central character of which was a dog called Blacky. Among the most popular completion-tests are the R.I.S.B. (Rotter Incomplete Sentences Blanck), in which 40 phrases have to be completed by the subject, and the "Test of Insight into Human Nature," with a series of plots that again the subject has to complete. Also widely used is the Rosenzweig P.F. (Picture Frustration Test) devised between 1947 and 1949, which analyzes the individual's reaction to a set of embarrassing, unpleasant and difficult situations. The particular situations are represented in 24 illustrations, in each of which appear two or more persons. One of the persons (on the left) makes an observation, the words framed in a balloon. The subject, identifying himself with the other person (on the right), has to write a suitable remark in another balloon, left blank for this purpose.

A test which has come in for much discussion was devised by Szondi in 1952: 48 photographs of mentally ill persons are shown to the subject, he is asked to pick out the person for whom he has the greatest sympathy, and the one for whom he has least. In 1942, Karen Machover created the "Draw-a-Person-Test for a study into the personality of young people. The subjects are given a sheet of paper and pencil, and asked to draw a figure, then another of different sex, and finally to invent a story about them. Lowenfeld's "World Test," adapted for both young people and adults, makes use of some three hundred objects: miniature houses, persons, cars, animals, etc., around which a wealth of stories can evolve. Another series of tests consists of putting various jumbled elements, especially words, in the correct order.

In 1937, Stern devised his "Clouds" test, the subject having to provide a subjective interpretation of different cloud formations. In 1949, Baumgartner created two tests, consisting of a catalogue of 430 book titles, from which the subject had to select his ten favourite titles; the other test was based on a selection of 190 proverbs, the objective being the same. In 1962, Jacqueline Boyer presented her "Metamorphosis Test," in which the subject was asked who he would like to be, and what he would not like to be, explaining his reasons.

Psychological tests, now widely used in psychodiagnostic practice, are not the subject of this book as such. This brief recital of some of the most famous should serve to convince the reader how much games-tests are the by-product of of those technical methods and experiences of the past. Besides, I am convinced that games-tests, ephemeral or lighthearted though they may at first appear, by virtue of the liberating effect they can have on the subject, have a role to play in the practice of psychoanalysis.

My aim in this book has been to devise games that can lead to a better understanding of our personalities and those of our fellow beings. Can you think of a subject more fascinating?

Explanations
If in the blank space you thought of writing "It's your fault. You've always wanted to show it off," it shows a tendency to lay the blame for your mistakes on others.

If instead you intended to write "Sorry, it was an accident," it means you shy away from blaming anyone, even yourself. If on the other hand, you would have written "What can I do to make you forgive me," it means you readily accept responsibility for whatever happens.

Table to register your choices in order to establish your psychological characteristics

Alongside many of the explanations of the games-tests, geometric signs appear: a square, circle, rectangle, diamond, or a triangle, sometimes black, sometimes white. Readers interested to know how they have fared in their overall scoring should therefore make use of the table below, and tick off the signs (white or black) that correspond to the explanations throughout the book that match their choices. The black and white symbols signify two contrasting aspects of character, one of which (the symbol which occurs least) will be discarded in the final count. Once you have completed all the test-games, the table on page 150 will indicate your psychological type.

△	△	△	△	△	△	△	△	△	△	△
▲	▲	▲	▲	▲	▲	▲	▲	▲	▲	▲
□	□	□	□	□	□	□	□	□	□	□
■	■	■	■	■	■	■	■	■	■	■
○	○	○	○	○	○	○	○	○	○	○
●	●	●	●	●	●	●	●	●	●	●
◊	◊	◊	◊	◊	◊	◊	◊	◊	◊	◊
♦	♦	♦	♦	♦	♦	♦	♦	♦	♦	♦
▯	▯	▯	▯	▯	▯	▯	▯	▯	▯	▯
▮	▮	▮	▮	▮	▮	▮	▮	▮	▮	▮

Explanations
The correct couplings are as follows:

1) space	2) sex	3) heat
4) tenderness	5) thirst	6) anger
7) fear	8) repose	9) noise
10) affectation	11) doubt	12) adoration
13) scream	14) dance	15) ocean

If you got all the couplings, it means you are endowed with an exceptional imagination.

A score of 14 to 8 still keeps you high in the imagination ratings.

If you scored 7 or under, your imagination is poor.

Picture games

A girl is reading

Test game 1

Take a close look at this picture of a girl seated at a table reading, then make a snap choice of one of the following four suggestions.

[1] The girl has stopped reading because she suddenly feels like going to a discotheque.
[2] Someone has knocked at the door but she does not feel like being disturbed.
[3] Her reading has brought back memories of a previous love affair.
[4] She has decided to accept an interesting job-offer abroad, which will mean her leaving home and her friends.

Now that you have chosen one of the four hypothetical suggestions, you must also imagine the sequel.

What will the sequel be if you have chosen 1?
[A] At the last minute the girl changes her mind and goes into town to do some shopping.
[B] She goes to a discotheque but spends a miserable evening.

What will the sequel be if you have chosen 2?
[A] The girl pretends not to be home.
[B] She opens the door, having resigned herself to receiving the unexpected visitor.

What will the sequel be if you have chosen 3?
[A] The girl regrets the past and feels sad.
[B] She knows that by making a phone-call she could rekindle the relationship, but she does not do so.

What will the sequel be if you have chosen 4?
[A] The girl makes a list of friends and acquaintances to whom she could turn in any eventuality.
[B] That same evening she announces her final decision to the person she is in love with.

(for the psychological explanation of this and the following test games, turn to pages 31–40)

The space-ark

Test game 2

Imagine that you are a modern-day Noah. Warned of the coming of a second flood, you have to accommodate the greatest possible number of animals in your mighty space-age ark. Eventually, it seems the space-ark can take no more and 14 animals are still left on earth. These are: 1) the ant, 2) the butterfly, 3) the camel, 4) the horse, 5) the eagle, 6) the elephant, 7) the dog, 8) the koala bear, 9) the lion, 10) the giraffe, 11) the ox, 12) the seagull, 13) the gazelle and 14) the monkey.

At most, Noah can take on board the space-ark – and save from extinction another seven animals. If it were you, which animals would you choose to save?

(turn to test game 2, page 31)

Write your own scenario

Test game 3

1 A young man finds himself alone in the big city

2 He meets a girl

3 So one day . . .

4 In the end . . .

With the aid of the four illustrations above, you can piece together a short tale of boy meets girl. Each of the last three drawings, however, contains an empty balloon. Write your own balloon, using, in each case, one of the two sentences given below.

2A **Boy:** We could start a business together.
or
2B **Boy:** Yes, I know. But we love each other. That's what counts.

3C **Girl:** It seems everyone's against us.
or
3D **Girl:** They might still be useful to us.

4E **Boy:** This whole thing has got me down.
or
4F **Boy:** It's another experience to add to the list.

(turn to test game 3, page 32)

Test your sexuality

We are now going to invite you to take part in a sexuality test – sexuality is part and parcel of our human nature. The test involves eight pairs of colour photographs which are to be found at regular intervals throughout the book. When you come across a photograph, like the one opposite, look at it, then turn the page and look at the second photograph. Choose the one in each pair you find most to your liking. This first photograph (opposite), for example, we shall indicate as A, and the photograph overleaf B. Which one do you instinctively prefer: A or B? Choose the photograph for its form, colour(s), and for what it evokes in your mind. The photos have been chosen deliberately with these objects in mind. So choose which of the two photos is most to your liking, purely on instinct. Mark down your choice: A or B.

Pitfalls

Test game 4

Our path through life is full of pitfalls, not necessarily made for us by other people. Sometimes we make pitfalls for ourselves, without consciously intending to, and then we complain about things which are already beyond our ability to remedy. Possibly, if we knew ourselves better, we could avoid certain stumbling-blocks. So here we invite you to answer the 13 questions below, choosing, in each case, just one answer from the eight suggested.
Use the table overleaf to note down the letters and numbers you have chosen and then, on page 32, be prepared to find out about some basic aspects of your character.

[1] How do you feel about one of your lesser vices such as smoking or drinking, etc?
— could be looking for trouble B4
— if it really is a lesser vice, so what? A3
— what would life be without the odd flaw? B8
— a means of not letting things get on top of you B6
— a dash of spice in the daily round A1
— a social hazard A7
— innocent folly A5
— straying from the straight and narrow B2

[2] Which opinion do you take into account most?
— your moral sense B2
— yourself A1
— an expert A5
— your superiors A7
— those looking after you B8
— logic A3
— the majority B4
— your nearest and dearest B6

[3] How do you react when you find you have a slight temperature?
— call a doctor B4
— consult someone close to you B8
— curse A1
— retire to bed B6
— resign yourself B2
— arrange the most urgent things that need doing A7
— do not make too much of a fuss A3
— wait and see how things develop A5

[4] What do you think about your first natural and normal sexual experience?
— pleasant natural act A1
— slightly clumsy experience that needs refining A3
— tangible sign of maturity A5
— the marvel of giving oneself B8
— deeply-felt upheaval B2
— new force in one's life A7
— exciting breaking of a taboo B6
— start of a lot of problems B4

[5] What is God for you?
— the creator of life B2
— something which, in practice, there is no need of A3
— a form of gullibility A1
— a prop B4
— the supreme authority B8
— father B6
— something associated mainly with childhood A5
— if he had power over everything, life would not be as it is A7

[6] Talking on the telephone, which of these sensations do you experience most?
— curiosity as to what the conversation might trigger off B8
— a desire to scream inside and unburden yourself A7
— apart from the convenience, nothing special A5
— relief that you can hide your real emotions B4
— an acute sense of distance and, perhaps, time too A1
— a slight fear of this instrument which can catch you out B2

— an instinct to reveal more of yourself than you would otherwise B6
— a sense of distaste at not being able to talk face to face A3

[7] How do you think you have behaved with your parents?
— they've gone their way, I've gone mine A3
— loved them, at the same time recognizing their failings A1
— have always (or would like to have) seen them as my educators B2
— so-so A5
— perhaps never understood what they expected of me B4
— have disappointed them B6
— have always respected them A7
— have always obeyed them B8

[8] How would you feel, alone in a dark wood?
— small, and afraid like a child B6
— prepared to put my courage to the test A7
— like to have someone with me B8
— a respect for nature A1
— worry about losing my sense of direction A3
— a desire to describe the experience in words, painting or some other artistic means A5
— feel closer to God B2
— unsafe B4

[9] Choose one of these adjectives to describe your most secret and inadmissible sexual fantasies
— guilty B2
— contradictory B4
— natural A1
— disgusting B6
— impractical A7
— necessary A3
— liberating A5
— dangerous B8

[10] You are waiting to be seen by an important person from whom you have to ask a great favour. Which of these attitudes fits you, or might fit you, moments before entering the room?
— touch a good-luck charm B2
— think ill of the person for treating me as an equal A1
— feel it's hopeless B4
— pray to my loved ones, even the departed B6
— try to convince myself that I can carry it off A3
— repeat over and over to myself what I shall say to the person A5
— put on a humble face B8
— try to think of someone more important than him A7

[11] Which one of the following could be a secret you have or might have?
— something to do with childhood A5
— have so many I can't differentiate. B4
— would not reveal under any circumstance A3
— a recurring sin B2
— something to do with sex B6
— fear of death A1
— a desire to turn things upside-down B8
— some weakness or other A7

[12] You are involved in a mysterious event for which there is no logical explanation. Which one of the following would best sum up your reaction at the time?
— afraid B4
— must be a prank A1
— thrilling stuff B6
— it's the times we live in A7
— like someone to explain it for me B8
— the main thing is not to worry about it A5
— it makes you think B2
— no rhyme or reason to it A3

[13] Which noise or sound are you happiest listening to?
— a city awakening A3
— running water B6
— nature's voices A5
— music I like at the moment A1
— the ringing of bells B2
— an old record B4
— the blare of trumpets A7
— the sound of the doorbell B8

Give your choices below
*Beside each boxed numeral, mark in the letter and number which correspond to your choice. Then add up the letters (**A** and **B**) and the numbers (**1**, **2**, **3**, etc.).*

[1] ____________ [8] ____________
[2] ____________ [9] ____________
[3] ____________ [10] ____________
[4] ____________ [11] ____________
[5] ____________ [12] ____________
[6] ____________ [13] ____________
[7] ____________

Total letters ____________
Total numbers ____________

(turn to test game 4, page 32)

At dawn a boat appears

Test game 5

A boat is about to pull in to this deserted shore. Who is/are on board?
Choose one of the four suggested answers, that you feel instinctively is the right one.

1 A few trippers on a day's outing, stopping to partake of an early breakfast.
2 A girl and a young man are seeking solitude on this deserted beach.
3 A solitary fisherman.
4 A small group of skin-divers in search of marine archaeological remains.

Now that you have made your choice of one of the four hypothetical suggestions, imagine what the sequel will be.

What will the sequel be if you have chosen 1?
A When the trippers depart, they also leave behind their rubbish.
B When they have eaten, they make a bonfire of all their debris and start to dance around the fire.

What will the sequel be if you have chosen 2?
A The two young people decide not to make love but instead to collect rare shells to give to their friends.
B Although attracted to each other, they do not make love out of respect for someone or something they hold dear.

What will the sequel be if you have chosen 3?
A After several vain attempts to land a fish, the angler uses a stun-explosive in order to change his luck.
B The fisherman lands an exceptional catch and takes some fish to a poor family in the nearby village.

What will the sequel be if you have chosen 4?
A With their finds the divers open a small museum which attracts tourists to the place.
B Having discovered this peaceful place the divers contact a tourist agency which recompenses them for the tip-off.

(turn to test game 5, page 33)

Whatever became of Little Red Riding Hood?

Test game 6

Everyone knows the story of Little Red Riding Hood who is tricked by the wolf who has already gobbled up her grandmother. Have you ever wondered what happened to her afterwards – in other words after the hunters have killed the wolf and removed the grandmother safe and sound from its belly? What fate awaited Little Red Riding Hood, and what was her life like in the years that followed?

Here are four different sequels, which are also illustrated in the pictures; choose the plot which instinctively appeals to you most.

[1] Little Red Riding Hood persuades her grandmother to make a will after such a frightening experience, and inherits the little house at the edge of the wood and all the surrounding land.

[2] Now that the wolf is no more, Little Red Riding Hood organizes a group of girls and boys of her own age to run errands and carry parcels through the wood – strictly business, of course.

[3] Little Red Riding Hood organizes things in such a way that her mother, who has lived alone for years, marries one of the daring hunters who helped kill the wolf.

[4] The hunters make use of the experience and cunning of Little Red Riding Hood to lure other wolves in the area to their doom.

2

4

But to get to know certain aspects of your personality a little better, you must go one step further and imagine what happened to Little Red Riding Hood after the developments described in the four imagined sequels above.

What happens if you have chosen 1?

[A] Little Red Riding Hood puts her grandmother in an old folks' home to avoid having to walk through the wood whenever she feels like visiting her.

[B] Although she is now rich, Little Red Riding Hood does not manage to shake herself free of her mother and gets used to the idea of growing old with her.

What happens if you have chosen 2?

[A] Little Red Riding Hood takes it upon herself to manage the income from errands run by her colleagues, and so no longer has to walk through the wood – in short she puts her feet up, grows a little fat, and lives the good life.

[B] After a while the other children tire of their job and Little Red Riding Hood is left alone to run all the errands through the wood. She has never forgotten what happened to her, but cannot afford to turn her back on the money she earns which enables her to look after her mother and her grandmother.

What happens if you have chosen 3?

[A] Little Red Riding Hood's relationship with her stepfather soon becomes unbearable, because he is a violent man. So the girl manages to persuade her mother to leave him and go back to living alone.

[B] Once installed in the house, the stepfather has Little Red Riding Hood to wait on him hand and foot, but she does not mind because at least there is a man about the house.

What happens if you have chosen 4?

[A] Little Red Riding Hood falls in love with the son of a hunter, and persuades him to elope with her, to get away from her poverty-stricken life.

[B] Little Red Riding Hood strikes up a friendship with a smuggler who lives in the wood, and helps to hide him, bringing him food stolen from her grandmother.

(turn to test game 6, page 34)

Consider these two situations

Test game 7

A young man is announcing to his wife his intention to change jobs – i.e. to leave his present job and take up something different. He is confident about what he is doing but for his friends his decision has its worrying aspects, at least at the outset.

If you were in the wife's shoes, which one of these four answers would you give to him?

1 You've always been irresponsible.
2 I'll support you no matter what comes of it.
3 I hope you've already got something else lined up.
4 I'll get a job too – that will help out.

Two friends meet by chance after a gap of many years. One of them speaks the words in the balloon, the other . . .

Speaking for the other, what would your answer be?

A Right now. I can easily put off my appointment.
B I don't know. Not today. Or tomorrow. I'm always so busy.
C Now I know where I can find you, I'll be in touch as soon as possible.
D You must come to dinner. We can talk over old times.

(turn to test game 7, page 34)

A murder has been committed

Test game 8

While reading a newspaper your attention is caught by news of a mysterious crime. Below the headlines are the pictures of four people under suspicion, one of whom is the actual murderer. And while you are looking at the four Identikit pictures, you find yourself of your own accord choosing the face of the person who, in your opinion, has committed the crime. Without trying to attach logical explanations to your choice, which do you think is the face of the murderer?

[A] [B] [C] [D]

Now that you have chosen the face of the likely murderer, can you imagine, among the following hypotheses, the motive behind the crime?

[1] A sudden moment of madness.
[2] For money.
[3] For love.
[4] To get revenge for some wrong suffered in the past.

(turn to test game 8, page 37)

The portrait

Test game 9

If you could commission your portrait from a famous painter, how would you like him to depict you?

Now that you have chosen your favourite pose, which one of these backgrounds would you choose?

(turn to test game 9, page 37)

The empty bench

Test game 10

Sometimes situations or things are there waiting for us. In fact it seems as if they are waiting for us to bring them to life with our own feelings. This empty bench in a deserted park at dusk seems to be waiting for somebody. Who do you think will arrive and sit down on the bench?
Choose from these two possibilities.

[A] An elderly married couple who always come and feed the birds in the park at this time of day.
[B] A young couple who embrace each other.

Now that you have chosen, try to imagine the sequel to the scene.

What will the sequel be if you have chosen A?

[1] The elderly married couple is joined by three other couples of the same age, and they set to to draft the statute for an old people's club.
[2] The elderly couple records the singing of the birds on a small tape recorder.
[3] They enter into conversation with a young man who is on drugs and has asked them for money – he visibly needs some help.

What will the sequel be if you have chosen B?

[1] The young couple is joined by her father, who drags her home.
[2] The couple ends up making love on the bench.
[3] A group of people the same age as themselves surrounds them threateningly, and the young couple run off.

(turn to test game 10, page 38)

How do you answer this little girl?

Test game 11

You are baby-sitting for a married couple you know. Suddenly the little girl, aged 6 or 7, asks you the question in the balloon: "What is sex?"
Choose from the four suggested answers the one you might give, and the one you would never give.

[A] How about a game of hide-and-seek? It'll be fun.

[B] Sex is one of the basic things in life. But if you want me to tell you about it you'll have to stop playing. It'll take a little while and you'll have to listen hard.

[C] But where have you heard about things like that? They don't concern you for the moment.

[D] Ask your parents. It's their job to explain. The more you love someone, the easier it is to explain things.

(turn to test game 11, page 38)

An image in space

Test game 12

During a television link-up with a spacecraft orbiting in space, for a few moments your TV screen is filled with an unintelligible image of the cosmos.
What immediately springs to mind?
From the answers below choose two: the one that seems most in tune with your own feelings and the one which seems the most unlikely.

[A] The surface of a planet with strange shiny precious minerals.

[B] A slimy substance with mysterious eyes staring out at you.

[C] Dark, stagnant water in which are reflected distant rays of stars.

[D] A shell which contains a fire inside it which is harmless but infuses strength.

Having decided on your answers (the one which appeals to you most and the one which appeals to you least) now read the relevant psychological explanation.

(turn to test game 12, page 39)

The way you walk

Test game 13

Like any gesture or outward form of behaviour, the way we walk can also reveal aspects of our character. Here we have four elements of our gait – head, trunk, arms and legs. Try to single out which type you identify with your own way of walking from those you see in the drawings, and note down your choices in each case.

(turn to test game 13, page 39)

Explanations of test games 1–13

Test game 1 (A girl is reading)

△ If you have chosen 1 + A, you tend to direct your energies towards outward reality, displaying an open temperament which is free and adapts easily to any situation. You have a marked capacity for achieving your goals since you do not pay too much attention to doubts fed to you by others. You act confidently in awkward situations. In some cases you are unbiased and open-minded and this can push you into some abrupt changes of direction, causing problems for those close to you.

△ If you have chosen 1 + B, you are capable of taking immediate decisions when put to the test. But there is the risk of impetuosity too, and because of a certain impulsiveness you fail to take into account all the relevant assessments to grasp the roots of a situation. Your initial intentions are always brisk and generous, but may well not lead to concrete results because of a tendency to over-stretch yourself and you do not always manage to bring what you are engaged in to a positive conclusion.

▲ If you have chosen 2 + A, you have a thoughtful temperament, which means that you like a withdrawn life, preferring to be on the defensive. You are not keen on action when it involves facing up to reality, but you are egoistic enough not to rely on others. You have your fair share of shrewdness, enabling you to avoid awkward situations, and can be found casting clever traps for others from your safe corner, which often works to your advantage.

▲ If you have chosen 2 + B, you have a very intense inner life, which you do not wish to upset by putting it to the test of reality. As a result you lack certain qualities of adaptation to practical situations, and for this reason you adopt defensive attitudes which lead to a restricted social life. To make up for this, you are very thorough, as well as generous, which enables you to strike up intense and emotional relationships with the few people whom you regard as worthy of your trust.

▲ If you have chosen 3 + A, you have a sentimental temperament, which is why your sensitivity is always alert to the emotional aspects of situations. Add to this the fact that you have a pessimistic view of reality, which does not encourage you to widen your range of experience; in fact you have a tendency to keep it restricted. In this way you gain in sentimental intensity what you lose in breadth, and you often manage to give intelligent, if very personal, assessments.

▲ If you have chosen 3 + B, you tend to be somewhat idle. By staying enclosed in your own world, you eventually find it's to your convenience. Top of your priorities is peace and quiet, although in real terms this includes a quality of selfishness, and shyness too. You almost invariably see situations from a negative angle; you view things scornfully from a distance, through disenchanted eyes.

△ If you have chosen 4 + A, you are quite sure that your intelligence will effectively direct your actions vis-à-vis reality, and as a result you relegate the demands of feelings to a secondary position. You do not lack the courage to face difficult situations in life, trusting to your experience and the experience of others to see you through. But you often start off impulsively and this can make matters somewhat complicated as you are not always in a position to control the ultimate consequences of your actions.

△ If you have chosen 4 + B, you have plenty of common sense to meet every kind of situation with practical realism. As a rule you will succeed in your endeavours because you combine practical intelligence with a certain unscrupulousness, which enables you to use others for your own ends. You regard feelings almost as weaknesses, and so never get involved in situations which you cannot control with logic. But you must beware of a propensity to cynicism, a character flaw which can let you down.

Test game 2 (The space-ark)

□ If you have chosen animals 2 (butterfly), 4 (horse), 7 (dog), 8 (koala), 10 (giraffe), 12 (seagull) and (13 (gazelle), or if there is a prevailing number of these animals (at least 5), you have a strong emotional makeup and your behaviour is bound up essentially with your emotional life. You are very sensitive to everything that governs and works on the emotions, and as a result you appear impulsive and even inconstant. The fact that you link your experiences mainly to feelings causes you a certain anxiety, because you are not always capable of using reason to govern your instincts. You have a lot to give in your personal relationships, but those who rely on you cannot always be sure of your judgement.

■ If you have chosen animals 1 (ant), 3 (camel), 5 (eagle), 6 (elephant), 9 (lion), 11 (ox) and 14 (monkey), or if there is a prevailing number of these animals (at least 5), your behaviour is based mainly on reason, and you try hard to attach as little importance as possible to instincts and feelings. You have a thoughtful temperament, so your behaviour is on the whole balanced, constant and responsible. You have no major cause for anxiety because your strong sense of logic instructs you how to be confident and calm. Others may sometimes find you a bit dry, but you are basically very dependable.

If there is no marked disparity between numbers 2–4–7–8–10–12–13 and numbers 1–3–5–6–9–11–14 in the animals you have chosen, in other words if you have 4 numbers in one group and 3 in another, you tend to waver between the emotional and the logical, between sentimental choices, and those dictated by reason. Such a contradictory state of mind does not make for personal serenity. It means you are impulsive but of a reflective nature too, constant and inconstant, responsible and irresponsible. Your friends never get bored with you, even though they may find it requires quite an effort to keep up with you.

Test game 3 (Write your own scenario)

■ If you have chosen slogans A–D–F, you are mainly concerned with making the most of opportunities continually offered by reality to people like you who are invariably on the alert. For this reason you are practical and forceful, efficient, even aggressive, when called for. Whenever possible you try to turn whatever comes your way to your own advantage. You are shrewd and never give too much away to others.

■ If you have chosen slogans B–C–E, you are one of those idealists who are less concerned with material advantages than with the enrichment of your interior life. So you are always consistent in your basic choice, which is invariably to make use of situations in order to learn, and know yourself, to probe deeper, to give your imagination free rein. Sometimes you appear slightly naive and often spend money as if it were no object, but where ideas are concerned you are unrivalled. There is the risk, however, that in the long run some of these ideas may border on the abstract.

■ If you have chosen slogans A–C–E or B–C–F or B–D–E, you are interested in developing concepts which advance knowledge and you are not overly concerned with prosperity. But you are nonetheless very interested in success. You have little time for those idealistic individuals who never come to grips with reality. You are yourself an idealist, but you are keen to translate your ideals into practice, and when this occurs you combine fantasy with a quality of concreteness. You are always ready to bring a shrewdness and aggressivity to that trusting naivety which is your fundamental, constant quality. For these reasons you are capable of giving form and weight to your ideals, however abstract they may appear, presenting a very stimulating impression all round.

□ If you have chosen slogans A–C–F or A–D–E or B–D–F, you are basically a practical person, keen on material success. But you also have ideals and these enrich your practical side with just the right degree of imagination. Essentially you are a strong person concealing your naivety behind various positive, efficient and aggressive attitudes. And "weaknesses" of this kind do no harm even to those who prefer the attractions of reality.

Test game 4 (Pitfalls)

Explanations as to the choice of letters A or B
◊ If your choice shows a prevalence of A, you are accustomed to relying almost exclusively on your own abilities. You have a sober temperament, at least in that you do not resort to palliatives to instil a sense of security. You believe that self-sufficiency comes from within, and there is no point in looking elsewhere. You are intelligent and mature, to the degree where you are also reasonably optimistic, because you see no point in dwelling on what might have been. You have a tendency to adopt an independent stance, not allowing yourself to be affected by childhood inhibitions, superstitions or false beliefs. Because of this you often assume authoritarian attitudes which demonstrate your intolerance towards all forms of weakness or emotional dependence. You always want to be sure what you can realistically expect of any given situation – in short, you are anything but a daydreamer.

⧫ If your choice shows a prevalence of B, you have need of something or someone on whom you can always lean because you see yourself as being too weak and uncertain. Sometimes you may become involved with some minor vice, which becomes for you a palliative whereby you can ease your inner tensions. At other times you become dependent on grand ideas which seem to shelter you from any kind of insecurity. You are attracted by everything that is mysterious and unknowable because it seems that reality is too unpleasant to be the only world in which one can live. At times your real dimension is day-dreaming. You are very attached to the past, in particular to your childhood, either because you feel those days to be a mythical period, or because you regret that your childhood was not as reassuring as you think it should have been.

Explanations as to the choice of numbers
Choices with a predominance of A:
– If number 1 predominates with A, your independence from any form of logical and emotional subordination shows its strength in the negation of all forms of religion or superstitious beliefs. Your logic works above all against transcendental concepts of reality, which is why you oppose all forms of dogmatism and spiritual reliance.

– If number 2 predominates with A, your independence stops short at the threshold of the unfathomable. You are sufficient unto yourself as far as reality is concerned, but when you venture into the realm of the mysterious, you feel a need to use some form of superstition or religion as a crutch. Perhaps you are afraid, essentially, of death, which for you represents the very negation of reality; as a result, you try to reject it in any way you can.

– If number 3 predominates with A, you have an independent and confident character. Independence and confidence combine within you to form a single attitude which makes you both positive and authoritarian. In situations dominated by logic you tend to prevail. On the other hand you display a certain lack of warmth or heart in situations where an extra emotional element is required.

– If number 4 predominates with A, you are not self-sufficient enough to escape from certain forms of insecurity. At times your independence stops short in the face of something which makes you unsure what to do, and this may give you considerable anxiety. Basically, not everyone can be a hero, and sometimes a little fear can make you more human.

– If number 5 predominates with A, you have a sense of independence which derives from a deep feeling of maturity. At heart you do not depend on anyone and anything. You have come by this attitude as a result of sometimes difficult experiences, which have made you more confident than many more overtly authoritative people. You can be depended on.

– If number 6 predominates with A, you are fairly independent in situations where the past does not impinge. Your weak point, however, is an over-attachment to certain past values, especially to do with your childhood, whether a truly happy one, or whether you simply wanted it to be so. Within you an eternal child lies dormant who is always ready to come perilously back to life.

– If number 7 predominates with A, you are so detached from all fetters of dependence that your vocation is, or might be, to wield your authority over others. You have the calling of a leader, and this attitude does not always take the rights of others into account.

– If number 8 predominates with A, you are hiding behind certain fundamental contradictions, because you force yourself to be self-sufficient and independent, but sometimes allow yourself to be dominated by other people, or by some notion to which you cannot reconcile yourself rationally. Your attitudes are often uncertain and you appear restless, worried and dissatisfied because it is not easy to reconcile your taste for freedom with an instinctive surrender to some form of authority.

Choices with a predominance of B:
– If number 1 predominates with B, you like being dominated by an idea or a person, but solely where practical matters are concerned. When, however, the mysterious or superstitious threatens to undermine your independence, your response is one of total rejection of all forms of illogicality. In short, although you look for props to lean on, this attitude does not apply to the unfathomable and the irrational. In your view, even when face to face with the incomprehensible, one might as well forge ahead on one's own: at such moments one cannot be of much help either to oneself or to others.

– If number 2 predominates with B, you are dependent above all on the realm of the irrational. When you have to venture into the more mysterious aspects of life, you look for some kind of support, and end up blending superstition with reality. The mystic qualities of the world, which defy explanation, for you also extend to day-to-day reality, an attitude which may seem to make your existence easier, but in fact only makes it more complex.

– If number 3 predominates with B, your attitude is one that is only apparently contradictory, because you look for supports which, once found, will enable you to display an enviable sense of security. You are in fact only being human. You feel weak, but with help forthcoming from someone or something, you rediscover the confident attitude of someone whose ideas are quite clear. Few of us are born heroes, but there are those, like you, whose heroic qualities can manifest themselves in the service of some ideal, or of someone whom you look up to.

– If number 4 predominates with B, you are in constant search of outside support, but even with this, you still do not manage to feel confident and secure. Reality worries you in many of its aspects, in particular where feeling and emotion alone do not live up to the occasion.

– If number 5 predominates with B, you like to lean on someone or something, but such support must be present and concrete. For example, you do not like to depend on the past, and you eschew childhood memories, which leave you with a sense of sterile consolation. What you really like taking on is reality here and now, where regrets are to no avail. You are more mature than your dependent attitudes might have others believe.

– If number 6 predominates with B, you are very dependent on the past, your childhood in particular. For you, whether actually lived or merely longed for, childhood represents a constant reference, which reveals a basic immaturity in you. You want to lean on someone or something, and you are under the illusion that these props have the same flavour and colour of other bygone, mythicized days. You are essentially a dreamer.

– If number 7 predominates with B, you display a curious attitude. This is why, once you have derived confidence from some prop or other, you also reveal a strong sense of authority. This means that within you there is a latent bully ready to spring out.

– If number 8 predominates with B, you have neither a great deal of independence, nor authority. You prefer living sheltered by some idea or dominant personality, which is why you have not much of yourself to offer. By way of consolation it should be said that not all weaknesses are reprehensible. The essential thing is that you manage to choose the right props.

Test Game 5 (At dawn a boat appears)

○ If you have chosen 1 + A or 3 + A, it means that you see yourself as the center of any situation. In most cases you follow your instinct, which tells you always to derive the maximum personal advantage, even if it is to the detriment of others. For this reason you are not concerned with ideas which might help to keep your egoism in check, as this would be tantamount to weakness. You are happy with yourself as you are, preferring to give in to your impulses, which never prevent you from taking what you consider the only viable path; in other words, your own interests.

○ If you have chosen 1 + B or 3 + B, it means your impulses are paramount, and therefore, inevitably, you think only of yourself. But you do not act out of malice because this egocentricity is a natural disposition, which makes you shrink from mean behaviour and even constrains you to think on the grand scale. Essentially you are strong and genuine, even though those close to you know that they will have to subordinate themselves to your egocentricity. Nevertheless, you have the stature of someone who knows his own worth tackling situations with determination, and without sentiment.

● If you have chosen 2 + A or 4 + A, you do not always place yourself at the center of the universe; in fact on many occasions you try hard to reconcile your own interests with the needs of others, especially if there are ideal reasons which help you to get the better of your instincts. Basically, you reckon that all forms of spiritual enrichment are crucial in binding you in some way to others, and to tone down your own primitive egoism.

● If you have chosen 2 + B or 4 + B, you are not a true egoist, because you try hard to understand and respect the needs of others. You are fond of whatever might enrich you in a cultural sense, and keep your cruder impulses at bay. However, you are weak, and do not always manage to act with the necessary determination. In some instances you joust quite nimbly, to appear to be something which you are not.

Test game 6 (Whatever became of Little Red Riding Hood?)

◊ If you have chosen 1 + A or 2 + A, you are capable of regulating your existence on your own, at least in that you are self-sufficient when it comes to major sentimental or ideological forms of conditioning. You are mature as a character and your attitude towards the past is one of disenchantment. All this gives you a basic sense of confidence which can make you appear quite authoritative. You often have the impression that people close to you stay enmeshed in ideas and emotions which may constitute distractions from predetermined objectives; when this occurs you try to unburden yourself of what you regard as cumbersome baggage. Your somewhat sanguine temperament does not always permit you that vital sense of objectivity when it comes to making judgements, and in some cases your actions can be clumsy, sometimes barely justifiable. With a character such as yours, pride is always lurking in the background.

♦ If you have chosen 3 + B or 4 + B, you have a tendency to put yourself at the beck and call of an idea or feeling, without realizing that you are to some extent neglecting what your real needs are. Your markedly melancholy temperament forces you to look for props; you do not always manage to be sufficiently mature to face up to reality on your own, not least because you allow yourself to be conditioned by the past, in particular certain emotional experiences pertaining to your childhood. All this often makes you rely on others, to the extent that you humble your own more concealed and genuine personality. You should have more faith in your own potential and resort more often to your own sensitivity and your rich store of emotion.

If you have chosen 1 + B or 2 + B, you are living contradictory attitudes because you set off with great verve thinking you can handle things on your own, only to end up finding yourself affected by feelings and ideas which sometimes lead you off the right track. In effect, you are self-sufficient only up to a certain point, beyond which there is always a kind of subordination to someone or something. You feel yourself to be mature and responsible, but every now and then you allow yourself to be influenced by the past and by your childhood experiences. As a result your view of life ends up by being slightly distorted, because by starting out from a stance of basic optimism, you end up from time to time in a state of pessimism which cannot be properly explained. When you take refuge in cynicism, even of a cleverly ironical brand, you do not feel satisfied because you know that you can only achieve success when you do not allow yourself to be beset by doubts.

If you have chosen 3 + A or 4 + A, it strikes you as convenient to accept from the outset a state of subordination, and then to try to rebel against it, so as to find a state of self-sufficiency which does not always turn out to be all that convincing. When it comes to tackling new situations you feel insecure, not least because you allow yourself to be affected by the past, in particular by childhood experiences. But by putting yourself to the test, you find within yourself a sense of security and maturity which you had not properly taken into account to begin with. In such cases you might feel like turning everything upside-down, to entrust yourself to a harsher kind of authoritarianism.

Test game 7 (Consider these two situations)

□ If you have chosen 1 + A or 2 + A, you have an impulsive temperament, in other words you are driven to act in a spontaneous and immediate way, without worrying too much about the consequences. Naturally enough, your decisions are short-lived, and just as easily as you take them you are ready to change them, at the risk of contradicting yourself. Similarly, feelings and emotions do not endure for long in you, if anything they tend to fade fast. As a result others appear to see you as instinctive and wavering, although you lay the blame for your behaviour on fantasy, which seems ever poised to excite you. You are basically changeable and unsettled. But fickleness is not always a flaw, when reality changes its forms so frequently.

□ If you have chosen 1 + B or 2 + B, you do not think a great deal before taking a decision, as a result you risk colliding with obstacles which would have been fairly easy to pinpoint

Opposite and overleaf appear the second pair of photographs, which we spoke about earlier as part of your sexuality test. Remember you have already made your choice between photographs A and B. Now you must add your choice between photograph I, opposite, and II, overleaf. Here again make your choice instinctively. Note down your choice, and add it to your previous choice between A and B. The psychological explanations for whatever choice you make, A or B + I or II, appear on pages 180–1.

VII
LE CHARIOT

earlier with a little forethought. Basically, you are guided by instinct, and you are aware of this, but once you have adopted your attitudes, without thinking greatly about them, you defend them with a pigheadedness which others might find irrational and unreasonable.

□ If you have chosen 1 + C or 2 + C, you usually take your decisions in an immediate and spontaneous way, without thinking them over a great deal. But you are not unimaginative and predictable; you base your attitudes on a special kind of intuition, which rarely lets you down. Others in fact regard you as a practical person, capable at first glance of coming up with accurate assessments. At heart, despite your impulsiveness, you take your experience into account, as well as that of others, before plunging into a judgement, and this acts as your saviour in many situations. Then, when it is time for action, you do so suddenly, with a great deal of practical sense, and time and again you manage to hit the nail on the head.

□ If you have chosen 1 + D or 2 + D, you have an impulsive temperament and you often resort to your imagination in order to assume attitudes which are capable of leaving others dumbfounded. Your intuition is not immediate and spontaneous, in fact it is complicated by many factors which come from some remove deep within you. You pour forth words and projects with the greatest facility, not least to confuse the ideas of others. Those close to you cannot count too much on your consistency, and must, above all else, be prepared to believe in you implicitly.

■ If you have chosen 3 + A or 4 + A, you tend to reflect before you act, and to avoid following your initial instincts, trying at all times to anticipate the consequences of your behaviour. But you are not capable of remaining faithful to your decisions for long; if anything you are prepared to change them without much prompting.

■ If you have chosen 3 + B or 4 + B, you are above all reflective, and thus suspicious of fantasy, your own or others' because it makes you feel divorced from reality, and this merely confuses your ideas. But you defend your ideas with a stubbornness sometimes verging on the excessive. In your view one should never trust one's instinct; however, by dint of being rational at all costs and always keeping one's head fairly and squarely on one's shoulders, one can end up dissatisfied. With oneself and in relations with others a little flexibility does no harm. Otherwise how could one cope with one's feelings, with all their contradictions?

■ If you have chosen 3 + C or 4 + C, you have an ability to think before you ever take a decision, and so you never expose yourself to too much risk. You are simple and linear in your arguments, taking practical considerations into account. At heart you enjoy understanding the character of the person you are dealing with, and as a rule you store up the experiences of others, as well as your own. You are suspicious of extreme whims but you do not deliberately shun them. At times you recognize that instinctive judgements can also be valid.

■ If you have chosen 3 + D or 4 + D, you attach major importance to reflection when decisions have to be taken. But you also pay close heed to your ideas, so it is above all towards yourself that you direct your thoughts – as well as towards your experiences and – why not? – your own talent. As a result others regard you as not only a little hidebound in your verdicts, but also authoritarian. And the fact that you enjoy complications comes out especially in your emotional life, where you are never prepared to give yourself completely. Does this holding back on your part not seem somewhat excessive to you?

Test game 8 (A murder has been committed)

If you have chosen A + 2 or A + 4 or D + 2 or D + 4, you set yourself at the center of everything, and make every effort to ensure that reality about you revolves around you. You prefer to follow your instincts rather than allow yourself to be checked by feelings. For this reason you appear to be strong and determined, but your weak point is a mistrust of culture which, in your eyes, almost invariably involves uncertainties, if not outright surrender. Whenever you yield to your natural aggressivity, you are genuine and do not in any way resort to falsehood to display your good points.

● If you have chosen B + 1 or B + 3 or C + 1 or C + 3, you have a tendency to compare your instincts with the demands of external reality. In a word, your egoism is rational and reasonable, and also takes the rights of others into account. For this reason you always try to grasp and investigate all aspects of a particular problem before giving rein to your impulses. You are consequently interested in everything that has to do with culture, seen as an instrument of improvement. But at times an excess of logic makes you too opportunistic and forces you to choose the path most advantageous to yourself. Culture, if used for over-individualistic ends, can become an instrument of camouflage.

If you have chosen A + 1 or A + 3 or B + 2 or B + 4 or C + 2 or C + 4 or D + 1 or D + 3, you are in a constant dilemma between wanting to impose your own demands and the opposite tendency of considering the interests of others. Your ability to adapt to circumstances could be considerable, if you manage to exploit your egoistic instincts and rational intentions in accordance with the occasion. But if you fail to keep a happy medium, you run the risk of appearing contradictory; sometimes using egoism and at other times a subtle respect for others. The risk is that others will fail to understand you and that you will have a problem in judging yourself on the basis of your proper merits.

Test game 9 (The portrait)

△ If you have chosen B + 1 or B + 2 or C + 1 or C + 2, you are very sociable and enjoy being among other people because you always see yourself as outstanding. In new situations which stimulate you, you plunge in with great boldness, at times even with foolhardiness. Basically, you do not count the cost of having to affirm yourself, and this continual measuring up against others is the most conspicuous aspect of your temperament.

▲ If you have chosen A+3 or A+4 or D+3 or D+4, you are not very sociable; if anything you enjoy your reserve, so that at times you appear shy to those close to you. You have a basic sense of pessimism which makes you regard reality in a bitter light, and prompts you not to trust others. As a result you tend to over-estimate yourself and your inner world.

▲ If you have chosen A+1 or A+2 or D+1 or D+2, you are reserved and not particularly sociable, especially on initial contact with others, but subsequently, if at ease and stimulated, you can become open and good-natured. In other words, you start in a mood of slightly egoistic idealism, and end up with a sense of realism which borders on enthusiasm. These contrasting types of behaviour do not surprise you, because you know yourself well, but they often unsettle those close to you.

△ If you have chosen B+3 or B+4 or C+3 or C+4, you enjoy taking on others as well as reality, when situations first take form, after which your initial enthusiasm starts to fade and give way to a certain pessimism, making you turn in on yourself, to the point of appearing proud and shy simultaneously. Your initial enthusiasms flag without someone or something to revive them. But others are not always prepared to fire them.

Test game 10 (The empty bench)

■ If you have chosen A+1, you are confident in your inner abilities, wanting your life to be marked by loyalty to certain ideals. You face up to reality; if anything you try to impress your own thinking on reality. For this reason you regard the path of our existence as being in constant motion, so that one should not give overdue consideration to past values. Your imagination forces you to fight prejudice and conformity. Following the logic of progress is, for you, of primary importance.

■ If you have chosen A+2, you live by ideal models rather than concrete realities. You are concerned first with understanding things, in order to achieve them, and the values on which your existence is based are consistent. In some cases you tend to dogmatize and permit no discussion about things you feel sure about. What militates most against your ability to realize things – in itself not tangible – is a powerful imagination which makes you chase Utopias, which provide the illusion that you can overlook reality.

■ If you have chosen A+3, you act in accordance with your ideas and do not readily become involved in contradictions because your normal attitude is one of consistency. You are an idealist, concerned with understanding and investigating every problem and situation as they occur, and you also have the imagination required to make changes, when called for in order to live up to your ideals at all times. Sometimes you may be slightly unbending, but only in the defense of your standpoints; and you may end up by appearing a little naive. But others close to you need never expect contradictory surprises.

□ If you have chosen B+1, you are more interested in practical well-being than in a deep grasp of problems. You can be positive and practical, which enables you to operate successfully in practical situations. You are also something of an opportunist, and because of this you like to keep your options open. On the whole you tend to remain static rather than pursue new ideas, and the views of the majority score most with you, given that you align yourself with the moral code shared by the society around you.

□ If you have chosen B+2, you proceed with a marked sense of what is both practical and achievable. As far as ideas and models of behaviour are concerned, you do not strive for them because you find those of the majority ready-made, and you adopt them unquestioningly. You are also quite an opportunist when it comes to adapting them to differing circumstances, almost invariably to your own advantage. You are efficient to the point of shrewdness; in other words, an achiever who is not too concerned with idealistic notions.

□ If you have chosen B+3, you conduct yourself with a great deal of realism, being concerned with well-being more than with abstractions. You have a strong practical sense which presupposes an efficient approach to the accomplishment of your plans. You are, however, a pronounced opportunist, a factor enabling you to adapt to every contingency, which you try to exploit to your own advantage.

Test game 11 (How do you answer this little girl?)

□ If you have chosen A or C and discarded B or D, you are basically an emotional person, and thus very sensitive; but you spontaneously react in a negative way to stimuli from outside. An unforeseen situation will often fill you with anxiety, because you are insecure and lack self-esteem, as well as esteem for others. You are impulsive, failing to appreciate the importance of the responsibilities that crowd in on you, to the point where you do not realize the harmful effects caused by your state of insecurity. You do not operate in a logical manner, and cannot but admire anyone who does. It's as if the realm of the emotions, whose dominion you are under, was quite unknown to the rest of mankind.

■ If you have chosen B or D and discarded A or C, your capacity for logic is such that you are always well-balanced in your judgements and unswerving in your decisions. You have a well-adjusted measure of self-esteem, and exist on the whole in a state of confident serenity. You have a marked sense of responsibility, which makes you suspect those who rely solely on emotions and show themselves to be impulsive and insecure. Those close to you can count on your capacity to think things over, even if, at times, you show a slight coldness.

If you have chosen B and discarded D, or chosen D and discarded B, you have a tendency to measure everything with the yardstick of logic and reflection, but you also contradict yourself by submitting to your emotions and sentimental insecurities. You thus live in a state of constant tension which in some respects makes you open and human. If, from the outside, you appear balanced and realistic, within you are carrying on a continual struggle against your impulses and certain forms of irresponsibility.

If you have chosen A and discarded C, or C and discarded A, you are an emotional person who aspires all the time to become logical and reflective. Your temperament is impulsive, changeable and insecure, but as an ideal you also aim for self-control, security and calm. You realize that you act irresponsibly at times, even though the need for responsible behaviour is always present within you. Basically, you are contradictory, like a great many people, which makes you appealing.

Test game 12 (An image in space)

◊ If you have chosen A and discarded B, you have an inner sense of security which makes you self-sufficient in that your rational and emotional capacities do not need to lean on anything or anyone. Those who base their own attitudes on any form of reliance annoy you.

◊ If you have chosen A and discarded C, you are self-sufficient, refusing to let your attitudes be influenced by anything or anyone. You need nothing beyond your feelings and logical ideas. In particular you despise anyone who displays too much attachment to childhood memories, in this concealing a tacit rejection of your own early experiences; the result is a certain aridity of character.

◊ If you have chosen A and discarded D, you show a developed security which does not depend on factors extraneous to your emotional and rational experience. You are critical of those who do not show a certain attachment to their own childhood experiences, which shows that you take your own past into account to some extent. This makes your self-sufficiency seem less arid. Basically, however, your attitudes embrace certain contradictions.

♦ If you have chosen B and discarded C, you display a basic insecurity, due to the fact that you feel more at peace if you can lean on certain ideas, not your own, or on someone capable of reassuring you. But you are averse to any attitude which might make you reliant on the past, in particular childhood experiences, which have probably left a negative mark on you.

♦ If you have chosen B and discarded D, you constantly need to lean for support on something or someone to find a degree of confidence and security. You are particularly attached to your childhood experiences, and probably tend to over-estimate them thus revealing a certain immaturity.

♦ If you have chosen C and discarded D, you reveal a certain basic insecurity, to overcome which, you revert preferably to past experiences, in particular those of your childhood, which you feel to be a mythical, happy period of your life. Yours is basically a pessimistic outlook on life.

♦ If you have chosen B and discarded A, you are essentially insecure, often needing external props both in terms of sentiment and reason. People who demonstrate their self-sufficiency attract you on the one hand because you need them, and annoy you on the other because you regard them as lacking in warmth, a state of affairs which only intensifies your pessimistic outlook.

♦ If you have chosen C and discarded A, you are very attached to past experiences, in particular those of your childhood, while displays of self-confidence in others irritate you, and you derive some consolation from the thought that those who have no need of others are deficient in feeling.

◊ If you have chosen D and discarded A, you reveal a high degree of security, which may even appear slightly cynical because in many instances you totally dismiss experiences that may have affected you in your childhood. There is a further contradiction in that you tend to resent people like yourself who make plain their self-confidence. It may well be that your security has the odd crack in it, either in the emotional or the logical sphere.

♦ If you have chosen C and discarded B, you show a strong attachment to past experiences, in particular those of your childhood. To some extent this attitude shows a sign of immaturity, not least because, fundamentally, you look down on those displaying insecurity and the need to depend on things or people.

◊ If you have chosen D and discarded B, you possess a strong sense of security, which makes you reject any conditioning from the past, particularly if it has to do with your childhood. Your maturity shows through clearly in the fact that you are irked by anyone who reveals a dependence on something or someone, either in the field of emotions, or of rational ideas.

◊ If you have chosen D and discarded C, you possess an enviable sense of security, free of any conditioning by the past, your childhood in particular. This self-sufficiency is revealed even more clearly by the fact that you rebel against any form of logical or sentimental reliance, especially when rooted in the past.

Test game 13 (The way you walk)

▲ If you have chosen A+1+C+3, you lack enthusiasm when dealing with unpalatable external realities because, deep down, you are idle and pessimistic. You prefer to stay shut away in your own isolated, melancholy thoughts.

▲ If you have chosen A+1+C+4, you are not very sociable, preferring to stay shut within yourself. The result: you almost always come to pessimistic conclusions. Nonetheless, you are not a type to sit around twiddling your thumbs; in fact you become seriously involved once your interest is stirred, especially in a cultural or emotional sense.

▲ If you have chosen A+1+D+3, you do not like becoming over-involved in practical situations, preferring to let reality pass you by, in favour of your own subjective assessments. Your judgements on cultural or sentimental levels are often positive; you retain a basic optimism despite a marked hesitancy in social contacts.

If you have chosen A+1+D+4, you are not in the least sociable, your reserve being very much in evidence when in contact with others. You do, however, seek actual involvement when a situation excites you, especially so when your intellectual or emotional sensibilities are concerned. There is no doubt that you are a wealth of contradictions.

▲ If you have chosen A+2+C+3, you seek to avoid over-involvement with reality, not least because your basic attitude is one of pessimism, which tends to damp down your enthusiasm. You are contradictory above all in your relations with others; at times you open up to them, while at others you stand aloof in stubborn withdrawal.

If you have chosen A+2+C+4, you have many inner contradictions, which you must take into account every time you have to face up to reality. Sometimes you become actively involved, at others you become a prey to pessimism: you give up before you put yourself to the test. In your human contacts too you are enigmatic; you switch from unsociable and even cantankerous attitudes to a sudden exuberance of spirit. The result is that others fail to understand you, and often you fail to understand yourself.

If you have chosen A+2+D+3, you have qualities and flaws which, at the best of times, tend to balance out, and, at the worst, lead you into deep contradictions. On the one hand you are basically an optimist, which leads you to confront situations with a certain aggressivity. On the other you do not like getting too involved, or at least not for too long. In your contacts with others, too, you sometimes appear open and free, at other times unsociable, immersed within yourself.

△ If you have chosen A+2+D+4, you hold all the best cards in your dealings with reality. You enjoy taking on situations head-on, and you do so with a fundamental optimism which almost always makes things easier for you. Your weak spot lies in human contacts since, to begin with, you are free and open, but in the long term you withdraw within yourself, preventing others from getting close to you.

▲ If you have chosen B+1+C+3, you are not really one to take on reality, preferring to stay aloof, to think your thoughts, which almost always lead you to pessimistic conclusions. As a result you appear quite withdrawn in your human contacts.

If you have chosen B+1+C+4, you are ready, keen even, to pit yourself against reality; at times, however, victory goes to the pessimistic streak which co-exists alongside your natural aggressivity. In such cases you invariably restrain your initial enthusiasm. You are also contradictory in your contacts with others, switching from a phoney bonhomie to the most stubborn kind of reserve.

If you have chosen B+1+D+3, although you have a good deal of optimism, which can trigger off your natural aggressivity, you do not always manage to find within yourself the energy necessary to bring to fruition even your fondest enterprises. Added to which is a certain contradictoriness in your contacts with others, who inexplicably find you sometimes sociable, at other times virtually unapproachable.

△ If you have chosen B+1+D+4, you have a self-confident attitude in your approach to reality, basically because you are an optimist, a decided asset in dealing with any new situation. You are also very sociable in your human contacts, even if you have to overcome a certain reserve, always latent within you, which at times can express itself quite unjustifiably.

If you have chosen B+2+C+3, you have a great need for others, which helps for human relations, which in your case are open and spontaneous, at least to begin with. But in the long term, pessimism asserts itself and many of your good intentions hit the dust. You are also idle, reluctant to face up to reality, and often disappoint or disillusion those who initially trusted you.

△ If you have chosen B+2+C+4, you show determination in confronting any situation. You enjoy a good fight, appearing open and sociable. Some may reproach you for a certain fundamental pessimism, which can cause your enthusiasm to waver. You have found by experience that an element of mistrust is necessary if mistakes are to be avoided.

△ If you have chosen B+2+D+3, you inject a great deal of vitality into your human contacts so that you appear open, sociable, free-giving. You are basically an optimist, which explains why most people feel at ease with you. You could achieve so much more were it not for a streak of laziness and a tendency to retire within yourself.

△ If you have chosen B+2+D+4, you have all the qualities needed to cope with reality and achieve maximum success. You have no hesitation in confronting new situations although at times you do so with a certain foolhardiness which, however, is not altogether to be despised. You are basically an optimist, the best antidote to discouragement, which means you oppose difficulties with constructive realism. In human relations you are open and sociable, an enviable asset in both practical and emotional situations.

Psycho-tales

One other way of shedding some light on certain aspects of our character is to subject events and patterns of behaviour to judgements that are at once instinctive and rational. For this purpose, we have made up four tales. You should read these stories as you would any fairy tale, in a mood of child-like abandonment that leaves the imagination free to range where it will.
When you have read them, you will learn more about the way a simple story can be interpreted as a "psycho-tale."
What it amounts to, is that you will be asked to answer a number of questions relevant to the events or characters in each story. You do not have to rack your brains to find the answers – it will be simply a choice of yes, no, or do not know. The important thing is that you will come to recognize various traits of your own character. But do not try at this stage to anticipate which ones because it would spoil the element of surprise. As in all games worthy of the name, these tests work best when you approach them without preconceived ideas.

Mutiny in the kitchen

Psycho-tale 1

The castle of the powerful Roderick was often the setting for a scene which made everyone feel uncomfortable. When there was a guest at his table, Roderick would inevitably ask him at the end of the meal:

"And what do you think of my fare?"

"Marvellous! Exceptional! Particularly the game," was the more or less stock reply each time. Roderick would insist, barely able to conceal his anxiety:

"And what about my wines?"

"To be frank, sire, they fall below the standard of your excellent food."

This unanimous verdict about the inferior quality of his wines made Roderick see red. He was a great glutton, and virtually lived for food. And to think that some time ago now Roderick had taken on as his head chef a wizard, a pastmaster when it came to casting any manner of spells.

"How come you never manage to make good wines?" Roderick asked him at the end of every meal. And the wizard would invariably answer:

"Wines are not my strong point, your lordship."

This confession infuriated Roderick who threatened to heap terrible punishments upon his wizard who, in turn, would retreat back to his kitchen, humiliated. The kitchen was like a huge smoke-filled cavern with fires here and fires there, where the wizard paced solemnly to and fro as if it were his kingdom, which in fact it well and truly was. The situation struck him as humiliating because he had a first-class honours degree in wizardry, even though he had now stooped to being a wizard with a wooden spoon, rather than a silver wand. And this insoluble problem of the wine troubled the wizard terribly. Every day he tried out some new brew with his stills, but he never managed to come up with a halfway decent wine.

One day a stranger sat down at Roderick's table. When the question about his host's wines was asked, he replied:

"Kind sir, your wines do not do justice to your fare."

Then seeing Roderick look mortified, he went on:

"But I am acquainted with the noble Rufus, who has some exceptional vintages."

"Where does he live?" Roderick asked anxiously.

"Far from here."

"I could send an envoy to him. Do you think he would grant me an audience?"

"I fear not. He is extremely jealous of his wines because there are none like them in the world."

Roderick hunched his shoulders, looking disconsolate. But the stranger went on:

"There may be a way of getting hold of his wines."

"How?"

"I know that he has been a widower for some time, and that he is on the lookout for a young wife who will make his old age easier to bear."

"I've got a daughter," Roderick burst out. The guest smiled.

"I've been lucky enough to meet her, while I was entering your castle, and I must say, she is very beautiful. If you could arrange such a marriage, you could exchange your specialities, your exquisite wild game, and Rufus's matchless wines. Your dinner tables would become truly worthy of the gods."

Roderick leapt at the idea, and straightaway dispatched a delegation to the noble old Rufus, offering him his daughter in marriage, and praising her youth and beauty. The noble Rufus replied that he would gladly accept Roderick's daughter as his wife, provided he could glimpse her delicate features before signing the marriage contract. Roderick instantly issued orders to seek out the finest of painters to paint his daughter's portrait. She was of such a gentle nature that she would not dream of going against her father's wishes.

The news that a skilled painter was being sought soon spread throughout the land, until it reached the ears of Lasius, a young and handsome noble, with not a penny to his name. One day he had gone hunting in secret in Roderick's estates where he had seen the noble lord's daughter pass close by him on horseback. In a trice, he had fallen head over heels in love with her.

The idea came to Lasius that if he could pass himself off as a painter, he would be able to approach Roderick's daughter and even declare his love for her. So even though he had never wielded an artist's brush in his life, he got an elderly whitewasher to teach him a few tricks of the trade, and then with admirable nerve he presented himself at Roderick's castle, leading an old nag laden with canvases, brushes, paints, pots, oils and other strange things to help him in the tricky art of painting.

When he set eyes on the handsome, brazen young man come to paint the portrait of his daughter, Roderick hesitated at first, but the portrait was needed urgently, and so far his scouts had only managed to come up with a few second-rate daubers. So, resolved to keep his eyes wide open and his wits about him, he ordered a room to be prepared for the young man, where, in person, he took his daughter for the first sitting.

When he saw her, Lasius felt his heart miss a beat, as she was even more beautiful than he had remembered; and she too felt herself instantly attracted to the young man.

"Start immediately," said Roderick, sitting down on a high-backed chair.

Lasius approached the maiden and led her over to the large window on the far side of the room so as to position her in the best light.

"What is your name?" he asked.

"Mantea, and yours?"

"Lasius."

"Are you a good painter?"

"I shall never manage to depict your beauty in all its loveliness. I have never seen the like of it before."

"Don't make me too beautiful, I beg you."

"Why not?"

"I must go away from here and wed an old man, and I don't want to. In fact if he finds me ugly he won't go through with the wedding."

"You can trust me. I'll save you."

"What are you waiting for, young man?" Roderick broke in with impatience, not least because he could not hear what the two young people were saying to each other.

Lasius had to start painting, but because he did not even know where to start, he took a canvas and patiently painted it pink all over, stealing mischievous glances at Mantea every so often, which she returned with her gentlest of smiles.

After an hour of this interplay of the most tender glances, Roderick lost his temper, because the result so far was simply a canvas covered all over with pink.

"Might I ask what you think you're up to, young man?" he finally asked Lasius grumpily.

"I'm painting your daughter's portrait, sire."

"I know. But where is my daughter?"

"I'm just getting the background ready. My art is a very delicate one; it needs a lot of patience."

And because Roderick never had much patience, he spent less and less time each day watching over his daughter Mantea, and on some days did not turn up at all, busy as he was with his affairs of state, better described as hunting and eating.

Lasius meanwhile had achieved what he had had in mind. The two young people had been able to spend whole afternoons together, with no one to disturb them, and little by little Mantea had fallen in love with him as he charmed her with his words of love.

One day, entering the room where Mantea was posing, Roderick stole a glance at the picture in the hope of finding it almost finished. Instead, when he compared it with the last time he had had a look at it, he saw that the only difference was a small flaxen mark.

"Do you mean to tell me," he asked, very hot and bothered, "that that flaxen mark is my daughter?"

"It is a lock of your daughter's hair," Lasius replied.

"So after sitting for ten days, you're still only on the first lock of her hair?"

"Art takes its time, your lordship. Anyway, I had to start somewhere. I chose her hair, but if you'd rather, it's all the same to me, I'll rub it out and start from the other end. Her feet."

Roderick felt his head swimming with one of those fits of rage which left him drained of strength, so he tried to calm himself a little.

"The portrait of my daughter must be finished in twenty days. Otherwise I'll throw you into my darkest dungeon, along with your wretched brushes and your miserable canvases."

"The truth is that I cannot paint in this room."

"So where would you like to paint?"

"Outdoors. By the light of the moon. Your daughter has a special complexion which only moonlight can bring out properly. If you want a faithful portrait, you must let me paint in the moonlight."

Roderick fell for the blackmail, but resolved to keep an even closer eye than before on things. But when the two young people were together under the moon he could not prevent them finally declaring their love for each other. The moon can be a great help at times like this.

One night, Roderick surprised them from a distance while they were kissing in the moonlight, by now oblivious to everything and everyone. There and then he thought of running his sword through this upstart painter, but checked himself and retired to his chamber, wondering what to do. Mantea's portrait was too important to him. He would have to find a solution which would give him the best of both worlds, namely, the portrait and Mantea's wedding to Rufus. He thought and thought, and sent for the wizard in the morning.

"I feel like eating the moon," he said as nonchalantly as he could. "Serve it at table tonight."

While the wizard turned pale, and leant against a chest of drawers, unable to refuse his master's request, Roderick smiled, thinking that in this way he would catch out either the wizard or the young lovers.

For his part, the wizard waited until evening came and the first pale glow of the moon appeared in the sky. Then he went into the woods, recited a magic spell, and two very tall fir trees bent their tops until they touched the ground together. He sat himself down on the two treetops, then uttered another spell, and the two fir trees let their tops spring skywards again, catapulting the wizard towards the moon.

So it was that at supper that night the wizard presented his master with a handsome slice of moon. Roderick tasted it and said:

"Not bad at all. But why didn't you cook me the whole moon?"

"Despite my magic skills, I was not able to remove the whole moon from the sky," the wizard confessed. "It must be attached to the sky with something special. So I decided to take a piece at a time, and I shall serve it up to my lord and master every evening."

Roderick nodded, showing that the idea had his full approval. In fact he was happier eating the moon a little at a time, because he was not that keen on the taste, it was very spongy and tasted a little of plaster of Paris too.

"The main thing," he said, "is that you bring me the whole moon in the end."

"Sooner or later you will see for yourself that not a sliver remains in the sky."

So for several evenings running a piece of moon was served up at Roderick's table. High up there the moon was now just half a moon, then no more than a slice, and eventually it vanished from the sky altogether, and the sky grew dark and threatening.

Mantea and Lasius no longer had an excuse to see one another and Roderick made the most of this situation to order the young painter to paint his daughter in the courtyard, by sunlight, in full view of all the windows in the castle.

Lasius, however, refused to accept defeat and thought of ways to get his revenge, by dealing a blow at Roderick in his tenderest part, his stomach. While the wizard was absent for a moment, busy working on some other brew of wine, he went to the kitchen and spoke as follows:

"Your tyrant Roderick soon will not need you any more, and he will sack the lot of you. He has started eating the moon, soon it will be the sun's turn, and who knows where it will all end. You will have no jobs, there will be no moon or sun, and heaven knows what else will be missing. Rise up and starve your tyrant to death, before he does the same to you and your families."

Lasius undoubtedly had charm, even if he had spoken slightly out of turn, and his words sounded so convincing that when the wizard returned to the kitchen to prepare the next meal, he found himself faced with the most incredible pandemonium.

The whole kitchen refused to lend a hand. The fire would not light, the pots and pans would not heat, the spits would not turn, the knives would not cut, the grinders would not grind, the choppers would not chop, the beaters would not beat, the strainers would not strain, the corkscrews would not pull, the colanders would not sieve and not even the cream would stiffen, while the milk got into a positive frenzy.

The wizard hastened to Roderick and in desperate tones said:

"Your lordship, there's a mutiny in the kitchen."

Roderick went weak, but he summoned up his courage. "I'll send in my soldiers," he shouted, and that is just what he did.

But the troops did not even manage to force an entry into the room, because everything rose up against them. The flames from the fire licked over anyone trying to get through the door, the spits flashed like swords beneath the noses of the soldiers, the pots and pans started to shoot tomatoes, potatoes, nuts and anything else they could find, the taps gushed forth boiling water, the choppers chopped, the rolling-pins cudgelled, the beaters hit out, the graters grated, and even the cats who had lived for years off kitchen leftovers started scratching and clawing.

The soldiers were pushed back and no one could get into that huge room which was now under orders from Lasius and his gastronomic allies. The mutiny went on for a long time, which meant that the kitchen could not be used for many days.

Deprived of those supreme delights of the meal table and terrified by the idea of dying of hunger, Roderick got used to feeding on grass, wild fruit and even roots from the fields. Reduced to a permanently famished skeleton, he declared himself defeated and Lasius dictated his terms.

The kitchen would return to normal if all its implements were treated with due considerateness, if no one was dismissed, and if there was a constant supply of scraps for the cats. Furthermore, Roderick had to agree to the marriage between Mantea and Lasius.

Roderick had to give in to these demands and he tendered his surrender. The wedding took place straightaway, as soon as the form of surrender had been duly signed; the chaplain, who had retired to bed expecting to die of hunger (because he had trouble digesting grass) was reinstated. The wizard set to with a will, now that the kitchen was once again working at full capacity, and in no time at all a great banquet with a hundred courses was prepared.

The funny thing is that the aroma of those hundred platters no longer did anything for Roderick. First he had ruined his taste buds by eating the moon, then he had got used to the flavour of grass and wild fruit. As a result he became a

CUCINA

convinced vegetarian, much to the delight of all the wild game in the area. Now he would not drink so much as a sip of wine, and so he forgot about his craze to find a wine worthy of his table.

In the kitchen things became much less frenetic than they had been, and everyone in the castle grew happy and contented again.

But Mantea and Lasius were still waiting to go on their honeymoon, because the moon had completely vanished from the sky and the alternatives proposed to them by a wise man in the castle had all been turned down. They could not work up much enthusiasm for a spongecake-sun or a marzipan Milky Way instead of having a honeymoon.

The wizard was summoned before Roderick to be given the most extraordinary order he had ever heard in his life.

"Put the moon back where it belongs."

After nearly fainting, the wizard ran straight to the kitchen, and with a dash of imagination, a helping hand from all and sundry, a little bit of luck, and another little bit of luck – just as happens in real life – he managed to invent a beautiful yellow cake to put up there in place of the moon.

The cake turned out quite well, except that there were no baking-pans large enough in the kitchen, and the wizard had to make the moon in pieces, fitting them together one by one.

But that was enough for Mantea and Lasius. They started their honeymoon straightaway, even though there was only a slice of moon in the sky to start with, then a half-moon, and finally a full one.

So they spent a few days like this in sheer bliss, and then suddenly one night they saw that a slice was missing from the moon. Roderick who had noticed this too, instantly summoned the wizard before him.

"What's happening up there?" he asked the quaking wizard.

"I have realized that by being put up there like that in pieces the cake breaks every so often."

"But it's not good to have a moon which isn't round."

"Your lordship, I should warn you that another slice will fall out, then another, and then the whole moon will vanish from the sky."

"Then I shall have you hanged," intoned Roderick, who now wanted nothing better than the prolongation of Mantea and Lasius's honeymoon, not least because they had promised him a grandson.

"I shall put it back up there, I promise," groaned the demoralized wizard. Roderick had a think about it and then said:

"You are a wizard, but even you will no longer be here one of these days. Who will worry about putting the moon back when you are dead?"

The wizard replied without a second's hesitation:

"I shall leave those following after me the recipe for my cake and all the vital magic spells."

"But your successors will also die."

"The ones to whom I'll leave the recipe will never die."

"And who might they be?"

"The lovers, your lordship. When lovers see first one slice of the moon fall from the sky, then another, and another, until there is no moon, they will see to it."

Since when, that is how things have been, just as the wizard had predicted. Today the moon still breaks into pieces every so often and we can see only half a moon, then a thin slice, and finally nothing at all. But there is always a lover somewhere on earth who manages to reenact that old magic and put the moon back together a little at a time. Then first a slice reappears in the sky, followed by half a moon, and then the moon's whole friendly face.

And so it will be forever. Love cannot do without the light of the moon; just like Mantea and Lasius who from that day on lived together in as happy a state as is possible on this earth; because the moon solves many things, but it cannot think of everything. The rest we have to do for ourselves.

Here are some questions based on the psycho-tale you have just read. Answer them without thinking twice about it, marking your choice: YES, NO, *or* DO NOT KNOW

1. Can one who lives more or less only for food, as Roderick does, have artistic taste? YES NO DO NOT KNOW
2. Does one, recognizing a woman's beauty at first glance, as the stranger does with Mantea, possess innate artistic taste? YES NO DO NOT KNOW
3. Can one learn how to do something artistic in a short time? YES NO DO NOT KNOW
4. On the other hand, is what Lasius says true when he remarks that one needs a lot of patience to do something artistic? YES NO DO NOT KNOW
5. Can a special complexion like Mantea's be brought out by the light of the moon? YES NO DO NOT KNOW
6. Do words of love sound more beautiful if heard by moonlight? YES NO DO NOT KNOW
7. Would you like to have a kitchen as strange as the wizard's? YES NO DO NOT KNOW
8. Do the phases of the moon, which cause it to appear and disappear, by turns in the night sky, make the moon more interesting? YES NO DO NOT KNOW

(for an explanation of this and the following three psycho-tales, turn to pages 67–68)

The girl with the crazy legs

Psycho-tale 2

A long time ago there lived in a village a beautiful girl called Dionea, who was extremely clever at making pottery. She lived alone with her father Manfred in a little cottage right in the middle of the village – her mother had died in childbirth. Since Dionea had started making pottery Manfred had discovered that he was something of a wizard with magic gifts, and now the two of them lived by helping all the villagers in their own village as well as from neighbouring places around. People came from here, there and everywhere and one would say to Dionea:

"Would you make me a tabby cat?"

"What's the use of that?" the girl would ask.

"I've got too many mice in the cellar. I want the cat to frighten them so I get rid of them."

Then in the twinkling of an eye Dionea's nimble fingers made a handsome tabby cat of clay. Once finished, she took it to Manfred, and with a magic spell he brought the tabby to life.

On another occasion a farmer arrived and said to Dionea:

"Would you make me some bees?"

"What for?"

"I want to make a new hive so that my children can have some good honey."

Fifteen minutes later the bees were ready and then it was Manfred's job once again to bring them to life.

In short, Dionea and Manfred satisfied the wishes of everyone who came to them asking to have some kind of animal, as long as there was a good enough reason for the request. Someone would come wanting a mule to help with his work; someone else would want a pair of cows to have milk, and someone else would simply ask for a dog with gentle eyes, as a companion.

In this way Dionea and Manfred produced many useful and handsome animals which roamed through the village and neighbouring parts, carrying out the task which nature had invented for them in the best possible way. Of course if someone came asking for a horse simply for the sake of mounting it and being high-handed in some way or other, Dionea and Manfred would refuse his request. And they would also not lend an ear if someone wanted a few more sheep than his neighbour, simply to spite him. Manfred was a good wizard and Dionea was his obliging daughter with the golden hands. And everyone around them wished them well.

One day a little old lady, whom no one had ever seen before round those parts, came to Dionea. And the old lady said:

"Dear girl, would you make a beautiful creature with a hundred eyes and a hundred legs?"

"What for?"

"You see, I live in a large house, although it's quite modest. And I need an animal to watch over it who can see into every room, and close doors and windows for me when the wind blows them open."

Dionea set to work straightaway, not least because she was excited by the idea of making an animal that no one had ever seen before. And in a matter of minutes she had made a strange creature with a hundred eyes and a hundred legs, which was certainly no beauty to behold. Then the girl called her father so that he could bring to life that curious creature invented by her there and then. When Manfred set eyes on this oddest of creatures which almost filled the entire room, he was a bit dubious about whether to bring it to life or not, but the little old lady insisted.

"I am old and in poor health. Every day it gets harder and harder for me to keep an eye on so many rooms. And then as long as a fortnight can go by before I manage to get up to the attic. And who is there to watch over my grain and my nuts?"

And she persuaded Manfred as well, so with his usual spell he brought the animal to life. But he regretted it straightaway, because the creature ran straight out of the house, breaking down the door, while the old lady cantered after it, guffawing with laughter.

From that day on the village lived through many a nightmarish moment. The creature gobbled up all the crops and stole all the farmyard animals, while the old lady grew fatter and fatter, and did not give a fig.

Dionea and Manfred were forced to make a decision, even though it went against all their principles. So the girl modelled ten fierce wolves and Manfred brought them to life, and then they set them loose against the creature. The fight was a long one, and the village was bespattered with blood, but in the end the wolves got the better of the creature, which they tore into a hundred pieces. Then, at a command from Manfred, the wolves slunk off into the woods to live the wild life ordained them by nature. As we all know, the world needs civilized people, but one or two wild things do not go amiss either.

When the old lady saw her creature torn to pieces by the wolves, she flew into a rage and ran straight to Dionea's house. When she saw the girl she stretched out her hands towards her and shrieked in a menacing voice:

Legs with no brakes, legs with no pity,
Make her wander from city to city.

All of a sudden Dionea's legs started to move all of their own accord. Dionea could do absolutely nothing about those unseemly movements. She tried shouting:

"Legs, stop! stop!"

But her legs started to jump up and down and then they ran right out of the house. Dionea shouted once more:

"Legs, take me back home!"

But her legs did exactly the opposite and in leaps and bounds they carried the poor girl towards the main road which led away from the village. Dionea saw that all was lost and called out to Manfred to come to her aid.

"Help me, papa, I am under a spell!"

In order to remove that evil spell Manfred needed to touch her, at the very least, but the trouble was he could not catch up with her because his legs were the legs of an old man, whereas Dionea's legs seemed as agile as those of a huge grasshopper.

"Stop, Dionea. Let me touch you," shouted Manfred, wearily dragging his legs along the dusty road behind Dionea. But the girl felt him being left farther and farther behind, until she could hear his voice no longer. By now her legs had carried her well away from the village, and still they went on running at their crazy speed, all of their own accord, and the girl could not tell them what to do.

So it was that in next to no time Dionea found herself far from home in unknown parts, still going wherever her legs

took her, still hopping and skipping, still running on those spellbound legs. If she told them to do something, they did exactly the opposite, and to stay still, without moving, the poor girl had to lie down on the ground and hold her legs tightly between her arms.

Because Dionea was a sensible, calm girl she did not lose her head. In fact she tried to get used to the strange life forced upon her by her spellbound legs. Wherever she went she made pretty animals of clay and then sold them, even though there was no one to bring them to life, because Manfred was not there to work his magic skills. In this way she was able to buy for herself the little she needed to live, and she slept wherever she ended up, but usually in haystacks or stables. Everyone who saw her and got to know her, even if only for a short while, now called her Crazy-Legs, and with every day that passed she felt more and more disheartened because she was unable to remove from her heart her homesick feelings for her father and their house.

One day, on her wearisome wanderings through whatever places her spellbound legs took her, Dionea came upon a handsome young man who looked as sad and downhearted as herself. In fact he was lying on the ground, unable to get up, no matter how hard he tried. He was a circus performer, and he had lost his companions who were travelling from village to village in their circus caravan. The young man had been riding behind the caravan on a mule, but the mule had suddenly shied because it had seen a large grasshopper on the ground, and the young man had found himself on the ground with both his legs paralyzed. The frisky mule had run off, and the caravan had also gone on its way because the young man's friends had not heard his cries for help. Now the young man was there on the ground, unable to move because of his legs being paralyzed, and he felt a great surge of despair welling up inside him.

"Happy you," he said, when he saw Dionea's legs all sprightly and skipping up and down.

"Happy, my foot," Dionea replied, "My legs are under a spell and take me wherever they want to go. I cannot tell them what to do any more."

"Some people have too much, and some too little," the young man said, scratching his head. "Life really is strange."

"We should exchange legs," Dionea said at the top of her voice, and as she spoke an idea was taking shape in her head.

So it was that she helped the young man to drag himself up into a sitting position; she propped him up against a tree trunk, then in turn she lay down on the grass close to him and held her legs tightly in her arms to stop them moving.

"I'll have a little rest too," she said, smiling warmly at the young man, who in turn looked hard at her as if he were seeing her for the very first time.

"My name is Malvo," he said. "What's yours?"

"I'm called Dionea," she replied, and the two of them struck up a natural conversation, as will happen between young people. It is between old people that friendship comes harder. Then Dionea produced some bread and cheese which she had managed to buy by selling a couple of her clay creatures, and she shared out the food with Malvo who thanked her warmly. At the end of their simple meal Dionea asked Malvo:

"Where would you like to go?"

"I want to find my circus companions."

"In what direction were they heading?"

"Towards the north."

Dionea had the idea that her house lay to the south and she remembered that her legs took her precisely in the opposite direction to the one she asked them to go in.

"What if I carried you on my back?" Dionea asked with a smile.

"Could you manage to carry me?" Malvo asked, his eyes opening wide with hope.

"Of course. My spellbound legs are so strong that I could carry a whole crowd of people."

"Let's be on our way then, Dionea. I'll be grateful to you for the rest of my life."

Without more ado Dionea hoisted Malvo on to her back, and happy as a bee Malvo shouted:

"Northwards, Dionea!"

"Northwards," the girl repeated, but her legs started to run and jump in leaps and bounds towards the south.

"North, north," Malvo protested. "This way we're getting even farther away from my friends."

"I can't do anything about it." Dionea replied, but she was beginning to enjoy herself, because things were turning out just as she wanted.

"But keep on saying where you want to go," she went on. "You never know..."

Malvo started to shout as loud as he possibly could. "North, you wretched legs, north I say!"

Dionea knew very well that her legs would do exactly the opposite of what was being asked of them, but this was all part of her plan. She did in fact live to the south, and if they carried on at this pace, running like the wind, her legs,

spellbound or not, would sooner or later bring her back home.

And that is in fact what happened. As night fell, Papa Manfred saw a girl coming towards the house in great leaps and bounds, with a young man astride her back, shouting ever more loudly as they approached:

"North, you wretched legs, north, I say!"

When the strange pair drew closer, Manfred's eyes – tired as they were – saw that the girl was none other than his very own Dionea. He ran towards her as fast as he could, and managed to touch her, and as he did so he uttered at the top of his voice a magic spell to break the one the legs were under. Straightaway the legs became no longer spellbound, and were once more calm and obedient to Dionea's wishes. She helped Malvo down from her back, propped him against a tree trunk and then at last hugged her father, Manfred, the tears running down both their faces.

Later on everything was explained to Malvo, including the trick invented on the spot by Dionea to bring her back home, and the young man, honest lad that he was, said: "It doesn't matter. I'm happy for you, Dionea."

The girl then turned to her father, and with a smile asked him if he could find a magic spell which could also mend Malvo's legs. All night Manfred thought about it, he could not sleep anyway because of the excitement of having found his daughter again. Early next morning, when the dew was still thick on the ground, he went to the woods, snapped off a branch of fir and returned home. There he tapped Malvo's legs over and over again with the branch, uttering a special magic spell all the while. All of a sudden the young man realized that strength was returning to his muscles and he jumped down from the bed, as happy as can be. He was overjoyed to rediscover the use of his legs and he thanked Manfred and Dionea over and over again. He was happy to accept their invitation to remain a few days before setting out again in search of his companions.

All too quickly, as happens with all good things, it was time for the young man to leave. Malvo had tried several times to say something very important to Dionea, but every time he seemed to run out of breath and could not get the words out. Dionea too would have liked to say many things to Malvo, but she said nothing because when there is too much to say people never know where to begin.

So Malvo departed and eventually found his friends and went to work in the circus once more. Dionea went back to making her pretty little animals and Manfred went on bringing them to life to meet the wishes of his fellow-villagers. But for all three of them their happiness was no longer what it once had been. Malvo no longer enjoyed working in the circus, and often he felt some mysterious force making him sigh from deep within his breast.

Dionea too found that she could not concentrate on her work, often staring out of the window at something far off that only she could see, until one day Manfred stood firmly in front of her and said:

"My dear daughter, make me some white doves."

"White doves? And what will you do with them Papa?"

"I want them to fly far away bearing an important message."

Dionea lowered her eyes because she felt troubled without knowing why, and before long she had made the most beautiful white doves that her hands had ever made. Manfred recited his magic spell and the doves came to life and started flapping their wings as if they wanted to fly far away. Then Manfred threw open the windows and they all flew off together, heading north, as light as so many dreams.

Malvo saw them fluttering down from the sky until he found himself surrounded by them, and they seemed to be inviting him to do something. He understood at once and without even saying goodbye to his companions he started out towards the south, with the doves leading the way.

When at last they looked into each other's eyes once more, Dionea and Malvo realized that they loved each other, without having to put it into words, and Manfred felt very pleased at what he had managed to do.

The story goes that from then on the two young people lived together forever and a day, and they seem to have been happy and contented too. But one can never have too much faith in the endings of stories.

Answer the following questions about the psycho-tale you have just read with a YES, NO *or* DO NOT KNOW.

[1] To do something artistic, like Dionea with her clay animals, is love necessary? YES NO DO NOT KNOW

[2] Are Dionea and Manfred wrong to trust the old lady? YES NO DO NOT KNOW

[3] Do you think our world is any worse off for having its wild creatures? YES NO DO NOT KNOW

[4] In order to live better on her own, do you think Dionea Crazy-Legs should have rid herself of her homesickness for her father and her home? YES NO DO NOT KNOW

[5] Is it true that friendship comes harder between old people? YES NO DO NOT KNOW

[6] If you found yourself in Dionea's and Malvo's shoes, separated from your loved ones, would you feel sad and leave it at that? YES NO DO NOT KNOW

[7] If, like Malvo, you were lured away by Dionea's doves, would you first say goodbye to your circus companions? YES NO DO NOT KNOW

[8] Do you find the "happy-ever-after" ending of many stories ridiculous? YES NO DO NOT KNOW

(turn to psycho-tale 2, page 67)

The green dog

Psycho-tale 3

A very long time ago there lived in a small village a handsome young man whose name was Bagnolph. He had just turned eighteen years old. He lived on his own, because he had no parents left, but he was happy enough all the same because nature had endowed him with a melodious voice and so on every festive occasion, when people gathered together, he would sing merry songs which he had written and composed himself. He was known for miles around, and was much sought after for his merrymaking gifts at banquets, weddings, christenings and other ceremonies, private or public. He made a good living and was everybody's friend.

One night, as Bagnolph returned home from a nearby village where he had been singing songs to mark the occasion of a wedding, he came upon a large white-haired dog. The animal, seemingly lost, made a great fuss of him as if it had found a parent again after many years.

"It must have strayed from its master," the young man mused aloud. The dog sat down on the ground, gazing up at him with two large, devoted eyes.

"Who knows where its owner might be," Bagnolph said to himself, and the dog stretched out a paw to touch him, as if it wanted to show that he was now its master.

"If, at least, I knew your name," mused Bagnolph, and the dog barked something in return though it was impossible to know what.

"I understand. Would you like to stay with me?"

The dog pricked its ears, cocked its head as if to say yes and panted to show how pleased it was.

"You seem to agree it's a good idea. That's settled then. I'll call you Chop."

At these words, the animal leapt up and down for joy as they made their way towards Bagnolph's home.

From that moment, Bagnolph and Chop became inseparable. The companionship of a dog, for someone who could hardly remember when he had not lived alone, came as joy unalloyed; for a dog, even more than the most loyal of humans, can be a man's best friend.

How was Bagnolph to know that his troubles were only beginning? He realized there was something odd about Chop when he took him along to the local market to buy himself a pair of shoes.

"These are the finest shoes in the whole market," said the shoe vendor, when Bagnolph picked up a pair which looked as if they would fit him perfectly. "I'm practically giving them away, and they'll last you a lifetime."

Suddenly they both saw Chop change colour, from white to green.

"Is this your dog?" asked the merchant, dumbfounded.

"Y-yes. As far as I know," stuttered Bagnolph.

"Why has he gone all green, when he was white just a

moment ago?"

"I don't know," murmured Bagnolph, and without buying anything he returned home, deep in thought, followed by Chop with his tail between his legs, pretending to sniff at ants on the ground. Meanwhile, his coat had turned to white once more.

The second time this happened was when Bagnolph had to go and see the doctor, because he had lost his voice.

"Take these tablets tonight before you go to bed, and tomorrow you'll feel as right as rain."

As the doctor spoke, Chop suddenly turned green all over, even though the doctor pretended not to notice, possibly because, like everyone who knows something, he wanted to make it seem that he knew everything and could not be taken aback by anything. But Bagnolph had a good think about it as soon as he was back home, and his suspicions were confirmed the following morning, when he realized that his voice was still hoarse, even though he had taken the pills which the doctor had given him just as he was told to do, before going to bed.

"I've got it," Bagnolph exclaimed in a flash, "Chop turns green when he hears a lie."

Chop lay curled up on the ground, with his head resting on his paws, and looking rather sad, as if to let his master know that his suspicion was right, and as a mere large hairy dog he was in no position to do much about it.

So it was that Bagnolph and Chop's troubles started. Soon in fact it was common knowledge that the white dog would change his coat from white to green once he heard anyone tell a lie. Chop accompanied Bagnolph to all the festivities where the young man sang his songs, and as chance would have it, these were occasions where people tended to tell the tallest of stories. So Chop reenacted his protean performance at most of these ceremonies, where there was always somebody making lavish promises about this, that and the other. Unfortunately his coat made no distinction between people and turned from white to green irrespective of whether the lie was uttered by pauper or prince.

In fact, one of the biggest lies Chop ever heard came straight from the lips of the prince's chief adviser. During the opening of the new drawbridge to the castle, the chief adviser publicly promised that within a year the taxes levied from the poorest subjects would be reduced. Poor Chop could not stop himself turning green, and he was immediately arrested for insulting a public official in the exercise of his duties.

Bagnolph did not want to abandon his dog, so he had himself locked up with him in a cell in the castle; then they both listened to the verdict together and heard themselves being exiled forever. Chop was immediately expelled from the village without any chance of lodging an appeal and Bagnolph was forced to take the dog into the woods and abandon him to his fate. But all it took was a lingering glance from Chop's moist eyes for the young man to decide on the spot to go along with him. He could not just leave him to suffer who knows what kind of fate. He preferred to go with him, leaving behind the quiet life which he had enjoyed up until that moment. Dogs always manage to make themselves loved, by fleas or by their masters alike.

While Chop waited in the woods, Bagnolph returned home to bundle up all his possessions, but to his great surprise he found none other than the prince's chief adviser in person waiting for him in his humble room, sitting in a chair flanked by two armed guards.

"I have come in secret," the chief adviser said in a solemn voice. "The prince wants to have the strange dog which turns green."

"But you've banished him for ever."

"As the property of the prince, the dog will automatically be pardoned."

"What will the prince do with him?"

"I should not really tell you, but it is not hard to imagine. A dog like that, which can detect liars, is worth a fortune to its owner. Especially if the owner is a powerful man like our lord and master."

"If the truth be told all the dog has done is bring me a mountain of trouble."

"You see? You do not realize how valuable a dog like that can be. But a prince does."

"What must I do?"

"You must hand the dog over to me. You will be allowed to go on living here in peace. We shall overlook the fact that you were once the dog's accomplice. You can thank the prince for his generosity."

"I shall go right away and fetch the dog," said Bagnolph, and he ran off to the woods where he found Chop who, meanwhile, had been seeking out truffles without even knowing how such a thing is done.

"Dear Chop, it looks as if someone has had their eye on you. Would you like to go and live in the prince's castle?"

Just then a leaf dropped on to Chop's nose and he shook his head energetically, and Bagnolph took this to mean that the dog was saying no.

"Well, my friend, let's be off. We'd better make a quick getaway, and cover up our tracks as we go."

Bagnolph and Chop ran off as fast as they could, and in no time were far away from the village and the prince's castle.

After being on the run for a few days, when they were sure that they were out of reach of the guards, Bagnolph decided to find himself a job. And partly because all he could do was sing and partly because he did not want to stay too long in the same place because he was afraid of the prince's spies, he joined up with a troupe of strolling players, who travelled about in carts with sets and costumes and by night recited tear-jerking dramas in town squares.

Bagnolph filled in the interval between one act and the next with his merry songs, not least to cheer up the tearful atmosphere which spread out from the stage into the audience from all those tragedies. Bagnolph was happy enough, and the strolling players were pleased with him too, because they had found a useful member for their company. The only one unhappy was Chop: he had to live day in day out in the midst of all the jealous tantrums thrown by these actors, and he became involved in all their lies even though he did not want to be. And he spent more time in his green coat than in his natural white one.

"What a performance you gave this evening," said one actor to a colleague coming off the stage, and Chop, who was curled up in the wings, turned completely green.

"Darling, you grow more and more beautiful," said a young actress to an older one, and once again Chop felt that accursed colour spread all over him. His was undoubtedly a dog's life: but a special kind of dog's life, one hastens to add.

One day Bagnolph found himself in a town on a festival

day and because his own show was not due until the evening, to kill time he wandered around among the merry-go-rounds and the fair stalls, followed as ever by the faithful Chop. For half an hour the young man had had his eye on a beautiful girl with a rather impish look about her, who might have been sixteen, or might not; he followed her at a distance of a few yards, looking for the right chance to talk to her. She too had noticed Bagnolph and as she found him a good-looking young man, she behaved like someone trying to hide in the throng, but at the same time ensuring she could be spotted. Eventually the two young people found themselves squeezed up against one another by the stall with the bearded woman, and Bagnolph spoke to her with the most bewitching smile he could muster.

"I'm sorry if I'm too close to you. But I can't help it. There are too many people."

"Don't worry. I quite understand," she replied, giving him a mischievous glance.

"I'd better introduce myself," he went on. "My name is Bagnolph."

"Mine's Prunella."

"What a lovely name," he said, and started to tell her what he was doing, inviting her to come and see the show that evening. During their encounter Chop had managed to find a spot among the throng where he could give his ear a good scratch. He felt ill at ease and did not know why.

Just then he heard a shout go up. "Stop, thief! Stop, thief! Someone's robbed me of my purse!"

With some difficulty, two guards forced their way through the throng and made for the old man who had shouted out.

"Do you know who robbed you?" they asked.

"Yes," and the old man pointed a finger at Prunella. "She did it. I'm sure of it."

Bagnolph squeezed Prunella's hand and shouted:

"That's not possible. She was talking with me."

Then things went from bad to worse, because the guards grabbed both Bagnolph and Prunella and hauled them away from the crowd, by now hurling abuse at them. Chop had in vain turned completely green at the old man's words, and now followed behind the unfortunate captives, his tail between his legs.

The judge before whom the guards led the two young people was a tall, frosty-faced gentleman.

"What's this dog doing here?" he asked at once.

"He's mine," Bagnolph replied. "He never leaves my side."

"All right, as long as he stays in that corner and does not misbehave."

Meanwhile Chop was his old white self again. Now he stared at the judge, letting just one of his ears flop down as was his custom in delicate situations. Then the guards came to the matter of the theft, saying that the thief was definitely one of the two young people. At the end of their statement the judge looked hard at Bagnolph and asked him:

"Did you steal the money?"

"Yes. It was me."

"No!" cried Prunella. "It's not true. I did it."

Chop hid his face between his paws, but still could not help turning green all over. The judge could not help noticing the change of colour.

"What kind of a trick is this?" he asked. "How has this dog suddenly turned green, and why?"

Bagnolph then explained it all to the judge.

"He does it when someone's telling a lie in his presence."

"So which one of you is not telling the truth? You, or the girl?"

"Me," the two young people said in unison.

The judge huffed and puffed.

"Very well. I shall have to sentence both of you."

Bagnolph and Prunella looked at one another and Prunella slipped her hand into Bagnolph's, who squeezed it hard. At that moment a third guard appeared dragging along a vagabond.

"Your honour," he said, "this is the thief. We found him with the purse in his possession."

The judge nodded to the guard to take the accused into another room, then he looked at the two young people and asked them in a stern voice:

"Well, you two, why did you each take the blame for stealing the money when neither of you had done so?"

Prunella was first to answer: "I was afraid that he was the thief, and I wanted to save him."

"Same here," Bagnolph added. "I was afraid she had stolen the money and I wanted to save her."

The judge gave them an impatient look and then said drily:

"Next time when you want to tell each other that you are in love, do not do so in a court of justice. It could well do you no good. Now, be off with you."

Prunella and Bagnolph made a dash for the door, followed by Chop, who was once more completely white all over, but

they were stopped in their tracks by the judge's voice:

"Just a minute!"

They spun round and saw the judge's finger pointing at Chop.

"Does that dog really turn green whenever he hears someone telling a lie in his presence?"

"That's the honest truth, your worship," replied Bagnolph.

"Doesn't it have its problems?"

"A few. But I'm very fond of him."

"He'd be a great help to a judge."

"But I would not give him away for all the gold in the world," said Bagnolph.

The judge gestured them to be off and the two young people ran from the court accompanied by Chop, who made it quite clear that he was delighted to be free once again.

From that day Prunella and Bagnolph never left each other's side, because they realized how much they loved one another. The strolling players were happy to put up an extra person in their caravans, and to make herself useful, Prunella, who happened to be able to play the flute, began to accompany Bagnolph with beautiful musical improvisations, while he sang. They were a truly handsome couple and because they were appreciated by everyone who saw them everything would have turned out for the best if, as usual, it had not been for the presence of Chop, complicating yet another situation.

Chop never left Bagnolph's side, not even when he took Prunella off to one side to exchange a few tender words, and this constant attachment started to become an embarrassment for all three of them.

"I shall love you all my life," whispered Prunella into Bagnolph's ear, and although Chop tried his utmost to stop himself, he could not help turning green all over.

"Have you ever made so many love vows to any other woman?" Prunella asked Bagnolph, and he hastily replied:

"Never, Prunella. Cross my heart. You are the first woman I've ever loved."

And dashing off as if he had just had an electric shock, poor Chop once more watched helplessly as his coat turned from white to green. In this way the poor dog's life with Prunella and Bagnolph became fraught with problems, until one day Bagnolph called the dog to him and spoke as follows:

"Dear Chop, as things are we cannot go on living together. You are fond of me, and I am fond of you. But between the two of us this wretched green colour keeps getting in the way."

To start with Chop let out a sort of whine, then his mouth dropped open.

"Yes, really," Bagnolph went on. "Indeed, you do everyone a good turn by showing us when we tell lies. But now I am in love, and Prunella loves me too, and love needs a few white lies now and then. Otherwise what other kind of love is there?"

And Chop, who was a clever dog as well as a sincere one, first had a good shake to tidy his coat and then walked away

with great dignity, nose in the air as if he were after a scent. And Bagnolph never saw him again.

But he did happen to bump into the judge, the same tall, stern-faced judge, who instantly remembered him and greeted him warmly.

"You can work for me," he said to the dog.

And Chop felt proud, as if he had been given an important mission. But to avoid any misunderstandings the judge added:

"You will show me who is telling the truth and who is lying. But the verdict will be my concern. Don't poke your nose into human goings-on too much, because you may end up understanding nothing at all. Just like me."

Chop nonchalantly snapped at his tail, as if trying to catch a particularly annoying flea. And the judge then summed things up:

"If you keep your end of the bargain, you will be well looked after. If you don't, I'll have all that white hair of yours shaven off."

Chop kept his end of the bargain and enjoyed himself thoroughly with the judge. And it would seem that little by little, as the years passed, his coat lost the habit of turning green.

A pity? Perhaps. But one cannot expect too much of a dog, not even a dog in a fairy tale.

Answer the following questions about the events and characters in the story you have just read, making an instinctive choice between YES, NO *and* DO NOT KNOW.

[1] Do you think it a good idea to have a dog like Chop showing you when people are not telling the truth?
YES NO DO NOT KNOW

[2] During family festivities is it a bad thing to tell the odd lie? YES NO DO NOT KNOW

[3] Would you do the same as Bagnolph and leave your native surroundings so as not to lose Chop?
YES NO DO NOT KNOW

[4] Would you ever feel like pursuing someone you like the look of at first sight, as Bagnolph does with Prunella? YES NO DO NOT KNOW

[5] Do you think that the old man in the crowd accuses Prunella merely because she is young?
YES NO DO NOT KNOW

[6] Is it impossible for a judge always to be fair?
YES NO DO NOT KNOW

[7] Is it a fact that love needs to tell the odd lie, as Bagnolph says? YES NO DO NOT KNOW

[8] Is it true that as the years go by one loses the urge to tell or know the truth, as happens with Chop?
YES NO DO NOT KNOW

(turn to psycho-tale 3, page 68)

The battle of the crumbs

Psycho-tale 4

In a castle in a faraway country there once lived a beautiful girl called Amaryllis. Good-natured friends would refer to her as plump. In fact everybody called her "Greedy-Guts" because she could never stop eating and always cleared the dinner table down to the last crumb.

Her mother, the princess Malvolia, was the very opposite of her daughter, thin and withered like a nail. Princess Malvolia hardly ever ate anything as she did not want to get fat, and when she did pop a morsel or two into her mouth, she always took the utmost care beforehand, consulting the court alchemist and choosing with his help the least fattening of foods. Of course she was always melancholy, and spiteful observers said that she sighed as much as she did "because people who don't eat have thin blood." But the princess, on the contrary, maintained that all her melancholy was caused by the fact of having her excessively fat daughter around her all day long.

"A fat woman," she would remark between sighs, "cannot have that regal look about her which a true lady of a castle should have."

The eighteen-year-old Amaryllis, however, was as merry as her mother was sad. She got on very well with her father, Prince Propertius, because he was of the same good humour, forever laughing and joking with his daughter since both refused to take life too seriously. Like all born potentates, Prince Propertius was not exactly rushed off his feet, and would spend his days playing tricks and jokes on all and sundry. Of course these pranks caused a great deal of mirth and, with the exception of Princess Malvolia, everyone joined in the laughter, including the victims.

One day it so happened that a certain Baron Brandon arrived at the castle, accompanied by his young nephew Edmund. The two were returning home, having spent some time at a spa, where the Baron had undergone treatment for his gout.

"As we are still a long way from home," the Baron said, when he spied the castle of Prince Propertius on top of a hill, "let's spend the night here."

"What will the food be like?" Edmund asked, with a trace of apprehension.

"We shall be treated as befits our noble rank, whoever the lord of the castle may be," replied Brandon somewhat arrogantly.

Propertius greeted Brandon and Edmund most warmly, if only because their arrival helped to jolt the monotony of everyday life. He had a tasty banquet prepared for them, to which he also invited as many of the local gentry as could be summoned in the time available. At table Brandon tried to eat as little as possible, because of his gout, but he could not resist the temptation of a choice pigeon roasted on the spit and containing in turn a small stuffed bird. He tucked into the pigeon, and was about to bite into the small bird when he saw two small bloody eyes staring straight at him.

Brandon turned deadly pale, while Propertius enquired of him:

"Is there something the matter, Baron?"

Brandon rose from the table and rushed from the banqueting hall into the first room he found open, where he deposited everything he had just eaten. When he rejoined the guests at the table, he had a dazed look about him; not only was he as white as a sheet, his face bore a message of doom for everyone around him.

"What has happened, Baron?" Propertius asked him once more.

Brandon pointed to his platter, where the two bloody eyes were still staring up at him.

"Those two eyes were inside my fowl. And they are still bleeding."

Propertius stretched out his hand towards Brandon's plate, siezed the two eyes and said with an angelic air:

"Two eyes, you say. They look to me like dog's eyes. And they are delicious."

In proof of which, he popped them straight into his mouth, and gobbled them down with relish, the red blood spattering his beard.

"You mean you like that sort of thing?" Brandon asked with disgust.

"Most certainly. My chef uses the very best marzipan to make them. What you thought was blood is only a red dye!"

At that juncture Propertius burst out laughing, and the mirth spread along the rows of guests. Before long the whole hall resounded with raucous guffaws. They all wanted to show how funny they found the whole thing. As the laughter subsided Brandon rose, pointed a finger at Propertius and uttered a sentence which, to judge from the tone in which it was spoken, seemed destined to be engraved in marble.

"Propertius, you are a clown."

It was the first time that Prince Propertius had ever encountered such a reaction to his practical jokes – for joke it was; as a rule everbody laughed at his jokes until they cried, and never had a bad word to say about them. He forgot that he had never tried his tricks on people who were not afraid of him.

Hearing himself thus described as a clown, Propertius soon lost the smile on his face and racked his brain for a fitting reply. But as almost always in such situations, he could think of nothing to save the occasion.

In the meantime Brandon had left the table and was preparing to leave the room, followed by Edmund. Propertius made a sign and Edmund was seized by two armed guards.

"What else does a clown like you have up his sleeve?" Brandon asked, staring fiercely into Propertius' eyes.

"I'm taking your nephew Edmund hostage," the Prince answered, with the air of someone who knows exactly what he is up to. "Just in case you feel like getting your revenge for a very innocuous joke. A joke which, everyone agrees, came off superbly. Everyone except you, that is."

"Keep my nephew, then," said Brandon with a sardonic smile. "All he's good for is chasing after women. But watch out. You'll be hearing from me before long."

So saying, he stomped out. The embarrassed silence that fell over the assembled company was shattered by a resounding guffaw. It was Edmund who, although held in the grip of the guards, was bent over double with laughter.

"And what have you got to laugh about?" Propertius asked, worried that he was about to lose control of the situation.

"I've never seen my uncle in such a rage. It's really funny," mumbled Edmund, half choking with laughter. Then he added:

"But then I've never seen a more clownish clown than you either."

"Take him away," screamed Propertius, "and lock him up at the top of the tallest tower."

That was how the evening ended, but it had a very sad aftermath, although a predictable one, seeing that powerful men were involved. Baron Brandon mobilized his army and besieged the castle of Propertius, thus embarking on a bitter battle, the outcome of which was anyone's guess.

Of course, the siege changed things for everyone at the castle. Prince Propertius lost his customary good humour and his desire to play tricks when the battle seemed to be going in favour of the hateful Brandon. Because he did not have the makings of a general, Propertius paced to and fro through the rooms of his castle, trying to look busy, and thinking that this would instil courage into his besieged subjects. Princess Malvolia grew more and more melancholy and half-starved, because she now added to her usual fasting the idea that the siege was nothing less than a holocaust. The only person having fun was Greedy-Guts Amaryllis because it was the first time she had been in a siege and seen so much military finery – all the armour and trappings of war only served to amuse her.

One day, when the siege had become a virtual stranglehold, during one of his brisk walks through the rooms of the castle, Propertius found his daughter sitting at table before the remains of a feast she had been eating, finishing off a mountain of crumbs which she so adored. Faced with the sight, the Prince's eyes darkened, not least because the siege had caused him to lose his appetite.

"How come, Greedy-Guts," he shouted, "that you can sit here stuffing yourself while our castle is under siege by the enemy?"

His daughter replied calmly:

"Do you want this silly war to be over?"

"Of course I do," thundered Propertius, and the tone of his voice seemed to lend him greater authority.

"Then you must use your brain. Leave it to me," Greedy-Guts said, getting up from the table.

"Are you going to do battle, then? On your own?" Propertius sneered.

"Not on my own, no. Get your soldiers ready to make a sally, at once."

All Propertius could do was to pretend to choke with rage, but if the truth be told he had confidence in his greedy daughter, and hurried off to order a general sortie from the castle without delay. His job, he saw as being to jolly the simpletons along.

Meanwhile, with great composure, Greedy-Guts gathered up the small mountain of crumbs she had scattered across

the table and went on to the battlements to shake out the tablecloth on the heads of Brandon's troops below at the very moment when Propertius's soldiers mounted a surprise attack across the lowered drawbridge.

The effect of the crumbs scattered over the enemy camp was decisive. In fact all the horsemen of Baron Brandon were thrown from the saddles, because each and every horse found a crumb lodged in its nostrils, and this unbearable irritation drove all the steeds crazy. The enemy artillerymen could no longer take aim and fire, because crumbs fell into their eyes, and more crumbs lodged in the ears of the foot soldiers, and so on and so forth. The soldiers were forced to scratch their ears, and could thus no longer hear their orders. What is more they could no longer march because scratching one's ears is best done standing still.

In a word, the enemy camp was thrown into confusion, so much so that Baron Brandon was forced to sue for peace. In the peace treaty which then ensued he renounced all idea of revenge, agreed to take back his nephew Edmund, who had spent the whole siege locked away in the tallest tower in the castle where the air was the most rarefied in the whole massive structure. Propertius was thoroughly fed up with looking after a young man who did absolutely nothing, ate even more than his daughter Greedy-Guts and spent all day long singing and laughing at the top of his voice.

Life at the castle resumed its normal pace, but oddly enough Greedy-Guts Amaryllis started to grow sad, and everyone was well aware of it, because not only did she find it a struggle to laugh, but she also started to grow visibly thinner, even though she went on eating as she had always done. The only person who was happy about her loss of weight was Princess Malvolia.

"At last you begin to look like a true lady, with a nice slender waist," she said to her skinny daughter.

But her contentment was short-lived, because while Greedy-Guts lost weight everywhere else in her body, she became strangely fatter around her waist, and particularly around her tummy. The court alchemists and astrologers were duly consulted, and after lengthy secret meetings they made the following prediction:

"Greedy-Guts – we beg pardon – the Princess Amaryllis, will get back to her normal state when something has come to pass."

"What sort of something?" Princess Malvolia asked anxiously.

"We cannot say. It is not written in the stars or in the retorts."

Finally the court physician was summoned and, because he was highly qualified, he gave his answers in Latin. His most important utterance was translated for Malvolia and Propertius, and it went something like this:

"Greedy-Guts, er, I beg pardon, Princess Amaryllis is sorely in need of some moon-baths."

In the end, after a minor nervous breakdown, Princess Malvolia forced Propertius to take a grip on the situation, because his daughter's tummy had grown into an enormous paunch, like a balloon, and even the way she walked had become somewhat awkward. So the Prince summoned his daughter before him, for a heart-to-heart talk.

"Greedy-Guts, . . . I'm sorry . . ., Amaryllis, what is happening to you?"

"I'm expecting a baby, papa."

The noise which echoed though the castle was caused by Princess Malvolia falling over. She had been eavesdropping in the next room, and had fallen into a dead faint on the hard floor. Propertius more or less lost the power of speech, but he managed to ask, in a voice which sounded even to him like someone else's:

"And who is responsible for this state of affairs?"

"Edmund," the girl confessed calmly, and to hear her say so seemed the most natural thing in the world.

During those hot, tedious days when the castle had been under siege, Greedy-Guts had been in the habit of visiting Edmund in his tall tower, because the air was so pure up there; what is more, he sang so well, and he always made her laugh too. You can understand that by spending so much time together the two young people had taken the odd liberty – it seemed the odd one too many.

Possibly as much to be seen to be taking some immediate action as anything else, Propertius had the guard who had connived at these illicit meetings between the two young people sentenced to be hanged, and it was only at the last minute that Greedy-Guts managed to arrange his escape. From then on, having been banished from the castle forever, the former guard never forgot the lesson of his fate: that you expiate your own guilt in making others pay for it.

Edmund readily consented to the marriage-of-amends. "Yes," he admitted, "I'm very fond of the cooking at the castle."

Baron Brandon found some excuse for not attending the wedding, and sent a duly prepared representative who, to take revenge for those eyes made of marzipan, secretly filled the organ pipes in the church with flour. As a result, instead of strains of the wedding march, the bride and groom were accompanied down the aisle by huge clouds of flour which powdered the lavish costumes of everyone present.

Straightaway Propertius declared war on Baron Brandon, but the situation sorted itself out with the birth of a son to Greedy-Guts and Edmund, called Sugarplum. So the castle once more echoed with general merriment, Sugarplum's laughter included, for he was after all born to two joyous parents.

The only person who went on sighing in the castle was Grandma Malvolia, but you can't please everybody.

Answer the following questions about the characters and goings-on in the story you have just read, with a YES, NO, *or* DO NOT KNOW.

1. Is physical appearance important in life?
   YES NO DO NOT KNOW

2. If you arrived at the castle of Prince Propertius, would you have behaved like Brandon and Edmund?
   YES NO DO NOT KNOW

3. If you had been in Edmund's shoes, would you have laughed at Brandon and Propertius?
   YES NO DO NOT KNOW

4. If on the other hand, you found yourself in Brandon's shoes, would you have declared war on Propertius?
   YES NO DO NOT KNOW

5. Was Greedy-Guts wrong in poking fun at the finery of the warriors, their armour and weapons of war?
   YES NO DO NOT KNOW

6. Does the idea of an army being defeated by crumbs irk you? YES NO DO NOT KNOW

7. Would you behave as Malvolia did on hearing that her daughter was pregnant? YES NO DO NOT KNOW

8. If you had been invited to the wedding of Greedy-Guts and Edmund and found yourself covered in flour, would you have lost your temper? YES NO DO NOT KNOW

turn to psycho-tale 4, page 68)

We are back once more with the sexuality test. Opposite and overleaf is the third pair of photographs: C and D respectively. Again you are to decide which of the two photographs, C or D, you prefer, relying on instinct rather than thought in making your choice. The psychological explanations for whatever choice you make, appear on pages 180–1.

Explanations of psycho-tales

Psycho-tale 1 (The revolt in the kitchen)

Give yourself 5 points for every YES, no points for a NO, and 1 point for every DO NOT KNOW. Add your points together and find out how you score in artistic sensibility.

Score: 0–10
Artistic sense is not your strong point, and your eye is not critical enough to take in at first glance the most interesting things from the point of view of beauty. You are probably distracted by more material interests, and by being attached to reality, you have forgotten that there also exist things which have no concrete value, but which are brimming with existential suggestions and stimuli. Good taste and an aesthetic sense can nevertheless be cultivated with a heightened awareness and the help of others. Try to attach more value to instinctive enthusiasms and indefinable feelings. Perhaps this is where the secret of good taste lies for you.

Score: 11–20
You are attached to concrete things to the point where you do not realize how much beauty passes you by. Or rather, you do realize it, now and then, but you are so busy that you do not find time to pursue stimuli which do not necessarily lead to practical ends. You have a certain presumptuousness which leads you to think that you can do without things that are beautiful but useless. Are you not afraid of becoming too materialistic? A little more artistic sense would not adversely affect the way you behave – in fact, the reverse.

Score: 21–30
You have a good aesthetic sense and you are fascinated by many sorts of stimuli, as long as they correspond to certain canons of good taste. Sometimes you even forget about reality, to chase after other refined and aesthetically satisfying experiences. You also display a little snobbery, at least when it comes to beauty, because you tend to look down on those who do not have your aesthetic sense. You must convince yourself, however, that something is missing from art if it forgets to serve everyone. Your life is certainly not tedious because if on the one hand there is a lack of beauty around you, you feel a need for it; on the other, when you find it, you live through moments that are indescribably emotional.

Score: 31–40
You have such a well-developed aesthetic sense that your judgement about the beautiful is usually correct, so you like to surround yourself with things that are harmonious in every way. But you run the risk of becoming too abstracted from reality and of appearing slightly inhuman. The truest art is art that has to do with life. At times a little more humility would help to heighten your awareness and persuade you that even the most general kind of judgement contains a modicum of truth. Your life is certainly not easy, even though it is extremely stimulating, because you are looking for beauty everywhere, and this can bring the odd disappointment.

Psycho-tale 2 (The girl with the crazy legs)

Give yourself 5 points for every NO, no points for every YES, and 1 point for every DO NOT KNOW. Add up your score and find out, by reading below, what your capacity for love is.

Score: 0–10
Your capacity for love is rather sparse. Or rather, you love yourself too much to be able to give to others the love they deserve. Your self-centeredness, which is nurtured above all by your egoism, makes you even suspicious of friendships, an attitude which leads to a general mistrust of people and situations, so you appear pessimistic to the point of cynicism. You do not hope for anything better in the future, but in your eyes this is a sign of strength rather than weakness. An open-mindedness or freedom from prejudice ensures a certain degree of success, but the price you have to pay is almost invariably solitude.

Score: 11–20
You have no great feelings of love, your habitual attitude is one of egoism. You do not trust others and pessism comes so naturally to you as to seem the only real thing on which to build your own reality. But every so often you are seized by doubts: you think that somewhere love must exist for you, and stirrings of trust and friendship make their presence felt, only to be as quickly extinguished as you revert to your abitual aloofness. You have to force yourself to understand that love is not a right, but a feeling that has to be earned and sought for.

Score 21–30
You have a reasonable capacity for love, but it needs almost continuous reviving. Sometimes you forget that in order to give and receive love you have to exert yourself, to partake, to show enthusiasm. It is true that one can also love in silence, but shouting it to the rooftops comes more naturally in some cases. The hearth of your emotional capacity is alight, but you must never tire of stoking the fire, and you will see how hope and optimism also flourish. Certainly, those near you cannot grumble about your emotional capacities, which are definitely above average.

Score: 31–40
Your capacity for love is such that, for you, love is the driving force of the universe. You have great trust in others, and consider friendship to be a particular form of love. You are convinced in fact that love is a force which can unite everyone, in certain respects at least, which is one reason why you involve yourself in many collective undertakings. Hope and optimism come naturally to you, are in fact your most enviable strengths. But your weak point could be your naivety, which acts as a screen before your eyes, so you see a reality which does not exist. Remember that true love, the love that endures, needs clarity of vision above all else.

Psycho-tale 3 (The green dog)

Give yourself 5 points for every YES, no points for every NO, and 1 point for every DO NOT KNOW. Add up your score of points, and then, by reading what follows, find out how young – or old – you are at heart.

Score: 0–10
Your true age, that is, the age within you, which has to do with attitudes, ideas and feelings, is rather advanced. You are old, in the sense, at least, that by eschewing any form of enthusiasm, you almost invariably present an attitude of disillusioned cynicism. The truth does not interest you that much because you feel that reality consists mainly of lies. You mistrust major values such as friendship or loyalty and, if you do sometimes feel a stirring of love, it is never a lively, buoyant feeling, but rather a serious, dark and even slightly tormented one. You can appear apathetic, even lazy, which constitutes a form of confidence for yourself and for those who like you, given that you use your brain, and almost never your instincts. Basically, you do not like anything new.

Score: 11–20
Your true age, your inner age, that is, is quite advanced, if one considers the serious attitudes you adopt, your conformist ideas and your controlled feelings. You are basically a pessimist and you mistrust grand ideas, because the experiences which you have had have often led to bitter results. You are afraid of the truth, because you regard it as a two-edged weapon, and loyalty and friendship seem to you to be luxuries that few can afford. And yet, at times, you feel like taking a headlong leap, saying to hell with logic, and escaping from the monotony of day-to-day things. In effect you can grow a bit younger in an inner sense, if you make better use of your enthusiasms, which tend to run out of steam.

Score: 21–30
You are sufficiently young in your inner self still to have plenty of potential generosity or dynamism to make use of. You are not averse to things that are new, you are still capable of getting involved in situations with a certain impulsiveness, you like contact with other people and have quite a strong belief in friendship. You also enjoy fantasizing, and even involving yourself in the odd grand scheme which gives you a feeling of living. You feel a certain resentment towards the society around you, but you think, somewhat optimistically, that things can change, as long as truth prevails.

Score: 31–40
You are very young at heart, with the ability to alter your attitudes in the face of interesting stimuli. You are active, dynamic, even adventurous. Above all you are an adherent of the truth, which you see as the most genuine and authentic force in life. You tend to place too great a reliance in grand ideas and schemes which give you a sense of living, and you believe that, with a view to real progress, there are always things that need changing in society. You run the risk of shutting yourself off in an unwitting form of immaturity, cocooning you in fantasies and illusions which can never be realized. You are enviably young, all the more reason to acknowledge the need for certain curbs. Remember, enthusiasm is a rare jewel; but be careful not to overplay your hand.

Psycho-tale 4 (The battle of the crumbs)

Give yourself 5 points for each NO, no points for a YES, and 1 point for each DO NOT KNOW. Add up your score of points, and then, by reading what follows, find out your capacity for irony, or, if you prefer, your sense of humour.

Score 0–10
As far as irony and sense of humour are concerned, it cannot be said that you sparkle in either instance. There is an air of pessimism about you, which shows in a marked inability to enjoy many things in life. You take life far too seriously, as a result your convictions are granite-like, impervious to any criticism. You take yourself very seriously, judging others by your own harsh standards. Since, for you, life is either all black or all white, you lack any sense of subtlety. You are not much concerned with reality, to the point that you avoid measuring yourself against others, for fear of comparisons that might undermine your ego. In some respects you have a strong character, but you need to loosen up, to let yourself go, give in and relax more often.

Score 11–20
You can do with more laughter in your life. Learn sometimes to laugh at yourself a little more, and stifle some of those rigid attitudes which often get the better of you. With a little bit of effort you can achieve that proper balance which is often the most satisfactory yardstick in human affairs. Enlarge your relationships because you do not need much to become sociable and good company. Become more involved with the concrete aspects of reality too, without trying to look too deeply into them.

Score 21–30
You are on the right path to getting the best out of life. You have a healthy ration of optimism, backed up by a bounding vitality. You are quite at home in company and, when you feel like it, can be indulgent with others – just enough not to scare them off. You steer a skilful middle course between instinct and reason, which provides you with a good moral sense, but you also appreciate the worthwhile value of doubt, so you can laugh at yourself. You could still try to laugh a little more, and slightly more freely too. A good sense of irony, like yours, is always a sign of intelligence.

Score 31–40
Your sense of humour is such that inevitably you are popular and liked. Perhaps more to the point, you view life at its most positive, managing to see a glimmer of hope even in the gloomiest of situations. With such a constant store of vitality, you manage to enjoy many aspects of life which seem to pass by others, less perceptive. You also have a solid sense of morality, a keen awareness of what is just and unjust. A developed sense of affectionate indulgence enables you to appreciate why, in life, apparently conflicting things have the right to coexist. Because of a doubting nature you do not believe in much, and are even ready to ridicule yourself. Although you tend to see things for what they are, at times you let yourself be carried away on a wave of superficiality. Nevertheless you have all the qualities that make for serenity and peace. A sense of irony like yours is the most effective means of dealing with disillusionment.

Professional aptitudes

In this chapter we present ten aptitude tests, covering a variety of professions.
In this instance we are talking about psychological aptitudes, and not the reasons that lead one to adopt a particular profession – something altogether different.
To find out to what degree you possess these fundamental aptitudes, you have to answer a series of simple questions, choosing one of the two suggested responses in each instance.
You will note that we have not indicated in advance which profession is in question so as not to influence your choice.

Test 1

1 **Which do you like more?**
- a crickets
- b ants

2 **You have half an hour for relaxation. What do you do?**
- a read a best-seller
- b listen to a music station on the radio

3 **You are in a bar or café on your own. At the other end of the room a group of people is singing in chorus. How do you react?**
- a you are pretty bored by their showing-off
- b join in the chorus

4 **During a concert a soloist plays a motif which you find very emotional:**
- a do you think others share your spiritual experience
- b are you so entranced that you feel the soloist is playing just for you

5 **Somebody gives you a brain-teasing game. How do you react?**
- a start playing straightaway, trying your best to figure it out
- b soon give up because it bores you

6 **With a group of friends you are deciding how to spend the evening:**
- a you go along with what the others decide
- b come up with your own ideas, and keep on about it

7 **You are stuck in a lift with a stranger who suffers from claustrophobia and starts acting a bit strangely:**
- a you try to offer help, keeping calm yourself
- b lose your temper and tick the person off

8 **After many years you find yourself with some schoolfriends and suddenly someone suggests a competition, "like in the old days," to see who can throw a stone farthest**
- a you refuse to join in
- b join in readily

9 **Looking at an abstract painting, what strikes you most at first glance?**
- a the composition
- b the colours

10 **You have been abroad for some time, too long, perhaps, and you hear bad things being said about the place where you were born:**
- a you are suddenly overcome with homesickness and do not know how to react, so you stay quiet

b try to change the speaker's opinion by a reasoned discussion

11 **In the hush of a wood you hear a bird singing:**
a you try to see where the sound is coming from
b stop in your tracks with a lump in your throat

12 **You are alone in a compartment in a local train, as it trundles along making its usual rhythmic noise:**
a at some stage you realize you are tapping out the rhythm with your fingers
b you do not react in any particular way

13 **You have sent a famous conductor a composition of yours, and one day the great man writes a letter suggesting a meeting:**
a you start thinking at once what you should do
b you start dreaming of all the fantastic possibilities that might come of it

14 **You are in a relaxed mood, when from your neighbour's house comes the sound of a lively piece of music which reminds you of something or someone:**
a you listen intently so as not to miss a single note
b start dancing to the beat of the music

15 **In an otherwise magnificent view there is one thing which upsets the overall effect:**
a it ruins the whole effect
b you do not worry about it, or at least you do not let it adversely affect your enjoyment

16 **During an evening with friends, there is a lull when no one has anything to say, and everyone feels a little embarrassed:**
a with all the will in the world, you do not know what to do to change the situation
b you get the conversation going again, and manage to involve more or less everyone in it

17 **You are alone on the seashore before a vast expanse of sea:**
a for no reason you remember a person or emotion not necessarily connected with the sea
b you think about the sea, its mysteriousness, and its vastness

18 **During a conversation someone clearly knows more than you about your favourite subject. How do you react?**
a you cleverly try to switch to another topic
b listen with genuine interest

(what your choices mean aptitudinally: turn to page 88)

Test 2

1 **If you fold a sheet of newspaper in 4, forty times, what, at a rough guess, would be the thickness?**
a 80 cm (2 ft. 6 in.)
b the distance between the earth and the moon

2 **Which of these sentences sounds more affectionate?**
a I would like to thank you, my friends
b My friends, I would like to thank you

3 **You find yourself shipwrecked on an island with an uncivilized native with whom you cannot exchange words because there is no common language. How do you communicate?**
a by teaching the native your language, or learning his
b by inventing a mutual language

4 **What would you do if you had just reached the summit of Mount Everest?**
a set up a device to measure the altitude of the mountain exactly
b take a photograph of yourself

5 **You have gone to a party out of mere duty and you are bored. What do you do to enliven a not very stimulating evening?**
a eat and drink to pass the time
b try to get to know as many people as possible

6 **You need to earn a specific sum of money in just one day. What would you go for?**
a selling encyclopedias door-to-door with no guarantee of selling enough
b making holes in cardboard with a special machine for eight hours with a guarantee at the end of the day that you will have earned the money you need.

7 **In order, on a sheet of white paper:**
– draw a circle without using a compass
– divide the circle into four equal segments
– beneath the circle, about half an inch away from it, draw a trunk with no lid
– starting from the trunk draw four lines which end up at the top of the circle
Now, what have you drawn?
a not very sure
b a hot-air balloon

8 **Someone has decided to sell off a series of old family swords, but is not sure which of two**

slogans to include beneath the photo of one of the swords in the publicity brochure. Which one would you recommend?
a a sword like this has many uses
b a sword like this is of no practical use

9 **After several invitations, an internationally famous financier has agreed to come to dinner at your home. What do you do?**
a invite along your ten best friends
b invite no one

10 **Two craftsmen are blowing glass. In your opinion which one is making the objects most in demand?**
a the craftsman working with other craftsmen
b the craftsmen working alone in his own workshop

11 **While waiting to be received by a person of high standing in a drawing-room full of vases and knicknacks, you break one. What do you do?**
a break the news to the first member of the household to appear
b hide away the broken bits

12 **You have to spend your holidays in an isolated village. How do you behave?**
a enjoy the peace and quiet, and do nothing much
b take photographs and make drawings of beauty spots with the idea of mounting an exhibition

13 **How many friends of either sex can you rustle up in half an hour who would come straightaway to your house?**
a more than ten
b four or five

14 **On a stroll with friends you come upon a picturesque landscape and feel like taking a photograph. How do you set it up?**
a with no people in evidence
b with one or more friends in the foreground

15 **You are working on something which you find quite interesting. To finish the job, would you:**
a work throughout the weekend
b take a rest on Saturday and Sunday, and start again on Monday with a clear head

16 **Using a photograph of a child to advertise a new food, which of these two subjects would you choose?**
a a well-dressed baby
b an untidy baby

(what your choices mean aptitudinally: turn to page 88)

Test 3

1 **You come upon a child who is lost. What is your initial instinct?**
a to take it to the nearest police station
b try to find out where the child lives

2 **If you suddenly hear the word "root" mentioned what do you see before your eyes?**
a a tree
b the square root sign

3 **Which of these two telegrams would you rather receive?**
a the Nobel prize awaits you
b In honour of your eminent work our Academy has conferred upon you the Nobel prize in the name of the international scientific community and hereby respectfully invites you to the award ceremony

4 **If forced to, would you prefer to live:**
a in a futuristic city built on the seabed
b in a country cottage with no mod. cons

5 **Answer this question without making any written calculations: if a clock strikes 4 in 3 seconds, how long will it take to strike 10?**
a 6 seconds
b $7\frac{1}{2}$ seconds

6 **If someone in front of you says, "in my day," what do you instinctively feel?**
a a feeling of human solidarity
b a sense of boredom

7 **If you had to play either of these card games, which would you prefer?**
a bridge
b poker

8 **If an object on your desk, at home or at work, is not where it usually is:**
a do you put it back in its usual place
b not bother, and leave it where it is

9 **Do you prefer:**
a an abstract picture which stirs up a strong feeling in you, even though you do not understand it
b a realistic painting with a landscape which stirs up a mild feeling, and which you understand perfectly

10 **Which would you rather watch:**
a a patient wood-carver
b a machine producing metal rods at high speed

11 **Driving in a city which you do not know well, you fail to find the place you are looking for:**
a you rely on street-maps and your sense of direction
b keep asking the way

12 **When people tell you that wood is "living":**
a you remain basically indifferent
b feel a sort of thrill

13 **Would you rather get lost:**
a in a maze
b in a castle

14 **If you have to get your revenge:**
a you do so straightaway
b put it off

15 **On TV would you rather watch:**
a a long documentary
b a short play

16 **For mankind which do you consider more important:**
a the inventor of the compass
b the inventor of musical notes

17 **In an old palace would you derive more pleasure by discovering:**
a a carefully tended garden
b a garden growing wild

18 **If you had to give yourself a toy as a present, would you buy?**
a a box of paints
b a radio-controlled car

19 **If someone drags you into a discussion where you know that you are right:**
a at a certain stage you give up in the face of the stubbornness of the other person
b carry on without getting irritated

20 **If you had to make an interplanetary journey, which would you rather have with you?**
a a robot which hardly ever makes mistakes
b a colleague who might make mistakes

21 **To fill your free time would you rather:**
a play tombola
b do a complicated jigsaw puzzle

22 **In a given situation, do you prefer?:**
a to await the outcome
b anticipate events

23 **If you found a prehistoric graffito in the shape of a half-moon on a rock, what would you immediately think of?**
- a a clear sign of a love of nature
- b an undecipherable symbolic language

24 **You lose a needle in a haystack and must find it at all costs:**
- a you start looking straightaway
- b you split the hay into sheafs

25 **With your friends, how do you describe your car?**
- a by a nickname
- b by the offical make

26 **If people ask for your opinion, do you prefer to give it:**
- a if it is something interesting which you are not that familiar with
- b about something which is not interesting but which you know about

27 **Do you prefer:**
- a an egg today
- b the hen tomorrow

28 **Can you answer this question in 10 seconds without making written calculations or drawings**
- a in a Chinese box there are three Chinese boxes, each of which contains two smaller Chinese boxes and in each of these smaller boxes there are three even smaller boxes. How many boxes are there in all?
- a twenty-eight
- b twenty-four

29 **If you had to be a spy would you rather:**
- a decipher secret codes
- b intercept communications

30 **If a project of yours is rejected out of hand, would you rather hear:**
- a that it was too imaginative
- b that it was too inflexible

(what your choices mean aptitudinally: turn to page 89)

Test 4

[1] **Faced with a piece of wood, what might your reaction be?**
a that it only needed the genius of a craftsman to bring it alive
b your eye takes in its shape and colour

[2] **You see somebody handling an object with dexterous movements:**
a you envy him
b are indifferent

[3] **To outline a scheme to someone:**
a you use paper and pencil
b explain it in words

[4] **Instinctively you tend:**
a to do things quickly
b make progress slowly but well

[5] **If you get a detail wrong:**
a you try to put it right
b start all over again

[6] **If you lived in the jungle, would you rather:**
a be Tarzan
b live with a tribe

[7] **When you embark on something:**
a you are clear in your mind as to how it will end up
b improvise as you go along

[8] **For you dawn is:**
a above all an emotional experience
b merely a physical phenomenon

[9] **For the same amount of money, would you furnish your home with:**
a something 70–80-years old
b something modern

[10] **If an apple fell off a tree on to your head:**
a would you think of Newton and the law of gravity
b eat it

[11] **In an attractive landscape which do your eyes light on first?**
a the shapes
b the colours

[12] **Would you rather:**
a write a letter
b solve a mathematical problem

[13] **Would you rather:**
a do something enjoyable for nothing
b something tedious, but well paid

[14] **If you picked up a paper-clip:**
a would you twirl it round your finger
b bend it to form different shapes

[15] **Playing hide-and-seek:**
a would you rather hide
b seek your playmates

[16] **Knowing that in the end you will find yourself unemployed, would you rather:**
a work for 20 years for $50,000 a year
b work for 10 years for $200,000 a year

17 **If you were a Renaissance prince, would you prefer to have in your court:**
a a thousand people less capable than you
b ten people more capable than you

18 **Would you rather:**
a give a wrong order
b receive a right order

19 **When someone is introduced to you, do you think:**
a how he or she could be of help to you
b how you could help this person

20 **Would you rather have**
a a squirrel
b a beaver

21 **You see darkness as:**
a black, pure and simple
b a mixture of colours

22 **For the same reward would you rather:**
a spend a day mending a clock
b move something very heavy for one hour

23 **Which would you ask of Aladdin's magic lamp?**
a good health
b the ability to fly

24 **Hearing an echo in the mountains:**
a would you remain enchanted like a child
b try to find out where it is coming from

25 **With a barrel of water in the desert, would you**
a keep it for drinking
b exchange it for something useful

26 **Which do you see as more important?**
a hand
b foot

27 **Wold you rather:**
a sample a tasty dish
b watch a soap bubble

28 **Of the two, who in your opinion is more important:**
a the first artist to use colour
b the first artist to use perspective

29 **When you see a swinging light:**
a does it bring hypnosis to mind
b shades of Galileo

(what your choices mean aptitudinally: turn to page 89)

Test 5

1 **Which in your opinion has proved the greater benefactor to mankind?**
a Marconi, inventor of radio
b Stephenson, inventor of the steam engine

2 **Which attracts you more?**
a a well of clear water
b a water wheel

3 **Which hurts you more?**
a a slap
b a look of disdain

4 **Before a beautiful sunset what is your first instinct?**
a to recite poetry
b stay silent

5 **Which do you find more pleasing?**
a a peacock
b a duckling

6 **As a rule are you more at ease?**
a alone
b with other people

7 **An empty stage, a light projector, what significance have they for you?**
a as stage props
b a potential show

8 **Modesty apart, how much do you like yourself?**
a a lot
b not much

9 **In a field in June what first catches your eye?**
a ears of corn
b poppies

10 **Which annoys you most about someone talking?**
a wrong pronunciation
b grammatical mistakes.

11 **Recounting something that has happened to you:**
a do you tell it straight out, and invent nothing
b draw it out, laying it on a bit

12 **When someone pays you a compliment:**
a you accept it graciously
b suspect the motives of the speaker

[13] **Would you rather:**
a listen
b do the talking

[14] **If visiting a friend's house you use a coat-stand which has another coat hanging on it, what do you do?**
a look where to put yours
b see if you recognize the overcoat of someone you know

[15] **Would you rather be:**
a a small-town notable
b a senator

[16] **If a self-important person slips and falls down in front of you, luckily with no injury to himself, what would you do?**
a offer help
b burst out laughing

[17] **When you see an antique what first comes into your mind?**
a who its first owner was
b where you could put it at home

[18] **Someone you know has done something out of character. How do you explain it to others?**
a cannot understand it
b I know what's going on inside him

[19] **In love would you rather have:**
a fidelity
b experience

[20] **Would you have more fun:**
a wrapping the Coliseum in brown paper
b holidaying in the Bahamas

[21] **If someone talking to you has a nervous twitch:**
a do you have to stop yourself copying him
b hardly notice it

(what your choices mean aptitudinally: turn to page 90)

Test 6

1 **If you had a choice of holiday, would you:**
a spend three days in the Mato Grosso
b a fortnight in Venice

2 **As leader of a group, you make an error of judgement:**
a do you put the blame on those under you
b assume full responsibility yourself

3 **A car is advertised which runs on wine:**
a would you buy this prototype
b opt for a traditional model

4 **The most important world heads of state are attending a banquet, it is your job to seat them at table. Would you:**
a entrust the job to a career diplomat
b use your own judgement

5 **In a study of marital problems, would you:**
a fall back on direct experience
b consult books on the subject

6 **Would you rather:**
a thread a needle
b split a log in two

7 **In your view is charm a quality:**
a which can be acquired by training
b is innate

8 **On your way to an important reception you realize your shoes have different, if same-coloured, laces:**
a do you go home and change them
b ignore it, thinking no one will notice anyway

9 **You are asked to write a short note on Dante:**
a do you rely on what you already know
b consult at least one book on the subject

10 **A friend announces that he intends to devote himself to painting:**
a do you offer encouragement
b point out the inevitable problems

11 **You are on a first-time visit to a city famed for its historic buildings:**
a do you ask the palaces questions
b do the palaces ask you questions

12 **You have started a job which will take some days to complete; you feel tired by the end of the first day:**
a are you proud of what you have done so far
b demoralized by how much there is still to do

13 **Someone tells you a secret and asks you not to tell a soul. Although you know that to reveal it would be to the advantage of the person who has confided in you:**
a you tell everything
b keep mum

14 **If someone gives you a robot that can cook:**
a do you make use of it
b distrust it

15 **If one of these two activities excluded the other, would you rather devote half an hour a day to:**
a reading the papers
b having forty winks

16 **Would you rather:**
a win $10,000 in a lottery
b learn a foreign language properly

17 **If you found a crocodile in the bath:**
a would you telephone the police for help
b call the zoo

18 **If someone of roughly your own strength challenged you to an arm-wrestling match in public:**
a would you accept
b refuse

19 **Who do you think has been more useful to mankind:**
a the inventor of the hat
b the inventor of the wallet

20 **If you found yourself in a hotel high up in the mountains, where it rained nonstop for three days:**
a would you leave
b organize a treasure hunt

21 **How would you rather people thought of you:**
a as a logical person
b an original person

22 **If you were lost in the jungle with a group of trippers, to find your way:**

Continuing with the sexuality test: opposite and overleaf is the fourth pair of photographs, I and II respectively. Note which of the two photographs you prefer, and add your choice to the previous choice between C and D. *Explanations on pages 180–1.*

a would you follow someone else's orders
b take over command yourself

23 **Seeing a person for the first time:**
a can you identify at least three of his character traits
b find it difficult to type him straightaway

24 **If asked when the French Revolution started and you do not have an encyclopedia within reach:**
a do you blurt out the first date which comes into your head, hoping it is the right one
b say you would have to look it up

25 **If you met the yeti – the abominable snowman – on a Himalayan mountain track:**
a would you take flight in terror
b yell for your companions to come and have a look

26 **Would you rather:**
a win an international literary prize
b be the first person on Mars

27 **To be a good businessman:**
a you must never tell lies
b you must tell lies

28 **Glancing at a passer-by, how many details of his or her clothing would you remember the following day:**
a just one
b at least five

29 **During a journey in unexplored territory would you rather photograph:**
a a prehistoric mammoth
b a butterfly that has never been seen before

(what your choices mean aptitudinally: turn to page 90)

Test 7

1 **In your opinion what does one person plus another together make up?**
a two people
b a small group

2 **Confronted with a tempting sweet which healthwise it would be in your interests to avoid:**
a do you forego it
b succumb to temptation

3 **What does friendship mean to you?**
a has its ups and downs
b something to be cherished

4 **If you are bothered by a persistent fly, do you:**
a open the window to get rid of it.
b fetch a fly-spray

5 **If forced to tell your partner that you intend to leave him or her:**
a do you write a letter
b say it to the partner's face

6 **If you won $50,000 in a lottery:**
a would you invest it
b spend and enjoy it

7 **Someone of the same sex appears naked before you and asks you to rub suntan lotion over his/her whole body:**
a you feel embarrassed
b do so quite naturally

8 **Instinctively, when watching a boxing match or other sport, whose side are you on?**
a the winner's
b the loser's

9 **Which annoys you more?**
a a flaunted virtue
b a flaunted flaw

10 **If you had a son would you rather he married:**
a a beautiful but characterless woman
b an ugly but intelligent woman

11 **Which do you instinctively like better?**
a human beings
b animals

12 **Looking from a window you see on the window ledge opposite someone who looks as if he is about to throw himself off. Instinctively:**
a do you reason with him
b turn away, albeit to phone the police

13 **Do you prefer:**
a to carry out an agreeable order
b give a disagreeable order

14 **You see human beings as:**
a basically unhappy
b basically false

15 **Alone with a stranger in a train compartment, he starts talking to you:**
a you remain on your guard and feel annoyed
b launch spontaneously into a conversation

16 **Someone tells you he has made a particular gesture, having been prompted by some mysterious instinct:**
a you believe it
b remain sceptical

17 **Are you happier to be with:**

a someone who may be of use to you
b someone from whom you can learn

18 **You have to give a nasty medicine to a child:**
a you use persuasion
b force it down the child's throat

19 **Would you rather deal with:**
a someone extravagant
b any other kind of person

20 **If you have a hobby:**
a do you regret not having made it your profession
b feel contented that it serves as a means of escape

21 **Do you feel drawn towards things beautiful but useless?**
a very rarely
b often

22 **If a person starts to cry in front of you:**
a do you respond with a pat on the back
b get him or her to talk over their problems

23 **When someone talks to you:**
a do you show instinctive trust
b instinctive mistrust

24 **When talking to someone are you more concerned with:**
a making an impression
b allowing yourself to be persuaded

25 **How do you evaluate fear?**
a as something to be ashamed of
b a natural reaction

26 **You recognize goodness as:**
a a strength
b a weakness

27 **Which has more meaning for you?**
a a smile
b a tear

28 **Someone tells you he can climb the stairs of a skyscraper three at a time without stopping:**
a you try to justify his boasting
b despise him for showing off

29 **Would you rather:**
a act the realist with a dreamer
b cheer up someone who is down in the dumps

(what your choices mean aptitudinally: turn to page 91)

Test 8

1 **When you listen to your favourite music:**
a do precise images flood into your mind
b just vaguely defined sensations

2 **In Leonardo's famous painting, the Mona Lisa has one hand resting on the other:**
a is her right hand resting on her left
b her left hand resting on her right

3 **Would you have preferred:**
a Los Angeles in the mountains like Denver
b New York surrounded by the sea like Venice

4 **To make a mask you have at your disposal a piece of black material and a piece of white material:**
a you make a pirate's mask, using the black material for a blindfold and the white material knotted over your head like a handkerchief
b you make an African-type mask, with the black material covering the face with holes for the eyes, nose and mouth, and the white material wound round the head like a turban

5 **Which would you rather stroke?**
a a dog
b a piece of velvet

6 **Do you usually dream:**
a in colour
b black and white

7 **Watching a sunset do you think:**
a what tomorrow will bring
b what today has brought

8 **Would you rather be bored:**
a alone
b in a group

9 **In a restaurant would you rather order:**
a a dish you have never tried before
b one you are familiar with

10 **Which stirs you more?**
a a colour
b a piece of music

11 **When someone is introduced to you:**
a do you try to guess what type of person he or she is
b pay heed to what people say about the person

[12] **Would you rather learn to use:**
a the boomerang of the Australian aborigines
b the smoke signals of the American Indians

[13] **How do you react to another's gaffe?**
a make clear you recognize it as such
b make a joke of it

[14] **Ten people suddenly turn up for dinner:**
a do you take them out to a restaurant
b empty the icebox of its contents and make do with what you've got

[15] **What immediately attracts you in a face?**
a the overall expression
b the eyes

[16] **A less than famous painter friend offers to give you anything of his you care to choose. Which would you take?**
a his secondhand car
b one of his paintings

[17] **Do you prefer:**
a a flat landscape
b a hilly landscape

[18] **You have seen a piece of antique furniture which you would like to buy. To win over your partner to the idea:**
a do you take him or her to the shop
b describe the item in detail

[19] **You have made a mistake. What do you say to someone asking you to explain yourself:**
a even the best people make mistakes sometimes
b don't know how it happened

[20] **Standing before a famous monument like Westminster Abbey or the Empire State Building do you:**
a accept it as it is
b feel like changing it in at least one minor detail

[21] **You have set off by car for the weekend; on the way the engine develops trouble; road works force you to drive 60 miles out of your way, and it's started to rain cats and dogs. You've got a splitting headache as well:**
a do you carry on nevertheless
b decide to turn back

[22] **A large sheet of white paper has been left on a table:**
a do you wonder who might have left it there
b have a sudden desire to doodle something on it

[23] **When travelling, which are more important:**
a ideas you may pick up for future use
b the pleasureable sensations of a new environment

[24] **To mend a household gadget, you have taken it to pieces and don't know how to put it together again:**
a you keep on trying
b call in an expert

[25] **Would you rather:**
a be popular with a lot of people
b amaze just one person

(what your choices mean aptitudinally: turn to page 91)

Test 9

1 **You see someone talking to a plant. Does it immediately strike you as the action of:**
a a lunatic
b an expert

2 **Would you rather:**
a tire yourself out with some manual work
b be bored

3 **If you had to live in a community would you rather it was:**
a a groups of animals
b human beings

4 **When alone, do you prefer to sing:**
a outdoors
b indoors

5 **Watching a drop of water slide down a pane of glass:**
a do you wait and see where it will end up
b trace out a route for it with your finger

6 **Each change of season means for you:**
a a total change of clothing
b total change of habits

7 **Would you say a natural disaster such as a flood is the result of:**
a man's carelessness
b the violence of nature

8 **For want of other alternatives would you rather follow the advice of:**
a a proverb
b a computer

9 **Would you rather gaze at a very beautiful and striking face:**
a in a painting
b in a passer-by whom you will never set eyes on again

10 **You have felt more remorse when you have unintentionally**
a torn a page from a book
b pulled up a flower in a greenhouse

11 **When something goes wrong, do you lay most of the blame:**
a on yourself
b on fate

12 **A chicken for you is an animal which produces first and foremost:**
a chicks
b a tasty soup

13 **A white cloud floating across a blue sky means for you**
a an imminent change of weather
b an emotion

14 **Would you rather:**
a understand
b have a good time

15 **Would you rather eat:**
a a loaf of bread fresh from a wood-fired oven
b caviar fresh from the Caspian Sea

16 **If you saw two animals mating, would you exhibit:**
a curiosity
b disgust

17 **When you were a child did you prefer:**
a building a new toy
b breaking up an old toy

18 **Would you rather be involved in a project that is:**
a stimulating, with long-term results
b ordinary, with instant results

19 **If you were to be reincarnated, would you rather:**
a have the patience of an ox
b the liveliness of a cockerel

20 **If from far off you spied the outline of an isolated building in splendid countryside, what would you think it was?**
a a holiday home
b a farm

21 **Would you rather visit:**
a a spot you have not seen before in uncomfortable conditions
b a place you already know in comfortable conditions

22 **Which moves you more?**
a a baby crying
b a Beethoven symphony

23 **It rains after a long dry spell. Immediately you think it will:**
a spoil some project or other of yours
b bring relief to plants

Test 10

1 **After cooking, you have some leftover dough. What would you make with it?**
a some tarts
b a flower design

2 **Have you ever felt like:**
a moving a famous monument somewhere else
b giving it a complete cleanup

3 **Where do you think the word is headed for?**
a damnation
b better times

4 **Would you rather work:**
a from 6 am to midday
b 6 pm to midnight

5 **You meet an old friend who has acquired a set of obviously ill-fitting false teeth. Do you:**
a let your friend do the talking
b try to do most of the talking yourself

6 **What do you remember most about a place where you spent a holiday?**
a the smells, sounds and colours
b the arrangement of the rooms

7 **You prefer to see a city-square**
a full of people
b empty

8 **As a shape which appeals to you more?**
a a dry branch of wood
b a bean pod

9 **How do you visualize the functioning of the human hand?**
a as a sort of lever
b part of the body

10 **Would you rather live:**
a in the 19th century
b in the late 21st century

11 **How does a house with a windowless façade affect you?**
a as something unfinished
b not unfinished

12 **You are at home alone for a whole day:**
a do you stay in your dressing gown
b dress normally

24 **You are looking at an abstract all-green painting. Instinctively you think it is meant to represent:**
a some kind of material; an emotion.
b grass

25 **A human and a wild animal show some kind of understanding between them. In your opinion:**
a this is normal in certain circumstances
b totally abnormal

26 **Would you rather have:**
a a delicate hand
b a strong hand

27 **Would you rather spend most of your time:**
a indoors in comfort
b outdoors

28 **When you see a lovely flower in a meadow:**
a do you admire the colour and the scent
b try to remember the name

29 **Do you consider mankind:**
a rules nature
b is ruled by nature

(what your choices mean aptitudinally: turn to page 92)

13 **A rose looks better:**
a in a small garden
b in a decorative vase

14 **Would you describe today as:**
a the preparation for tomorrow
b the conclusion of yesterday

15 **Would you more readily rid a room of:**
a a cobweb on the ceiling
b crumbs on the floor

16 **Visiting a museum what is the first thing you feel?**
a excitement
b respect

17 **Out for a stroll in the country:**
a do you, where possible, take short cuts
b follow a meandering path

18 **What would you rather see inside a transparent glass cube?**
a solid shapes
b colours

19 **What does the word "cavern" convey to you?**
a gnomes
b damp

20 **Would you rather have:**
a an ordinary house which resembles its occupants
b an original house which does not resemble its occupants

21 **Would you rather use an old beam:**
a to fix the ceiling of an old country cottage
b mend an antique piece of furniture

22 **To fill the empty spaces in a library you have to buy a hundred books:**
a would you choose them one by one, irrespective of size, and colour of binding
b go for rows of books of uniform size and same kind of binding

23 **When you look at an empty stage what do you instinctively imagine?**
a receiving applause as an actor or musician
b filling it with your own scenes and characters

24 **Coming across a fine piece of material do you see it being used for:**
a a dress
b covering for a divan

25 **If a child asks you to come and play, would you prefer:**
a a game of hide and seek
b an educational pastime

(what your choices mean aptitudinally: turn to page 92)

Explanations of tests 1–10

Test 1

Using the table below, award yourself marks for each choice you have made. Then add up the two scores, "a" and "b." The total represents your degree of professional aptitude as shown in the aptitudinal diagram (below).

question	score "a"	score "b"
1	1	3
2	4	1
3	0	3
4	1	4
5	4	0
6	0	3
7	3	0
8	0	3
9	4	1
10	0	3
11	1	4
12	4	0
13	1	3
14	1	2
15	4	0
16	0	2
17	4	1
18	0	3

Total a + b ....

Check your total score with the aptitudinal diagram:

If your score falls within the light area (1 to 20), your aptitude for music is virtually nil.
If it falls within the middle area (21–40), your aptitude is at best mediocre.
If your score falls within the darker area (41–60), your aptitude for music is high.

Test 2

Using the table below, award yourself marks for each choice you have made. Then add up the two scores, "a" and "b." The total represents your degree of professional aptitude as shown in the aptitudinal diagram (below).

question	score "a"	score "b"
1	0	4
2	4	1
3	1	4
4	4	1
5	0	4
6	4	0
7	0	3
8	0	4
9	0	3
10	4	0
11	4	0
12	0	4
13	3	0
14	4	1
15	4	0
16	0	3

Total a + b ....

Check your total score with the aptitudinal diagram:

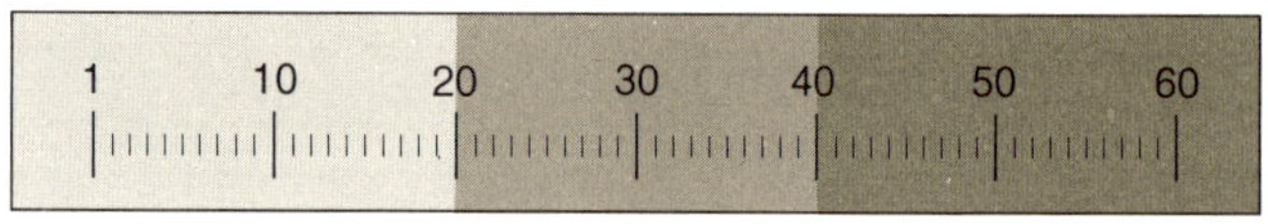

If your score falls within the light area (1–20), you have virtually no aptitude for advertising.
If it falls within the middle area (21–40) your aptitude is no better than mediocre.
If your score falls within the darker area (41–60) your aptitude for advertising is high.

Test 3

Using the table below, award yourself marks for each choice you have made. Then add up the two scores, "a" and "b." The total represents your degree of professional aptitude as shown in the aptitudinal diagram (below).

question	score "a"	score "b"
1	2	1
2	0	2
3	2	0
4	2	1
5	2	0
6	0	2
7	0	2
8	2	0
9	0	2
10	0	2
11	2	0
12	0	2
13	2	0
14	0	2
15	2	0
16	1	2
17	2	0
18	0	2
19	0	2
20	2	0
21	0	2
22	2	0
23	0	2
24	0	2
25	2	0
26	2	0
27	0	2
28	2	0
29	2	0
30	0	2

Total a + b ....

Check your total score with the aptitudinal diagram:

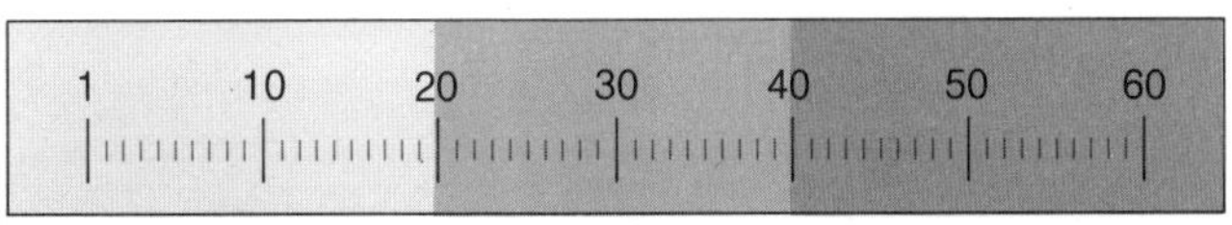

If your score falls within the light area (1 to 20), you have virtually no aptitude for computer programming.
If it falls within the middle area (21–40), your aptitude is no more than mediocre.
If your score falls within the darker area (41–60), your aptitude for computer programming is high.

Test 4

Using the table below, award yourself marks for each choice you have made. Then add up the two scores, "a" and "b." The total represents your degree of professional aptitude as shown in the aptitudinal diagram (below).

question	score "a"	score "b"
1	2	0
2	2	0
3	2	0
4	0	2
5	0	2
6	2	0
7	2	0
8	0	2
9	2	0
10	2	0
11	0	2
12	0	2
13	3	0
14	0	2
15	0	2
16	0	2
17	2	0
18	0	2
19	0	2
20	0	2
21	0	2
22	3	0
23	0	2
24	0	2
25	0	2
26	2	0
27	0	2
28	0	2
29	0	2

Total a + b ....

Check your total score with the aptitudinal diagram:

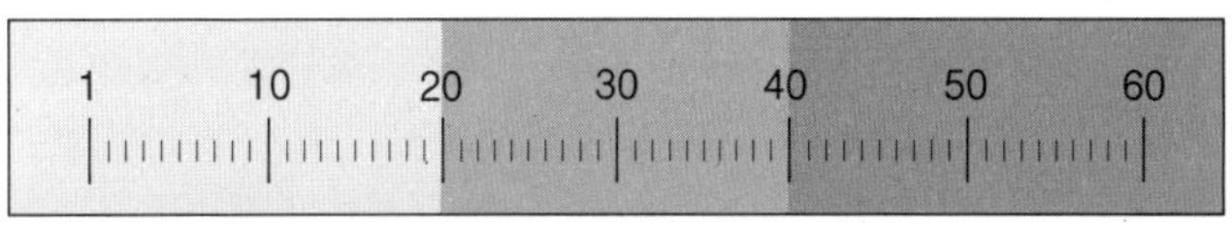

If your score falls within the light area (1–20), your aptitude for craftsmanship is virtually nil.
If it falls within the middle area (21–40), your aptitude is no better than mediocre.
If your score falls within the darker area (41–60) your aptitude for craftsmanship is high.

Test 5

Using the table below, award yourself marks for each choice you have made. Then add up the two scores, "a" and "b." The total represents your degree of professional aptitude as shown in the aptitudinal diagram (below).

question	score "a"	score "b"
1	3	0
2	3	0
3	0	2
4	3	0
5	3	0
6	0	3
7	0	3
8	3	0
9	0	3
10	3	0
11	0	3
12	3	0
13	0	3
14	0	3
15	3	0
16	0	3
17	3	0
18	0	2
19	0	2
20	3	0
21	3	0

Total a + b ....

Check your total score with the aptitudinal diagram:

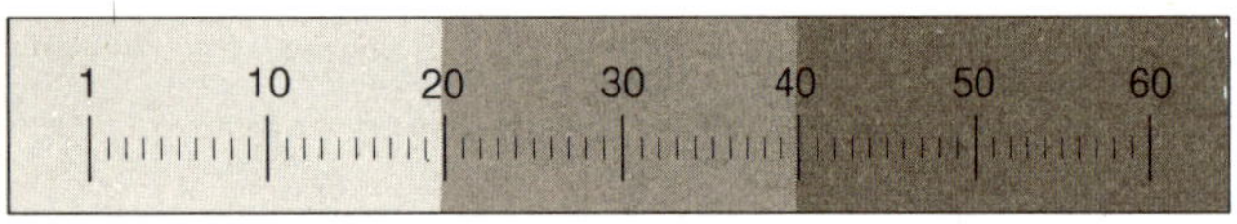

If your score falls within the light area (1–20), you are not made for the stage.
If it falls within the middle area (21–40), your aptitude for performing is no better than mediocre.
If your score falls within the darker area (41–60) your thespian aptitude is high.

Test 6

Using the table below, award yourself marks for each choice you have made. Then add up the two scores, "a" and "b." The total represents your degree of professional aptitude as shown in the aptitudinal diagram (below).

question	score "a"	score "b"
1	2	0
2	0	2
3	2	0
4	0	2
5	0	2
6	2	0
7	2	0
8	2	0
9	0	2
10	2	0
11	2	0
12	2	0
13	0	3
14	2	0
15	2	0
16	0	2
17	0	2
18	2	0
19	2	0
20	0	2
21	0	2
22	0	2
23	2	0
24	0	2
25	0	2
26	0	2
27	2	0
28	0	2
29	3	1

Total a + b ....

Check your total score with the aptitudinal diagram:

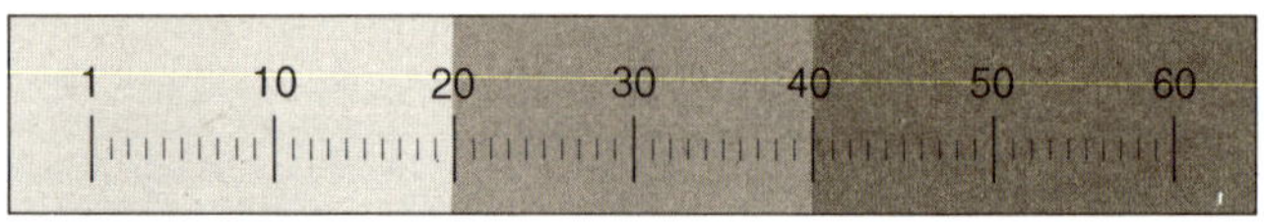

If your score falls within the light area (1–20), your aptitude for tourism is virtually nil.
If it falls within the middle area (21–40), your aptitude is no better than mediocre.
If your score falls within the darker area (41–60), your aptitude for tourism is high.

Test 7

Using the table below, award yourself marks for each choice you have made. Then add up the two scores, "a" and "b." The total represents your degree of professional aptitude as shown in the aptitudinal diagram (below).

question	score "a"	score "b"
1	0	2
2	2	0
3	0	2
4	2	0
5	0	2
6	2	0
7	0	2
8	0	2
9	0	2
10	0	2
11	2	0
12	2	0
13	0	2
14	2	0
15	0	2
16	2	0
17	0	2
18	2	0
19	0	2
20	3	0
21	0	2
22	0	2
23	2	0
24	0	2
25	0	2
26	3	0
27	0	2
28	2	0
29	0	2

Total a + b ....

Check your total score with the aptitudinal diagram:

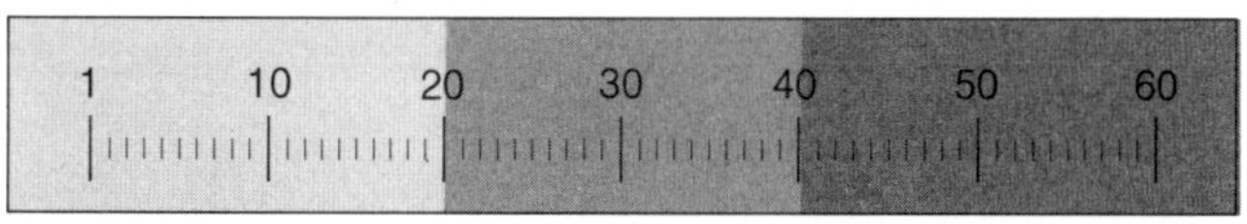

If your score falls within the light area (1–20), you have virtually no aptitude for a paramedical career.
If it falls within the middle area (21–40), your aptitude is no better than mediocre.
If your score falls within the darker area (41–60), your aptitude for a paramedical career is high.

Test 8

Using the table below, award yourself marks for each choice you have made. Then add up the two scores, "a" and "b." The total represents your degree of professional aptitude as shown in the aptitudinal diagram (below).

question	score "a"	score "b"
1	3	0
2	3	0
3	0	2
4	0	2
5	0	2
6	2	0
7	2	0
8	0	2
9	2	0
10	3	0
11	2	0
12	0	3
13	0	2
14	0	2
15	3	0
16	0	2
17	0	3
18	0	3
19	2	0
20	0	3
21	2	0
22	0	2
23	3	0
24	3	0
25	2	0

Total a + b ....

Check your total score with the aptitudinal diagram:

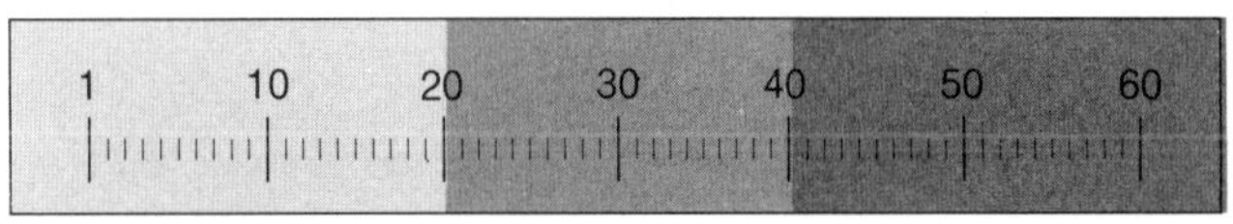

If your score falls within the light area (1–20), your aptitude for fashion is virtually nil.
If it falls within the middle area (21–40), your aptitude is no better than mediocre.
If your score falls within the darker area (41–60), your aptitude for fashion is high.

Test 9

Using the table below, award yourself marks for each choice you have made. Then add up the two scores, "a" and "b." The total represents your degree of professional aptitude as shown in the aptitudinal diagram (below).

question	score "a"	score "b"
1	0	2
2	2	0
3	2	0
4	2	0
5	2	0
6	0	2
7	2	0
8	3	0
9	0	2
10	0	2
11	2	0
12	2	0
13	2	0
14	2	0
15	2	0
16	2	0
17	2	0
18	2	0
19	2	0
20	0	2
21	2	0
22	3	0
23	0	2
24	0	2
25	2	0
26	0	2
27	0	2
28	0	2
29	2	0

Total a + b ....

Check your total score with the aptitudinal diagram:

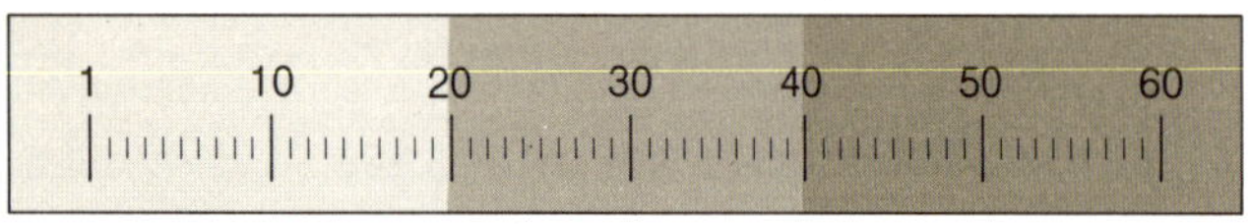

If your score falls within the light area (1–20), you have virtually no aptitude for agriculture.
If it falls within the middle area (21–40), your aptitude is no better than mediocre.
If your score falls within the darker area (41–60), your aptitude for agriculture is high.

Test 10

Using the table below, award yourself marks for each choice you have made. Then add up the two scores, "a" and "b." The total represents your degree of professional aptitude as shown in the aptitudinal diagram (below).

question	score "a"	score "b"
1	0	2
2	3	0
3	0	2
4	2	0
5	0	3
6	0	3
7	0	2
8	0	3
9	2	0
10	2	0
11	3	0
12	0	2
13	3	0
14	2	0
15	0	2
16	2	0
17	2	0
18	3	0
19	2	0
20	3	0
21	2	0
22	0	3
23	0	2
24	0	3
25	0	2

Total a + b ....

Check your total score with the aptitudinal diagram:

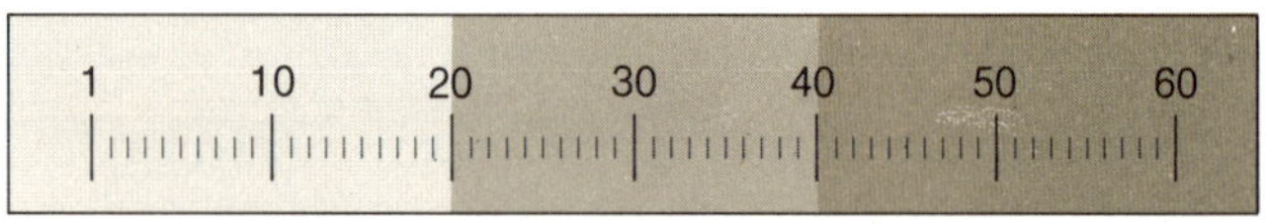

If your score falls within the light area (1–20), you have little or no aptitude for furniture design.
If it falls within the middle area (21–40), your aptitude is at best mediocre.
If your score falls within the darker area (41–60), your aptitude for furnishing is high.

Speech and character

In this chapter we examine the relationships between our way of speaking and our character. As we shall see, the links are very close and highly revealing.
We have attempted here to offer some practical suggestions as to how personality can be assessed by means of verbal communication, believing that a broad discussion of this topic is worthy of inclusion in this book because it can help us both to understand ourselves and our relationships with other people, even if it does not lend itself so obviously to "games" as do the mental tests associated with other areas of study.

The validity of speech patterns

It has always been recognized that speech and character are closely interrelated. A person who speaks in a weak, faltering tone and manner is assumed to be timid, whereas the traditional hero on the stage speaks out confidently with a strong, vibrant voice. People in a state of stress and excitement tend to spill out their words and raise the pitch of their voice, while lovers instinctively express their inner feelings in low, measured tones. It is for this reason that teachers of elocution and drama begin by impressing on their students the importance of the spoken word as the essential vehicle of thought and emotion.

The psychology of speech and language dates back to the 1950s, but prior to this scientists were already seeking to demonstrate the psysiological and, later, the psychological links between speech and character; they examined the relationship between speech processes and emotional factors, ways of thinking, social contexts and individual variability.

In 1912 Sievers distinguished four different types of speech articulation and hence four different psychological types, based on physical structure, rhythm, sound, emotional tension, etc. The four types suggested by Sievers were: 1) the abdominal type, sensitive; 2) the chest type, cold; 3) the descending type, energetic-cold; 4) the ascending type, energetic-warm.

In 1928 Drach listed four types with different speech propensities: 1) strongly impulsive, uninhibited; 2) strongly impulsive, inhibited; 3) weakly impulsive, uninhibited; 4) weakly impulsive, inhibited.

In 1934 Allport and Cantril, two American psychologists, established experimentally that traits of character and temperament can be more correctly deduced from the manner of speaking than from external characteristics.

Herzog and Bonaventura confirmed the validity of speech patterns and declared that they are particularly reliable in providing information about the sex, age, physical well-being, temperament, and even profession of individuals concerned.

Lersch wrote that in the course of a psychological session it is just as important to note the way in which a person speaks as it is to listen to what he or she is saying.

Rohracher maintained that each of us possesses an individual type of vibration that is derived from the voice and the manner of speaking, and that this has a special "expressive effect" on the listener.

A student of acoustics, Kersta, following up the enquiries begun by Gray and Kopp, demonstrated scientifically that every voice has its unmistakable impression, as clear as a fingerprint, and that this distinctive feature cannot be altered either by activities within the mouth and nose or by age. There is some truth in this assertion even though it has been subsequently shown by experiment that these vocal "prints" are influenced by many factors apart from the voice, such as tiredness, drunkenness and certain diseases. The surroundings too can affect the spectogram of the voice, depending on the point of origin.

Recently Joseph Matarazzo and his colleagues at Oregon University proved that every individual has stable speech habits, i.e. that he or she always speaks in particular ways and that each of these peculiarities explains something about the personality of the speaker and his or her feelings towards the listener. In this context it is an odd fact that the sentences we compose for speaking do not as a rule last more than thirty seconds; and if we happen to be addressing someone of a higher social rank and the latter agrees with what we have said, we then tend to lengthen the average duration of our sentences.

William H. Sheldon included the controlled and uncontrolled voice among the chief components of temperament; and it is now possible to measure the feelings, affectionate or otherwise, of a speaker addressing another person. This can be done by means of a filter which eliminates the higher frequencies of a recorded conversation – frequencies above 200 cycles a second in the case of a woman, and above 100 cycles a second for a man. In this form the words are no longer intelligible and only the vocal quality remains, from which it is easy to gauge the degree of sympathy or antipathy conveyed during the conversation.

Miller and McNeill, Moscovici, and Wiener and Mehrabian have all done detailed research on so-called paralinguistic communication, concluding that people communicate too through vocal intonation, by emphasis and by pauses.

More recently Walter Weintraub, of the University of Maryland, has devised a system for classifying certain traits of character, based on the way in which the subject under examination uses syntax, the frequency with which particular expressions recur, and the speed of delivery.

To sum up, the spoken word is the most direct way of expressing our inner thoughts and feelings; consequently it can throw light on our personality without the risk of obscurity or confusion as is sometimes produced by less direct and more problematical methods. A famous linguist, Whorf, declared that "speech is the finest play staged by man." As such we should be able to enjoy it in all its implications, even those normally concealed.

Before we begin looking into the associations of word and character, it is worth pointing out that the term "word" is used to indicate our method of expressing ourselves by speaking, and that it embraces two distinct yet inseparable concepts: voice and speech.

The voice is the sound emitted by our organs of phonation or vocalization, and this is essentially a natural, physiological process. Speech, on the other hand, is an organized sound, capable of expressing our inner needs and thus forming an integral part of our mental processes, so much so that it becomes a genuine means of regulating our behaviour. The celebrated Russian physiologist Ivan Pavlov wrote that speech is "the supreme controller of human behaviour."

In scientific terms, voice and speech are inseparable phenomena of a single physiological process, peculiar to ourselves, namely communication among all members of the human species. Communication through vocal sounds is an activity that develops in us automatically as a result of a neurophysiological maturing process. Thus we do not start to speak merely by imitating others; we speak when a physiological process, enabling us to communicate with others of our kind, is fully developed.

This propensity for speech usually begins at around the age of two years and continues to develop until about the tenth year. A normal ten-year-old child is well able to converse; after that the way in which he or she speaks will continue to alter, according to individual personality, until puberty, when the final change occurs. At this point there is no further development,

A tragic stage hero interpreted by a 19th-century actor. The confident bearing is reinforced by a strong, warm voice.

In this drawing a subject (Christopher Columbus) speaks to persons of higher social rank (Ferdinand of Aragon and Isabella of Castile) and endeavours in this instance to talk in as respectful a manner as possible, lengthening the average duration of his sentences, which in normal circumstances would each last about thirty seconds and no more.

for the speech pattern has reached maturity. At puberty, along with other neurophysiological changes, the voice likewise undergoes a profound alteration, because the larynx very rapidly increases its volume to its maximum size. In 15–20 months the diameters of the larynx grow by more than 20 millimeters, especially in boys, so that a predominantly high-pitched voice is transformed into one of much deeper tone.

The changes that affect the actual voice at puberty are more pronounced than those relating to speech itself, because the character of the latter is already precisely determined. After puberty therefore we are capable of exploiting both voice and speech to the utmost. Whereas up to this point they have tended to be used almost wholly instinctively, they now emerge increasingly as facets of our inner being, consciously adapted for our various expressive needs.

In the development of "words" every individual is subject, as in all other formative areas, to two fundamental influences – the genetic, transmitted by birth, and environmental, affecting virtually all aspects of speech. The voice, to a great extent genetically conditioned, is less likely to be influenced than speech, which is by its nature closely associated with the surroundings and with education. We have to accept our voice more or less as programmed by our chromosomes, but we can make individual corrections to our speech, moulding it to our moods, our culture and our inclinations. Yet both constitute the mirror in which we can read not only our momentary states of mind but also the basic foundations of our personality.

In this chapter we shall be considering four characteristics of the voice (register, volume, timbre and nasalization) and four characteristics of speech (diction, cadence, affectation and modulation). Each of these can be associated with some character trait, easily identifiable by the reader, who may find it of interest either for self-appraisal, or for a psychological assessment of someone else. So in this respect, our chapter on speech and character can rightfully be included as a subject for psychological games.

The register of the voice

When we speak, our vocal cords emit vibrations which continuously vary in intensity. The number of vibrations per second produced by the vocal cords determine the pitch of the voice, in somewhat the same fashion as the strings of a guitar. If the cords are slack, they give out a deep, hollow sound; if they are taut, they produce a high, resonant sound. If they are averagely tense, they give out a balanced sound, neither too deep nor too shrill.

In singing or in ordinary vocal modulation, this variable tone quality is known as "register"; this is high-pitched when the vibrations are at a maximum, deep when they are at a minimum, and medium when they are of medium intensity.

The different speeds of vibration of the vocal cords give rise to three fundamental types of voice: the so-called "head voice," which corresponds to the high-pitched register, the "throat voice," which is that of the medium register, and the "chest voice," which is associated with the deep register.

The head voice produces a high-pitched tone which seems to resound high up in the mouth and nose cavity, in contrast to the chest voice, which appears to resound lower down in the chest cavity. Midway between these is the throat voice, which seems to emanate from the higher throat region.

Every person has a natural predisposition, physiological in origin, towards a determined average number of vibrations, but as psychological development progresses this is likely to be adapted or become subject to various reactions. Thus there is a normal register which each individual adopts normally when speaking and this may be modified as the personality develops.

There are also certain states of mind which instinctively demand a particular vocal register. A painful confession, for example, whereby some secret is revealed, will tend to be made with minimal vibrations of the vocal cords, and thus in low, grave tones, reflecting the speaker's momentary shame or embarrassment. Similarly, in whispering words of love, the vibrations are likely to be slow, so that the voice conveys a feeling of complicity and intimacy. If, on the other hand, we get into an argument, we use rapid vibrations, and our voice, emanating from the head, becomes high-pitched and excited.

The true indication, however, of a character trait is the natural, normal vocal register, which is not altered by extreme states of mind and which results from the fusion of voice that has been determined genetically and speech that has been acquired in the course of social acclimatization.

(explanations on page 105)

The woman at the top places her hands between mouth and nose. The one in the middle touches her throat. The man below presses his hands against the upper part of his stomach. These are the areas from which their voice seems to come; thus they speak, respectively, with a head voice, a throat voice and a chest voice.

The volume of the voice

The volume of the voice depends on the amount of air expelled from the lungs, so that the sound produced will be strong, weak or average. It is one of the easiest characteristics to recognize since one is immediately aware of a person who speaks loudly in a high voice, or someone who speaks softly in a low voice. So there is not a great deal to say in the way of explanation about vocal volume.

By and large, a person who speaks in high-pitched tones is almost invariably determined, even excitable, the lungs being filled with air so that they can be used to fullest capacity. Such an individual tends to be a touch conceited or, by contrast, neurotic. On the other hand, a person who speaks in a low voice always has a minimal quantity of air in the lungs, letting it out from the mouth little by little, almost with an effort. The impression is of someone who is thoughtful, serious, even unctuous and patronizing.

(explanations on page 105)

It is easy to tell which of these two people is speaking in a high-pitched voice, with exaggerated facial mimicry, and which one is replying quietly.

The timbre of the voice

The celebrated seducer Giacomo Casanova, using all his wiles to engage the lady's attention, employs a voice that will be persuasive, full of modulation and variety.

Whether a voice is monotonous or varied depends essentially on the manner in which it is formed within the mouth and nasal cavities; this process involves the tongue, the palate, the soft palate, the nature of the tissues and the contractility of the walls of the mouth and nose.

To get some notion of the complexity of the operations involved in the formation of the voice, we should remind ourselves that more than a hundred muscles come into play, and that these receive instructions from the nerve centers at the rate of fourteen impulses per second. The outcome of all these complicated physiological and psychological operations is what we call "timbre;" in the present context this can be defined basically as the quantity and variety of stresses involved in vocal delivery.

What this means is that the voice can be used in either of two ways. If it is used so that a single constituent element or group of elements predominate over all the others, the result is an impression of vocal flatness and monotony. If, on the other hand, all the elements are combined and fully exploited, the voice acquires variety and conveys a sense of lively intelligence.

A monotonous voice lacks highs and lows, resonance and modulation: by and large, it fails to reap full advantage of the potential harmonic range. The effect is rather like an insistent, predominant musical leitmotiv which, endlessly repeated, generates boredom. It is the kind of voice we use when we mumble words independently of their meaning or when we are in a certain mood, as, for example, when making a mathematical calculation or abstractedly mouthing a prayer.

A varied voice, on the other hand, makes skilful use of highs and lows, resonances and modulations, like a series of variations on a musical theme. This is a voice that seduces, persuades and engages the interest, sometimes quite independently of what is being said.

A voice that is balanced between monotony and variety is reasonably modulated in some respects and unvarying in others. It does not respond sufficiently to inner stimuli and comes alive only when certain special states of mind arouse it from its habitual torpor.

(explanations on page 106)

Nasalization

The voice is said to be nasalized when the air needed to produce phonemes or speech sounds passes mainly through the nose, excluding, either wholly or partially, the mouth cavity. This phenomenon occurs either because of pathological conditions, which obviously have no relevance in the study of personality, or because the organs responsible for speech production have assumed particular positions, perhaps as a consequence of certain attitudes related to character.

Many people therefore speak "through the nose," the mouth playing very little part in voice production. The effect is a voice that tends to whine and often becomes tiresome; it has its origins in childhood but persists in the adult should it not have freed itself completely from certain forms of conditioning. By contrast, the voice that never seems to pass through the nose is dry, matter-of-fact, almost dull, without any hint of frailty or childish overtones. Midway between the two is a voice which produces words through the mouth and nose at the same time; this tends to be soft, sometimes seemingly affected, but always attractive, probably because it evokes tender memories.

This is perhaps a good opportunity to mention voices which have a strong sexual appeal or erotic quality. Sexual attraction in either the male or female voice is, in our opinion, also due to a particular type of nasalization, neither too much nor too little but just enough to soften the intonation, making such voices rather warmer than usual, so that the sounds seem to echo from deep down to thrilling effect.

The secret of a sexually alluring voice is not of course simply a question of nasalization, because there are other elements of voice and speech – deep chest register, low volume, varied timbre, skilful modulation and the like – which all combine to create its special appeal. Even so, although it is fairly easy to recognize the nasal quality of a voice with strong sexual overtones, it is virtually impossible to define the precise nature of a warmly sensual voice, to identify its exact constituents, or to teach tricks by which it may be acquired. The sexual appeal of the voice also appears to be part of our genetic inheritance, although it is the combination of our individual attitudes that subsequently determines its true character and helps to make it even more seductive.

(explanations on page 106)

The voice can have strong sexual overtones, especially if it is fairly deep, low in volume, varied, well modulated and with a particular kind of nasal quality.

Diction

Diction or enunciation, in the sense of style of vocal delivery, should ideally be clear, distinct and pleasing to the ear. A person with poor or careless diction has trouble in pronouncing certain consonants correctly; some of these tend to be distorted in normal speech so that the sounds cannot always be identified immediately, with the result that the meaning of words and sentences is often difficult to grasp. The reason that some consonants emerge in garbled, indistinct form is that in the course of producing vocal sounds some obstacle or impediment prevents the organs concerned from functioning normally.

Faults in diction obviously differ in detail according to the language involved. In English many people experience difficulty in pronouncing correctly the "r," "s," "t" and "th" sounds. Yet even these inaccuracies are not necessarily due to physiological defects, and many people who stammer or mumble their words, sometimes to the point of unintelligibility, are not invariably suffering from a congenital handicap.

Certain forms of poor diction may be due to insufficient or excessive salivation, which is a defect only if constant rather than temporary, since the salivary glands often stop functioning under certain conditions of stress. If there is too little saliva produced, speech tends to be dry and mumbled, whereas if there is too much, the words are literally spat or dribbled out.

Some faults of diction may be explained in the context of the surroundings, inasmuch as they are confined to a particular region, perhaps a single town, or maybe merely to a social class. In such cases any striking errors in pronunciation can be attributed to individual choice or upbringing and not in large measure to a physiological defect. Where such peculiarities are collective, they may develop into local jargon or slang, and obviously have no bearing on individual psychology.

(explanations on page 107)

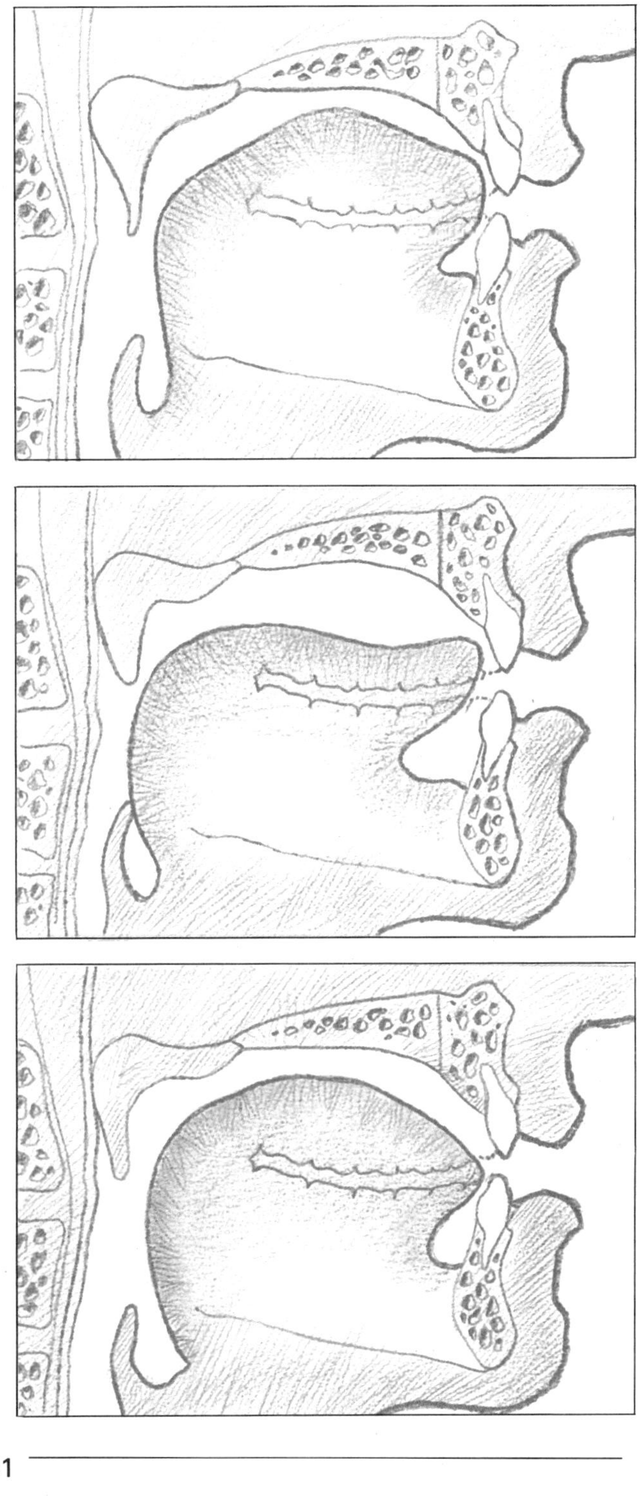

In the top figure the position of the tongue is shown when a palatal "c" is pronounced. In the center its position is seen when an "r" is pronounced; and in the bottom figure when an "s" is pronounced. The various defects of pronunciation are mainly due to a wrong positioning of the tongue.

Speech cadence

Each of us speaks at a constant speed, and this is described as our individual speech cadence or rhythm. It is determined not only by the frequency with which syllables and words are articulated but mainly by pauses between words, phrases and sentences; and this is to a large extent a matter of social background and surroundings. We all speak according to a precise rhythm of breathing, but even breathing depends on emotional factors or at any rate individual attitudes.

Certain emotions may temporarily slow down the movements whereby our speech is articulated, just as others may increase their frequency only for a limited period. Almost all adults can pronounce up to 500 syllables per minute in particular circumstances, yet certain painful or dramatic sensations may slow down speech to the point of arresting it altogether.

If what we are saying is complicated, the cadence is slower and more carefully thought out, whereas when we are expressing relatively simple ideas in normal conversation, using familiar terms and idioms, the words flow more naturally and at a higher rate.

Time also controls our thinking, in the sense that each of us organizes our ideas in our mind and then expresses them vocally within a consciously chosen time span. We punctuate our silence with sequences of verbal expressions according to a psychological pattern, delivered with an individual rhythm. So the cadence of the spoken word has a continuously organizing and regulating function; and this cadence varies with nation, language and, above all, individual. Thus it may serve to illuminate certain traits either of collective or individual character.

Some people habitually pepper the listener with an uninterrupted barrage of words, while others have a slower rate of fire, words and sentences being punctuated by intervals more or less deliberately contrived, and, provided these are not exaggerated, far less taxing for the recipient.

Speech cadence is therefore a sign of some trait of character, inborn and instinctive but subsequently conditioned by social environment and development of personality.

(explanations on page 107)

An Arab visitor to London asks a policeman for information. Which of the two do you think uses a slower vocal cadence? The answer will doubtless be evident, since every language has its own specific cadence, quite apart from individual differences.

Speech affectation

Affectation in speech is an artificial mode of expression in which particular words and phrases are given exaggerated emphasis, strung together in a way designed to buttonhole the listener and heighten the general impact of what is being said. The typically singsong manner of delivery seems to be contrived deliberately to draw attention away from the meaning and make essentially trite and commonplace ideas sound more important than they really are.

This affected method of speaking invariably aims at larger-than-life effects, as if each word were intended to seduce or inflame, shrouded perhaps in mystical significance.

Equally affected is the repeated use of strange, unaccustomed expressions which, when adopted by a restricted social group, become a form of slang. In this instance words appear to be employed not as a means of communication but as a proclamation of superiority and exclusivity, designed merely to make an impression.

Such a manner of delivery is a common fault among inexperienced actors, sometimes used simply as a way of obtaining a cheap laugh. Permissible in a comedy of manners, this cannot normally be condoned in naturalistic drama. It suggests that the actor concerned understands little or nothing of what is being said, and that the words are merely being polished as if they were somehow indecent. Good acting, like correct speech, seeks to express inner thoughts and feelings; and if there is something true and interesting to say, it should be said in the clearest and most direct manner, without resort to special trappings. It is worth noting that in the field of animal behaviour, trills, exaggerated warblings, signal bright colours and the like, are devices confined to the mating season!

Fortunately, it is quite easy to detect affectation in ordinary, everyday conversation. Apart from the tone employed, the speaker tends to adopt a boastful attitude, chin up and nose in air, as if disdainful both of the listener and the words being emitted.

There is also a form of affectation that goes to the opposite extreme, ostensibly timid and submissive but even more of a sham. The eyes are lowered, the lips pursed, yet the effect is, if anything, even more irritating. It may appear to reflect contrition yet it aims just as surely as the overtly conceited form of affectation to impress the listener, who is still being treated as an inferior. Furthermore, in comparison with the arrogant approach, it demands of its listener unconditional trust.

(explanations on page 107)

An actor portraying a comic character will heighten the visual caricature effect by using an exaggerated, affected type of speech.

Speech modulation

Some of us, when we speak normally, have a tendency to use certain words and expressions more frequently than others. As a rule these are exclamations, rhetorical questions, idioms and perhaps swear-words, adjectives with private significance, hyperbole and the like. They range from simple terms such as "right," "certainly," "absolutely," "believe me," "you know," etc. to more elaborate phrases like "isn't that right?," "do you know what I mean?," "it seems to me," "in a manner of speaking," "speaking for myself," "to be precise," and innumerable others.

In this context such expressions have virtually lost their original significance and here represent a form of modulation or inflection, a purely rhythmical treatment of a phrase. The speaker often uses them as a kind of verbal springboard for thought. Alternatively, they may provide a convenient way of pausing for breath and collecting one's thoughts.

When employed in this manner, even certain modish or obscene exclamations, when frequently repeated, lose their basic meaning and become a means of retaining the continued interest of a listener who seems not to be paying sufficient attention. Of course, conversational repetition does not consist entirely of arresting exclamations and hyperboles; more often they tend to be less conspicuous, almost involuntary, and sometimes so casual that they may go virtually unnoticed. Indeed, certain repetitions occur almost automatically, so that they are no longer proper words but more like vocal tics, subtle pleas for attention. What happens here is that the voice fades to a kind of mutter and air is expelled from the nose, so that what comes out is a succession of "ah," "eh," "er," "ih," "oh," "uh" and "um" sounds, variously intoned, or broken and incomplete consonantal sounds.

Many of us habitually modulate our sentences with these types of repetition and accentuation, almost as if the natural speech sounds were not sufficient to express our innermost thoughts with clarity and precision. When longer phrases are frequently repeated, they tend to sound like an attempt to create a kind of private language, more efficient than the speech commonly used by everyone.

In our opinion, the use of popular proverbs and idioms in conversation represents, in some measure, the psychological need we all feel to give a solid, indisputable foundation to what we are trying to say, providing confidence and reassurance. Since their meaning is so often vague and arbitrary, they do not bind or commit the speaker in any way.

(explanations on page 108)

It is very likely that these two youngsters, when speaking together, will use more repetitions and colourful exclamations than two adults. This is because certain modulations of speech, notably particular words and idiomatic phrases, frequently repeated, form the basis of a generational slang, which, once adopted, is hard to drop.

Explanations

Reading character from the register of the voice

Register
High-pitched: this is the head voice, produced by rapid vibrations of the vocal cords. The voice is shrill, often rising to a pitch of excitement. Since both the mouth and nasal cavities are fully involved, a few accompanying facial expressions are quite pronounced.

Corresponding character traits
□ Sometimes you tend to be satisfied with outward appearances. You are not too interested in delving deeply into the aspects of different situations, because you prefer to range widely, giving yourself as many options as possible, even if your objectives are somewhat vague. By and large, you go for quantity rather than quality. Basically you take a realistic approach, attracted by what you can actually see and touch. You are one of those fanciful, unpredictable people who on first acquaintance seem persuasive but who often turn out to be disappointing in the long run.

Register
Deep: this is the chest voice, produced by slow vibrations of the vocal cords. The voice is low and warm, coming from deep down. It tends to sound uniform, unemotional and deliberate, and any kind of facial expression is kept under tight control.

Corresponding character traits
■ You tend to look inwards and examine things closely. So you can be classified as an idealist rather than a realist. In your view, matters should be considered in all their aspects, however unlikely, since this is how ideas form and develop. Without individuals like yourself, there would be little progress in science and culture, from which everyone must benefit. Even so, your idealism can often prove burdensome to those close to you. You can be charming, but seldom amusing.

Register
Medium: this is the throat voice, produced by medium-speed vibrations of the vocal cords. Thus the voice never climbs too far up into the head nor does it descend all that much towards the pit of the stomach. It tends to be hard, dry and a bit harsh, not noticeably flexible or varied, lacking in elegance.

Corresponding character traits
You are one of those people who tends to waver between the superficial and the profound, uncertain whether to rush into things or to think matters out. Confronted by new situations, you cannot decide between the realistic and the idealistic approach. You are tempted by apparent realities such as success, but you are equally intrigued by the possibility of truths not immediately evident to the naked eye and requiring a greater measure of effort to be brought to light. You often feel anxious, because such conflicting attitudes are hardly conducive to peace of mind. It has to be said, however, that this is a dilemma that faces most of us – the inclination to accept the easy solution or the wish to probe more deeply into the question; in human behaviour, as in other fields, nothing is wholly black or white.

Statistically, in any research into character, extremes are rare, the majority somewhere between the two. In graphic terms the curve is bell-shaped, which is the norm both for psychological and physical valuations. Thus very tall and very short people are in the minority, most being of medium stature; and according to the studies of the psychologists Stanford and Binet, human intelligence is not distrubuted evenly among populations but conforms to the same statistical law, likewise represented by the bell-shaped curve of probabilities. Geniuses are therefore as rare as complete imbeciles, which in a sense is a comforting thought, but which tends to condemn humanity to a rather discouraging state of uniform drabness. Nevertheless, in considering human character in the widest sense, the fact that most people tend to fluctuate between extremes is perhaps more consoling, since rigid, inflexible attitudes are seldom constructive. So perhaps this midway position is healthy, inasmuch as it gives us a wide range of options, minimizing the possibility of fanaticism which throughout history has been the cause of so much cruelty and tragedy.

Reading character from the volume of the voice

Volume
High.

Corresponding character traits
△ You are a bit aggressive and so capable of exploiting all the dominant features of your personality. You are not content to accept things as they are and you enjoy competing with others. Always desirous of success, you are sometimes satisfied with making a temporary impression rather than leaving a lasting impact. Your practical abilities are considerable, but may be marred by a certain superficiality. What may appear to be bravery is more often adventurousness. Those living with you are seldom bored but may sometimes get fed up with you.

Volume
Low.

Corresponding character traits
▲ You are sometimes inclined to be compliant and rather than face reality uncritically you prefer to retire into yourself to examine it calmly. What you occasionally lose in breadth, you gain in depth, because you like delving into all aspects of a situation before committing yourself. You are serious,

thoughtful and unruffled, creating ideas rather than actions, slowly but deliberately. So your rhythm, basically, is relaxed and measured, and by reason of close analysis you manage to fend for yourself without recourse to others. This mistrust of reality and of other people leads to loneliness.

Volume
Medium, neither too high nor too low.

Corresponding character traits
You are uncertain whether to face facts or focus inwards, whether to rush somewhat heedlessly into a situation or to give it serious, detailed thought. The most obvious consequence of this uncertainty is lack of stability. Only when you do not allow this indecision to get the upper hand are you able to play your cards with confidence and come out the winner. Thus you may give the impression of unpredictability and you may even be accused of opportunism. Your Achilles' heel therefore is ambiguity.

Reading character from the timbre of the voice

Timbre
Monotonous: a flat, boring manner of speech, without variation or modulation.

Corresponding character traits
□ You have a frank, uncomplicated character and sometimes show a lack of eagerness. What motivates you most is an instinct for security. Essentially you are a realist although with a touch of ingenuousness. You tend to steer clear of obstacles so that your progress can be as trouble free as possible, and you regard fervour and excitement as pointless forms of extravagance, which prevent one from grasping facts. Unless such facts, as you interpret them, are broadly and easily comprehensible, they will not interest you. Your world may be limited but the most important thing is that it should be serene. Those close to you are unlikely to experience unpleasant surprises.

Timbre
Varied: a way of speaking in a lively manner, arousing the listener's interest, full of variation and modulation.

Corresponding character traits
■ You are a slightly complicated person and when you set yourself a target you do not necessarily pursue it in a straight line. As a rule you prefer twisted paths and vicious circles, as if protecting yourself against traps. You think a lot of yourself and are more than averagely intelligent, but this is sometimes negated by sudden impulses. Occasionally, you let these bouts of eagerness run away with you, to the detriment of your better judgement. You are not easily bored but sometimes you make heavy demands on those trying to keep pace with you. You also have artistic inclinations, but find it somewhat difficult to express them.

Timbre
Between monotonous and varied.

Corresponding character traits
You often find it hard to decide between simple and complicated choices, and as a result you swing from calmness to anxiety. When confronted with new situations, you manage to see certain aspects of the problem clearly but cloud others with complexities. Take comfort from the fact that most people come into this category, seeing everything as possible and nothing is easy.

Reading character from vocal nasalization

Nasalization
Excessive: a somewhat whining voice of someone who always speaks "through the nose," without having any particular physiological defects.

Corresponding character traits
♦ You still show slightly immature tendencies. When small, you probably began speaking "through the nose" because this form of intonation made it easier to get the affection that you felt you needed. Although you appear gentle and loving, you also tend to complain and moan a bit, perhaps expecting too much of yourself and failing to reconcile reality with your own emotional hopes and fantasies. The nasal quality of your voice is undoubtedly a mark of strong sensuality, which, nevertheless, is sometimes difficult to fulfil. You may be much loved but you are a little self-centered.

Nasalization
Absent: this is a dry, almost dull voice of someone who never adopts a nasal intonation and never gives way to any form of childish emotion.

Corresponding character traits
◊ You are a mature person in the sense of having successfully overcome problems related to childhood, not retaining any form of complex or inhibition. You are thoughtful, sensible, almost always logical, perhaps because you tend to be wary of instincts and emotions. Basically you are self-sufficient, for your attitudes and decisions are not dependent upon anything or anyone else. You are an achiever, often managing to achieve your objective, but you are liable to seem a bit insensitive.

Nasalization
Moderate: a voice with faint nasal intonation which makes it warm and soft, without affectation.

Corresponding character traits
You are often worried and unsatisfied because you enjoy going from one experience to another, even if these are almost always at opposite extremes. What really counts is trying, being involved, quite apart from concrete results. So you blow hot and cold by turns, torn between instinct and reason, sometimes succeeding, sometimes failing. Where love is concerned, you tend to depend initially on your partner to provide you with protective affection; but in the long run you are likely to free yourself of these shackles with some lack of consideration, confident of standing on your own feet, even where emotions are involved.

Reading character from diction

Diction
Clear, without defective pronunciation.

Corresponding character traits
◊ Your character is uninhibited and free of complexes, suggesting that the family and social environment in which you have grown up has been harmonious and without major shocks. This opportunity you were given to find a happy balance between your instinctive tendencies and outside reality has furnished you with a basically healthy equilibrium. As a rule you are straightforward and objective, and you are usually successful in overcoming quite painlessly the inevitable conflicts that sometimes arise between your subconscious self and external realities. Broadly speaking, you are self-reliant and self-sufficient, and this stands you in good stead when confronted with situations that may be full of tempting snares.

Diction
Poor, with signs of one or more pronunciation defects.

Corresponding character traits
♦ You experience some difficulty with relationships, probably as a result of problems encountered during your psychological development. Now that you have matured, you appear anxious and insecure, sometimes even irrational. At times you suffer from an inferiority complex and consequently you are not always able to cope properly with problems. You may overreact or become aggressive, feeling unjustly dominated and therefore seeking in your turn to impose dominance as a form of compensation.

Diction
Neither poor nor markedly clear, perhaps with a single, hardly noticeable, pronunciation defect.

Corresponding character traits
You have some inhibitions but do not necessarily let them get the better of you. Basically, you believe that you are what you make of yourself: nothing is too difficult to attempt. You are capable of going from the ridiculous to the sublime; and even if every decision costs you an effort, the chances are that it will be worthwhile. However, the fact that you hold many cards in your hand means that you may be a winner in the game of life.

Reading character from cadence

Cadence
Fast: a way of speaking smoothly and rapidly, without uncertainties and with as few pauses as possible.

Corresponding character traits
□ You are basically an emotional person and so, when you make a reasoned decision you tend to do it rather impulsively. You are intuitive rather than logical, but a feature of your emotional attitude to things is that you invariably retain some measure of self-control. Your speech is rapid, smooth and confident. Your emotional approach causes you no embarrassment and does not handicap you; thus it tends to be aggressive and overbearing, allowing others few openings that may unduly threaten you. You always aim to impress, implicate and sway other people.

Cadence
Slow: a way of speaking that is punctuated by frequent pauses, showing some degree of uncertainty.

Corresponding character traits
■ You rely mainly upon reason, liking to think everything out and tending to avoid emotional upsets. This tendency to play down the natural emotions – common to us all – has its cost. You need some kind of support when flaunting your logic in someone's presence; so you make use of pauses, sometimes feigning to search for words. By and large, yours is an exaggerated fidelity to reason, so that you often give the impression of being cold, rigid and inflexible; and sometimes your unbending logic inspires fear rather than enthusiasm.

Cadence
Moderate: midway between fluency and uncertainty.

Corresponding character traits
You are like a tightwire walker suspended between the extremes of emotion and reason. So although you hold all the winning cards in your hand, you do not always succeed in choosing the right one. You are determined to face situations rationally but you cannot dispense with instinct and are consequently troubled by uncertainty. In this, you are all too human, however, since most of us refuse to be attracted by extremes and hover somewhere in between, open to options.

Reading character from speech affectation

Affectation
Excessive: verbal communication conducted with aim to impress by means of exaggerated and uncommon expressions, slang, and a contrived, singsong intonation.

Corresponding character traits
○ You are sometimes inclined to overvalue yourself and try to conceal your shortcomings in the hope that the listener will be beguiled by the superficially musical quality of your speech. Basically, you are narcissistic, ever prepared to admire yourself and your ideas, and inclined, conversely, to underestimate those you are addressing. You may consider yourself unsatisfied and victimized in the circumstances into which you have been forced, so that you aim to climb higher in the social scale than your true merits can justify.

Affectation
Absent: a form of natural speech, without wheedling and superficial embellishments, employing no exaggerated expressions, slang terms or singsong intonation.

Corresponding character traits
● You have a proper and realistic opinion of yourself, which is always a sign of healthy balance. Furthermore, your taste for irony precludes you from adopting grandiose notions that

are unsuitable for all practical purposes. Sometimes you do not even take yourself too seriously, so much so that you undervalue your true merits. This is really a mark of sincerity, candour and unaffectedness, and these are your finest gifts. Since you can measure yourself without emphasis or exaggeration, you are not inclined to overestimate or undervalue others, so that you give an impression of fairness and not fanaticism. You do not let yourself become annoyed and angry, tending towards scepticism and cynicism, and thus you are not tempted by mystical or transcendental notions. Such characteristics enable you to clarify and simplify even the most complicated and awkward situations, especially in the area of emotional relationships.

Affectation
Moderate, between affected and natural: this is an essentially simple way of speaking, but now and then punctuated by some exaggeration, forcing of tone and singsong intonation.

Corresponding character traits
You are torn between the tendency to overvalue and, conversely, underestimate yourself, in other words, you swing between moods of euphoria and self-disparagement. In certain situations you think on a grand scale, at other times you fail to rise to the occasion. You know the value of liberty but are not always able to pursue it to the limits. For all these reasons you are slightly anxious and insecure.

Reading character from speech modulation

Modulation
Pronounced modulation of speech: a form of verbal communication with frequent and insistent repetitions, exclamations and idioms.

Corresponding character traits
□ You are somewhat insecure and even when speaking to others you have the need of reassurance. You want what you say to have the ring of truth but you are afraid of the other person's criticism. So, in order to appear persuasive, you resort to these verbal devices so as to obtain maximum attention and credibility. Basically, you are an emotional person who, when not feeling insecure, tends to be enthusiastic and optimistic.

Modulation
No speech modulation: a form of verbal communication without continual repetitions, exclamations and catchwords.

Corresponding character traits
■ Because you feel secure, your speech can flow smoothly without the need for rhythmical reinforcement to sustain your inner beliefs. You do not care if some aspects of your conversation are misunderstood because you are convinced that by and large your logic is sound and unassailable. In fact, you are so logical that you also indulge in cynicism. It is clear, without having to spell it out, that you are against all forms of exaggeration and hyperbole. Because your logical outlook is without illusions, this stands you in better stead with society than in your personal affairs, for as an individual you are likely to pay dear for your lack of enthusiasm. Indeed, indifference to passion often stifles your initiative in affairs of the heart.

Modulation
Averagely modulated speech: a form of verbal communication that resorts only now and then to repetitions, exclamations, catch phrases and the like.

Corresponding character traits
You hover between certainty and uncertainty, which means that you tend to be irresolute. You are subject to alternating emotions, because certainty so easily leads to uncertainty and vice versa; having touched the depths of uncertainty, you manage to find the strength to hang on to something stable. Nevertheless, the urge to act and the reluctance to do so seem to be simultaneous human instincts, just as inner contradictions tend in the long run to give spice and meaning to life.

We continue with our sexuality test: opposite and overleaf are photographs E and F respectively. Which do you prefer? Note, or remember, your choice.

Chart for comparative study of speech styles and character

To facilitate a comparison between methods of speech and character, the observations made in the preceding pages are here presented in chart form.

Characteristic of voice and speech		Corresponding psychological characteristic
Register	high-pitched, from head	superficiality, extroversion
	medium, from throat	fluctuation between superficiality and depth
	deep, from chest	tendency towards introversion and depth
Volume	high	aggressivity
	medium	fluctuation between aggressivity and compliance
	low	compliance, renunciation
Timbre	monotonous	simplicity
	between monotonous and varied	fluctuation between simplicity and complexity
	varied	tendency towards complexity
Nasalization	excessive	immaturity
	moderate	fluctuation between immaturity and maturity
	absent	maturity
Diction	poor	inhibitions and complexes
	between poor and clear	fluctuation between inhibitions and lack of inhibitions
	clear	no inhibitions and complexes
Cadence	fast	emotivity
	moderate	fluctuation between emotivity and rationality
	slow	rationality
Affectation	excessive	over-estimation of self
	moderate	fluctuation between over-estimation and true estimation of self
	absent	true estimation of self
Modulation	pronounced	uncertainty
	average	fluctuation between uncertainty and certainty
	absent	certainty

How would they have spoken?

At this point, having examined the eight most significant features of voice and speech as linked to personality, here is an interesting game which should prove entertaining for everyone, and which could perhaps be particularly useful for actors or would-be actors.

Choosing particular characters from history, fiction or mythology, how do you imagine they would have spoken in the light of what has been said in the preceding pages about voice and speech?

Here are a few suggested examples. It is then up to you to do the same with other characters of your choice, or with your own friends.

Hamlet
Register deep (tending to analyze)
Volume low (introverted)
Timbre varied (somewhat complex)
Nasalization moderate (part mature, part immature)
Diction poor (inhibited, with complexes)
Cadence slow (rational)
Affectation absent (true estimate of self)
Modulation pronounced (uncertain)

Madame Bovary
Register high-pitched (superficial)
Volume medium (part extrovert, part introvert)
Timbre varied (somewhat complex)
Nasalization excessive (immature)
Diction poor (inhibited, with complexes)
Cadence fast (emotional)
Affectation absent (true estimate of self)
Modulation pronounced (uncertain)

Harlequin
Register high-pitched (superficial)
Volume high (extrovert)
Timbre monotonous (simple)
Nasalization excessive (immature)
Diction clear (uninhibited)
Cadence fast (emotional)
Affectation absent (true estimate of self)
Modulation pronounced (uncertain)

Cleopatra
Register medium (hovering between superficiality and depth)
Volume high (extrovert)
Timbre varied (somewhat complex)
Nasalization excessive (immature)
Diction poor (inhibited, with complexes)
Cadence fast (emotional)
Affectation excessive (narcissist, megalomaniac)
Modulation pronounced (uncertain)

Sancho Panza
Register high-pitched (superficial)
Volume high (extrovert)
Timbre monotonous (simple)
Nasalization absent (mature)
Diction clear (uninhibited)
Cadence slow (rational)
Affectation absent (true estimate of self)
Modulation absent (certain)

Casanova
Register high-pitched (superficial)
Volume high (extrovert)
Timbre varied (somewhat complex)
Nasalization moderate (part mature, part immature)
Diction clear (uninhibited)
Cadence moderate (part emotional, part rational)
Affectation excessive (narcissist, megalomaniac)
Modulation absent (certain)

Dante
Register deep (tending to analyze)
Volume low (introvert)
Timbre varied (somewhat complex)
Nasalization absent (mature)
Diction clear (uninhibited)
Cadence moderate (part emotional, part rational)
Affectation excessive (narcissist, megalomaniac)
Modulation average (part certain, part uncertain)

Don Quixote
Register deep (tending to analyze)
Volume low (introvert)
Timbre varied (somewhat complex)
Nasalization moderate (part mature, part immature)
Diction poor (inhibited, with complexes)
Cadence moderate (part emotional, part rational)
Affectation absent (true estimate of self)
Modulation pronounced (uncertain)

Lucrezia Borgia
Register high-pitched (superficial)
Volume high (extrovert)
Timbre monotonous (simple)
Nasalization excessive (immature)
Diction poor (inhibited, with complexes)
Cadence fast (emotional)
Affectation excessive (narcissist, megalomaniac)
Modulation pronounced (uncertain)

Othello
Register medium (hovering between superficiality and depth)
Volume medium (part extrovert, part introvert)
Timbre medium (part simple, part complex)
Nasalization moderate (part mature, part immature)
Diction poor (inhibited)
Cadence fast (emotional)
Affectation absent (true estimate of self)
Modulation pronounced (uncertain)

Penelope
Register deep (tending to analyze)
Volume low (introvert)
Timbre varied (somewhat complex)
Nasalization absent (mature)
Diction between poor and clear (with some inhibitions and complexes)
Cadence moderate (part emotional, part rational)
Affectation absent (true estimate of self)
Modulation absent (certain)

Venus
Register high-pitched (superficial)
Volume high (extrovert)
Timbre monotonous (simple)
Nasalization moderate (part mature, part immature)
Diction clear (uninhibited)
Cadence moderate (part emotional, part rational)
Affectation excessive (narcissist, megalomaniac)
Modulation average (part certain, part uncertain)

Sappho
Register deep (tending to analyze)
Volume low (introvert)
Timbre varied (somewhat complex)
Nasalization excessive (immature)
Diction poor (inhibited, with complexes)
Cadence fast (emotional)
Affectation excessive (narcissist, megalomaniac)
Modulation pronounced (uncertain)

George Sand
Register deep (tending to analyze)
Volume high (extrovert)
Timbre varied (somewhat complex)
Nasalization absent (mature)
Diction clear (uninhibited)
Cadence moderate (part emotional, part rational)
Affectation excessive (narcissist, megalomaniac)
Modulation average (part certain, part uncertain)

Ulysses
Register deep (tending to analyze)
Volume high (extrovert)
Timbre medium (part simple, part complex)
Nasalization absent (mature)
Diction clear (uninhibited)
Cadence slow (rational)
Affectation absent (true estimate of self)
Modulation absent (certain)

"Do-it-yourself" psychology

In this chapter we have constructed a modern-day tale, consisting of twelve different versions, from which readers are asked to select the plot they prefer – the technique might be termed psychological "do-it-yourself."

In practice there are four interruptions in the course of the story. At each interruption the reader is faced with three tests, which serve two purposes: an immediate one, to discover at what point he should take up the story again, and the other, to provide an overall psychological insight into his own personality, through childhood, adolescence, adulthood and old age.

So each reader will indicate the plot he favours by his answers to the tests, which is why we have used the "do-it-yourself" tag.

The objective is to enable the reader to recognize the character-plot of his own life, or at least how it might be, if he remained true to his own character, no matter the circumstances.

A well-brought-up child

The cast is as follows:

Trevor Landen, *a second officer in the British Merchant Navy*
Solange Ranier, *a Frenchwoman*
Adam Benson, *an American*
Larry Benson, *his son*
Elsie Fammer, *an English waitress working in the Azores*
Hatty Glamps, *one-time fiancée of Second Officer Landen*
The captain *of the liner "Haiti"*
The owner *of a restaurant in the Azores*
A friend *of Mr. Benson*
Mr. Benson's lawyer

No sooner had he finished his meal than Second Officer Trevor Landen felt a keen desire to spend some time on his own, making the most of that half-hour which he was allowed before getting back to his duties. Not that the life of a second officer on board a luxury liner was particularly onerous; but there was not a great deal of leisure time, and Trevor found himself having too many things to ponder over in his moments of solitude. Even in his most sanguine moments, he was haunted by memories, and would ask himself what had really been the point of his going to sea, in a vain attempt to forget the past.

Trevor went up to the first-class deck for a brief stroll and suddenly saw a child, who could not be more than eight years old, who was trying to saw through one of the steel cables supporting one of the large lifeboats suspended overboard. He approached the child and with the most ingratiating smile he could muster said:

"Perhaps we'd best leave that cable alone. If we needed to use it..."

But he never got to finish his sentence because he suddenly felt a jet of liquid strike him full in the face. When he reopened his eyes he saw that the liquid was red and had not only stained his face but also his shirt, tie and the lapels of his jacket. Meanwhile, the child had run off, holding a toy water-pistol in his hand.

A thoroughly angry Trevor set off in pursuit. When he reached the corner of the deck he came upon the child, feet planted in a defiant attitude, standing not more than ten feet away. Trevor slowed his pace enough to give the child time to pull a wicked face at him. He lunged forward to grab the child, but he slipped on something oily and fell flat on the deck, while the diminutive trouble-maker once more made good his escape.

As the sun was setting, Second Officer Landen was once again on the first-class deck, leaning on the railing, gazing at the foaming waves created by the ship's bows. It reminded him of the soapy liquid which the child had squirted onto the deck a split second before he had reached out to grab him. How he would dearly have liked to have caught the child. But most of all he was thinking about his wrist which he had hurt quite badly in his fall, and which had had to be seen to in the sick bay. Suddenly he heard himself addressed from behind by a warm womanly voice:

"I beg your pardon. Could I have a word with you?"

Trevor turned round and came face to face with a young woman, who could not be more than about twenty-five, who gave him the friendliest of smiles. She was holding the hand of the odious child.

"This is my son, Larry. I know that he has been extremely naughty. I want him to apologize to you."

"It's nothing," Trevor replied with, this time, a genuine smile. "He's only a child, after all."

"That's precisely why he should be a taught a lesson straightaway," the young woman replied with a soft smile on her lips. She then took hold of the boy's ear and twisted it hard. Larry made a grimace, squirmed a bit and managed to blurt out a mangled: "I'm sorry."

"It's okay, Larry. Let that be a lesson to you."

Trevor did not know quite what else to say, but the woman drew closer to him.

"My name is Solange Ranier. I'm French. But Larry's father is American."

"Second Officer Landen, Madame, I'm delighted to make your acquaintance." And Trevor stiffened into a perfect salute to the peak of his cap, revealing as he did so the bandaged wrist.

"What have you done to your hand?" the woman asked with obvious concern, and Trevor suddenly realized that the little culprit had only told his mother part of the story.

"Oh, a small accident, part of the job," he lied.

"You have a beautiful ship," the woman continued, giving the impression that she wanted to engage Trevor in conversation. And Trevor, to tell the truth, did not find the idea altogether unpleasing.

From that moment the trio was often to be seen together. Larry would play at a slight distance while the second officer and the Frenchwoman strolled slowly up and down the deck, telling each other many of the things that had befallen them in their lives. In no time they had established such a degree of trust in one another that Trevor even confessed to Madame Solange the real reason, which he found so embarrassing to tell, why he had signed on as second officer on the liner sailing from Haiti to London.

"You see," he found himself saying one evening to Madame Solange, "I'm here because of a broken love affair."

"I thought as much."

"How come? Is it so obvious?"

"In France we have a saying: love is like the mumps."

"My fiancée left me," Trevor went on.

"Didn't she love you any more?"

"I'm not altogether sure. One evening I was taking my fiancée Hatty back home. We had stayed a bit late at a friend's house and there was nobody about. All of a sudden we were surrounded by four young hooligans. They'd had too much to drink and started bothering us. I did not feel like taking them on. I knew I was outnumbered, so I thought I'd use my brain rather than my fists. I said I'd picked Hatty up in a certain place where there were many lovely girls like her. I even offered them money to have a little fun and I gave them an address I made up. So the four of them left us in peace

and went away, thank goodness."

"It seems to me you handled the situation very cleverly."

"Hatty didn't seem to think so. When we got home, she accused me of treating her like a tart. She also told me I was a coward and that she never wanted to lay eyes on me again."

"And you never saw her again?"

"No. I signed on for this voyage immediately after we parted."

"I'm sorry, really I am."

"You're very kind."

On the night of Trevor's confession to Solange there was a force-7 gale and the passengers for the most part stayed in their cabins, and throughout the following morning as well, until the liner docked in the Azores. But in the Azores the passengers were informed that the ship would have to stay for twenty-four hours in the port of Ponta Delgada, for vital maintenance and repair work.

After this announcement Trevor found himself in his cabin getting ready to go ashore, as he had been given a few hours' shore leave. Suddenly Larry appeared at the door.

"My mother would like to see you," he said airily.

"Where is she?"

"In our cabin. Number 42." And the boy went off as if he had more important things to do.

In Cabin 42 Trevor found Madame Solange in bed.

"I've got quite a high temperature," she announced in a weak voice.

"I'd never have guessed," Trevor replied. "You look wonderful."

The young woman slid a hand from beneath the sheets and took hold of Trevor's.

"I have to ask you a great favour."

"I'm entirely at your service."

"As you can see, there's no way I can go ashore. And you're the only person I can turn to. I must tell you. Larry is not my son. His mother, who was my best friend, died a short time ago in Haiti. So it fell to me to bring the boy to his father, an American who lives in the Azores. They had been living apart for quite some time, the American and my dearest friend. But how can I, in my present predicament, take him to his father? I can ask no one except you to do this for me."

"Does his father know about all this?" Trevor asked, directing his gaze at the boy.

"Of course."

"Then there shouldn't be any problem."

The young woman had written down two addresses: one to take Larry to, and the other in case any difficulties arose.

"This is where you can find the Haitian consul," she added. "He'll give you all the help you may need."

She seemed to guess what Trevor was thinking because she added hastily:

"If Larry is not handed over to his father he will not be able to disembark in London: he does not have a passport. That's why he was passing for my son. He'd be sent straight back to Haiti, and that would present a lot of difficulties. His mother was a secret agent."

So it was that that same morning Trevor found himself knocking at the door of a modest villa, holding on to Larry, who was behaving oddly, in that he seemed to be half frightened, half enjoying himself. Trevor knocked several times, but no one came to open the door.

At this point we introduce the first break in our story, to allow for the first of four tests. The outcome of this test will determine which of the first three versions of the story you will now carry on reading. In other words, you will yourself have selected the plot that best reflects your own mentality. On completion of all four groups of texts, you will have obtained an overall picture of your personality.

Look for a moment at the façades of these two London houses. In which do you think Second Officer Trevor Landen would have been born? Do not think too long about the answer. In fact you should base your choice on an instinctive identification with the character in the story. You will need to note down, or remember, your choices as they will be discussed in their psychological implications, in the next chapter.

Either of these two drawings might well represent a dream. Which of the two images have you dreamt of more often? Or if you have never dreamt them, which would you like to dream of more?
Again, be sure to note down, or remember, the drawing you have chosen.

Compare these two pictures, each a portrait of a mysterious female ancestor of Second Officer Trevor Landen. Both women lived in the last century, and all they left behind were these pictures of their respective faces. Which of the two women do you think would have been Trevor's favourite ancestor? Of course, his preference would also be an instinctive one, because he has never known either of them, and he has never got to know anything about them either. Here again, try to answer without over-rationalizing your choice.

Before reading any further:

Add up the numbers of As and Bs you have chosen in the three tests, 1, 2 and 3.
If you have chosen 3 As, carry on reading version 1 of the story on page 120.
If you have chosen 3 Bs, carry on with version 2 on page 122.
If you have chosen 2As + 1B or 2Bs + 1A, turn to version 3 on page 124.
Your choices will be discussed in the next chapter.

A well-brought-up child (1)

Trevor finally lost all patience, when Larry, with the pretext of tying up a shoelace, bent down and found a way, heaven knows how, of slipping a live insect into the second officer's trouser leg. He yanked the young upstart none too gently to his feet, thinking meanwhile of ringing the bell at some nearby house to see if anyone knew anything about Mr. Benson.

He repeated the same question two or three times:

"Do you know when Mr. Adam Benson, who lives in that house over there, might be back home?"

The reply he got was invariably "No," and Trevor resigned himself to having to hang around for some time. Meanwhile,

tired of being on his feet for so long, and having to hold Larry in a vice-like grip for fear he might dart away suddenly, he directed their steps to a nearby restaurant where, seated at an outdoor table, he could keep an eye on Mr Benson's house.

No sooner were they seated than a corpulent gentleman emerged from the restaurant together with a waitress, and walked up to the table where Trevor was sitting with Larry. "We don't serve meals at this time of day," he remarked.

"Could you possibly bring us something to eat, though?"

"This is a restaurant, not a café."

"Do you know Mr. Adam Benson?"

"No. I'd appreciate it if you left this table."

So Trevor found himself wandering once more along the avenue, still holding Larry by the hand. He was getting close to desperation when the waitress ran up behind them.

"I heard you're looking for Mr. Adam Benson," said the girl, who as well as having a pleasant manner, was also extremely pretty, a fact which did not escape Trevor's eye.

"Don't be upset at the way my boss treated you," the girl went on. "He's the same with everybody. He's always scared of talking. It doesn't seem to matter what it's about. He comes from these parts, but I'm from England."

"I'm English too. What a relief to find someone from England. Actually, I just wanted to know one simple thing."

"Maybe I can help you."

"Do you know Mr. Benson?"

"Of course. He often comes to eat at our restaurant. And he's always very nice to me."

"You didn't by chance see him go out this morning? He had an important appointment."

"This morning? I know that Mr. Benson left home about two weeks ago. Since then I haven't seen sight of him."

"Two weeks ago?"

"Two weeks exactly."

"What kind of person is Mr. Benson?"

"A nice man. Very friendly and easy to get along with."

The second officer had the habit of pulling the lobe of his ear when he felt a bit on edge. Now, in order to do so, he slackened his hold on Larry's hand for a split second, and the boy seized the opportunity to dash off like a rocket. Trevor stood rooted to the ground, just long enough for the boy to be lost among the traffic. When Trevor started off in pursuit, Larry was nowhere to be seen.

After running in vain hither and thither, round one block after another, he hailed a taxi and made the driver circumvent the area where Larry had vanished, driving round in concentric circles, gradually widening the radius more and more. It was the same technique as used by ships when a man was lost overboard, but it did not really work in a town congested with traffic. After more than an hour of this, however, there was still no trace of the boy.

Trevor realized only too well what a fine mess he was in because, no matter how things eventually turned out, he had not acquitted himself at all well. It is no laughing matter to lose the son of a secret agent in a strange town, precisely at the moment when you are meant to be handing him over to his rightful father.

Trevor then remembered that Madame Solange had given him a second address, which he took out of his wallet as much to collect his thoughts as anything else. For he found it extremely embarrassing for an officer of the British Merchant Navy to present himself to the Haitian consul and own up to the fact that he had lost a child who had been entrusted to his care.

He then went back to Mr. Benson's house, rang the bell once again in the vague hope that the American had returned, and then, confronted by the same stubborn silence, he wrote a note which he pushed under the door.

"I have news for you about your son Larry. You can find me on board the 'Haiti' which is at anchor in the port." He signed it Second Officer Trevor Landen.

The idea now came to him of unburdening himself to the pretty, sympathetic girl from the restaurant; besides she seemed to be particularly interested in the whole business. He arrived at the restaurant, caught her attention through the window and beckoned to her to come outside. When she was standing before him, she seemed the only agreeable thing that had happened to him the whole morning.

"You haven't found the boy?" she remarked straightaway.

"No."

"Oh dear."

"Oh dear it is. Listen. If you happen to see Mr. Benson come back home, please let me know. You can find me at the port, on the 'Haiti.' I am the second officer on board. My name is Trevor Landen."

"And my name is Elsie Fammer. I'm from Liverpool," the girl said with a sort of curtsey.

She went back inside the restaurant, leaving Trevor with no alternative but to return to his ship, not least because he had in the meantime decided that the best solution was to go and see Madame Solange and tell her the truth about what had happened. Then he would put himself at her complete disposal no matter what decision she came to about what to do next.

When he tapped at the door of Cabin 42, one or two other doors were ajar as the cabin cleaners were already at work. Trevor tapped lightly, then because there was no reply, he rapped louder with his knuckles. Perhaps she had dozed off, in which case it would be a pity to disturb her, but the situation was such that he could not delay. The third time, as well as knocking on the door, he called out:

"Madame Solange."

A black steward suddenly emerged from a small side passage.

"Good morning, sir. The cabin is empty. I've just finished cleaning it."

"Nonsense," Trevor snapped, losing his temper. "The woman who has this cabin had a very high temperature. I saw her myself only a short while ago."

He instantly regretted what he had just blurted out, as he saw a thin and cunning smile spread across the black steward's face.

"I can assure you she's left her cabin, sir. I saw her leave myself," the steward added.

"And when was this?"

"An hour ago. It couldn't be more than that."

Trevor turned away and shut himself in his cabin. He poured himself a noggin of whisky to calm his nerves, and try to make some kind of sense of that most ill-fated morning. And he ended up by thinking that the whole thing would be laughable were it not for the fact that he was the person in the middle of the whole fine mess: a father who could not be found, a son who had vanished, and an invalid who had apparently undergone a sudden miraculous cure.

A well-brought-up child (2)

Trevor finally lost all patience, when Larry, with the pretext of tying up a shoelace, bent down and found a way, heaven knows how, of slipping a live insect into the second officer's trouser leg. He yanked the young upstart none too gently to his feet, thinking meanwhile of ringing the bell at some nearby house to see if anyone knew anything about Mr. Benson.

At that very moment, a man aged about thirty, wearing a rather loud jacket, was approaching the door of the house, holding a morning newspaper in his hand.

"Is it me you want?" he asked, inserting a key in the door.

"Are you Mr. Adam Benson?" Trevor asked cautiously.

"No. I'm his lawyer."

"So Mr. Benson isn't here?"

"He's out of town right at this moment."

"But he knew about this morning's appointment, didn't he?"

"Sure he did."

"Well then, can I hand the boy over to you?"

The lawyer frowned, directed a mystified look at Trevor, and said: "I think we'd better talk. Would you mind stepping inside for a moment?"

Trevor sensed that things were not going as planned, but by now he could not very well back out of the situation. He nodded his head and the lawyer walked ahead of him and Larry into a drawing-room furnished with a modern decor. He waved them to a seat on a divan, while he himself stretched out in a comfortable armchair and lit a foul-smelling cigar. He did not speak and seemed to be waiting for Trevor to make the first move. Trevor accordingly took the initiative.

"This is Larry," he said, nodding at the boy, whose hand he was still holding just to be on the safe side.

"Pleased to meet you both," replied the lawyer. "I've already noticed what a lively child he is."

"He sure is. He's no ordinary boy."

"He'll go far in life."

"Let's hope so. After all, he's Mr. Benson's son."

Not a muscle moved in the lawyer's face. He looked like Buddha, as he pulled on his cigar.

"My client does not have a son. He never has had children. He's happier with dogs, if the truth be told."

Trevor shot up from the divan, pulling Larry with him.

"What kind of joke is this?" he said, his voice raised.

"That's what I'm asking you," the other replied calmly. "I come back to Mr. Benson's home, where I'm staying as a guest, and what do I find but some stranger trying to pass the paternity of some lad on to my client. It's too silly for words."

Trevor loosened his hold on Larry's hand to point a threatening finger at the armchair where the lawyer was sitting.

"But just now you said you knew about the appointment?"

"I knew something vague about a business appointment. That's why I'm here, because I'm keeping an eye on Mr. Benson's financial interests. I'm not interested in matters of the heart, or any other romantic nonsense."

"Does your client also deny knowing a woman who worked as a secret agent in Haiti?"

"How the hell do I know? My client has never even been to Haiti. He can't stand the heat. And he's never had anything to do with secret agents."

"But he does at least know a Frenchwoman, Madame Solange Ranier?"

"Never heard of her."

Trevor felt he was about to choke with rage, and to relieve his feelings he took a couple of nervous steps to the side, then suddenly spun round in front of the lawyer's armchair.

"This is an absurd situation. I am asked to hand over this boy to his father, and I find him being rejected like an unwanted parcel."

At that moment there was a noise as the front door was suddenly flung open. Unseen, Larry had crept off towards the door, flung it back on its hinges, and was now staring straight at the two men with hate-filled eyes.

"Horrible people! I hate you both!" he called out as he ran off, slamming the door shut behind him. The lawyer did not turn a hair, but after a few seconds' bewilderment Trevor rushed off after the boy to try and catch him. But he had already let him get too far ahead and when he reached the main road, busy with traffic, there was no sign of Larry at all.

Trevor hailed a passing taxi and got the driver to drive around a bit, fast at first, and then more slowly, in the hope of finding the child. But he soon realized that it was an impossible task. So he had himself driven back to Mr. Benson's house, almost in the hope that Larry had thought better of it and gone back there. And if that was not the case, he would have to have words with that odious lawyer. But no matter how hard he knocked, no one came to open the door. The lawyer, obviously a phoney, must have left in a hurry to avoid any further trouble.

Trevor felt desperate. Not only had he failed to hand Larry over to his father, he had actually lost the boy, who had probably run off in despair when he heard himself being rejected by his father's lawyer. What had seemed a perfectly simple matter was now turning out to be nothing less than a fully-fledged family drama, with God-knows-what problems still to come.

Trevor noticed a restaurant close by the house with tables laid outside, and he suddenly had a very precise idea of what to do next. As he entered the restaurant, he was immediately approached by a young and very pretty waitress who said with a smile as lovely as her face:

"I'm sorry. You're too early for anything to eat."

Trevor found her instantly attractive, and friendly into the bargain. He spoke to her hurriedly.

"I don't want anything to eat. I just wanted to ask if you know Mr. Benson. Adam Benson. He's American and he lives in that house over there."

"I don't know any such person."

"Fine. Could you let me know, then, if you see anyone going into the house? I know it's an odd thing to ask of anyone but, please believe me, it's a matter of life or death."

"You can rely on me, sir. If I see anyone going into the house, I'll let you know."

"Thanks a lot. You can find me on the liner 'Haiti' down in the harbour. I am Second Officer Trevor Landen."

"My name is Elsie Fammer. I'm from England," said the girl, holding out her hand to him. He took it in both his and held it perhaps longer than he should have done.

"Thank you, Elsie. I am really most grateful to you. But most of all, I'm so glad I've met someone from England, someone so pretty and helpful."

The flush that spread over Elsie's cheeks was the first good thing to have happened to him, he thought, that morning.

After leaving the restaurant, Trevor decided to go back on board his ship and see Madame Solange. He remembered that he had the address of the Haitian consul, but as things stood, he thought it more logical to tell the Frenchwoman what was going on, because he trusted her – at least until she proved otherwise.

When he tapped at the door of Cabin 42, one or two other doors were ajar as the cabin cleaners were already about their chores. Trevor tapped lightly, then, because there was no reply, he rapped louder with his knuckles. Perhaps she had dozed off, in which case it would be a pity to disturb her, but the situation was such that he could not delay. The third time, as well as knocking, he called out:

"Madame Solange."

A black steward suddenly emerged from a passage.

"Good morning, sir. The cabin is empty. I've just finished cleaning it."

"Nonsense," Trevor snapped, losing his temper. "The woman who has this cabin had a very high temperature. I saw her myself only a short time ago."

He instantly regretted what he had just blurted out, as he saw a thin and cunning smile spread across the black steward's face.

"I can assure you she's left her cabin, sir. I saw her leave myself," the steward added.

"And when was this?"

"An hour ago. It couldn't have been more than that."

Trevor turned away and shut himself in his cabin. He poured himself a noggin of whisky to calm his nerves, and try to make some kind of sense of that most ill-fated morning. And he ended up by thinking that the whole thing would be laughable were it not for the fact that he was the person in the middle of the whole fine mess: a father who could not be found, a son who had vanished, and an invalid who apparently had undergone a suddenly miraculous cure.

A well-brought-up child (3)

Trevor finally lost all patience, when Larry, with the pretext of tying up a shoelace, bent down and found a way, heaven knows how, of slipping a live insect into the second officer's trouser leg. He yanked the young upstart none too gently to his feet, thinking meanwhile of ringing the bell at some nearby house to see if anyone knew anything about Mr. Benson. But the neighbouring houses were also deserted and this seemed quite unusual to Trevor. "Probably," he thought to himself, "they belong to wealthy people who only live here off and on. In fact they probably only use these villas for their vacations. But then who is Larry's father and what does he do?"

On the other side of the road Trevor noticed a restaurant with tables outside, and he decided to see if anyone there could help him in his dilemma. So he crossed over and sat down at a table, keeping Larry, who seemed completely uninterested in the whole affair, on a short rein close beside him. The boy's concentration obviously lay more in annoying his escort with nasty little pranks.

"Could we have something to drink, please?" Trevor asked the pretty, young waitress who had quickly emerged from the restaurant.

"We're not really a bar," the girl said smiling. "But for someone English I suppose I can make an exception to the rule."

"You're English too?"

"From Liverpool," she replied.

"Well, that gives me the courage to ask another favour of you. Do you know someone called Adam Benson? He's an American and he lives in that house just opposite."

"I'm sorry. I've never heard of him. What did you say his name is?"

"Adam Benson."

"No, never heard of him. I could ask somebody in the kitchen. In the meantime, what would you like?"

"A hot chocolate for me," Larry broke in cockily.

"In this heat?" Trevor remarked.

"Mind your own business," came the reply. "And don't be ridiculous."

"A glass of port for me, please," Trevor said, as he fiddled nervously with the ashtray on the table.

"Stop fidgeting," he heard Larry say. "It's annoying me."

"Would you mind telling me what you've got against me?" Trevor asked, by now reduced to a high state of embarrassment by the boy's insolence.

"If you don't know, think about it. We don't even know one another," the boy said nastily, pulling a face.

Trevor was searching hard for some scintillating reply to get his own back on the boy, when he saw a man of about thirty approaching the table, dressed in rather loud clothes.

"Excuse me, sir. A moment ago I was just passing and I overheard you say you are looking for Adam Benson."

"That's right. Do you know him?"

"I'm a friend of his," said the stranger with a disarming smile, and Trevor suddenly leapt to his feet, almost tipping over the table in his excitement.

"You know Mr. Benson?"

"I've just told you, I'm a friend of his. Maybe his best friend."

"Do you happen to know where I can find him?"

"He is not far. He'll be back soon. He sent me on ahead of him."

So intense was the relief felt by Trevor at the stranger's statement, that he could hardly get out the words he now uttered:

"Well, this is his son. Mr. Benson's son."

The man's face seemed to light up with a mixture of surprise and delight.

"Larry?"

"Yes. Larry. Don't you recognize him?"

"No. It's so long since I've seen him. The same goes for his father incidentally," said the friend of Mr. Benson, and holding back with difficulty a poorly concealed tide of emotion he pulled the boy out of the chair and hugged him tightly. Larry did not appear to be particularly moved by the encounter. In fact, over the shoulder of his father's friend, who was still hugging him, he made a face in Trevor's direction. Hiding his distaste for the boy, Trevor said:

"Come on, Larry. Haven't you anything to say to your father's friend?"

"Who knows what he is?" the boy answered back insolently. "What do you think I should say to him?" he added with a sneer.

"Well, I don't really know. You could ask him to take you straightaway to see your father?"

"Why do you think I should want to see my father in such a hurry?"

At this point Mr. Benson's friend intervened, and leaning towards Trevor, murmured a few words, which he clearly did not want the boy to hear.

"Wait for me here a moment," he whispered.

Trevor, alive to the situation, turned to Larry.

"Would you go into the restaurant and order another port for your father's friend. Ask the English waitress. She'll see to it."

Surprisingly enough, Larry rose and disappeared into the restaurant, and Trevor took the opportunity to ask Mr. Benson's friend for some clarification.

"What's this all about? Why should I wait for you here? Where are you going?"

"To Adam's house," said the American's friend, lowering his head as if ashamed of being overheard. "That house over there."

"I know that's his house. Won't you take your friend's son with you?"

"Just be patient for a moment. There's a woman in Adam's house. You know what I mean. Give us time to get her out of there. We don't want to upset the boy from the word go. Adam is very worried. He wants to establish a really good relationship with Larry from the start."

"But wasn't Benson expecting us? Hadn't somebody warned him?"

"Yes, he'd been warned. But he thought the appointment was arranged for tomorrow. He's a bit vague. And a bit muddleheaded too. That's why, when we heard the doorbell ring, we invented this little act on the spur of the moment."

Trevor could not conceal his disappointment. But the other still insisted:

"Just a little more patience. Let me sort this out and in fifteen minutes you'll see Benson. You know, with some women all it takes is a little money to persuade them to make themselves scarce."

Trevor felt his gorge rise at the blatant cynicism of this rather unpleasant man, and he only hoped that Larry's father was a cut above the friends he chose to have around him.

"In the meantime," the man went on, "and on behalf of my friend too, I should express how grateful we are for all you have done for Larry. We shall never forget how kind you have been. And Benson, sooner or later, will find a way of rewarding you."

Trevor shrugged, a gesture which the friend took to be a sign for him to go to the house.

"Thanks," he said, and hurried away towards the villa. He went inside, and closed the door behind him with obvious caution.

Trevor returned to his seat at the table, and the waitress emerged from the restaurant with the order, followed by Larry munching a packet of popcorn. Trevor decided to drink the port which he had ordered for Mr. Benson's friend, and Larry sucked enthusiastically at his hot chocolate. The second officer was glancing at his watch, when he noticed a powerful car pull into the curb right by their table. Two men emerged, approached the table, and without a word seized Larry and bundled him into the car. After an initial moment of consternation, Trevor dashed to help the boy, but he was left reeling from a kick on the shin, and fell to the ground in agony. The car pulled away with a screech of rubber, and vanished in seconds in the traffic.

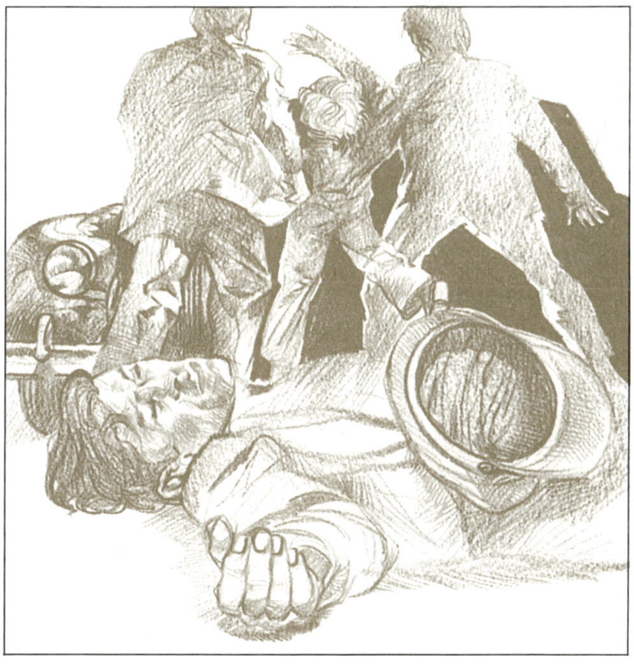

When he got back to his feet, Trevor was hobbling, and what was more important, he had been unable to identify the car's number plate because of the pain which forced his eyes shut. Nevertheless, he ran as best he could to Benson's villa to alert someone and get help. But despite his insistent knocking, nobody answered the door. The villa seemed abandoned once again. So Trevor returned to the restaurant, and the English waitress was the first to make clear that she had seen nothing from inside the restaurant, although she was clearly sorry about what had happened. Trevor nevertheless left her his address, then took a taxi, making the driver drive slowly round the town, hoping to see Benson's friend, if not Larry himself. He suddenly remembered the second note which Madame Solange had given him with the address of the Haitian consul, should there be any complications, but he did not really think it warranted disturbing the consul at this particular juncture.

First he wanted to get back to the Frenchwoman, who was the only person he trusted in this whole strange business. So he decided to direct the taxi to take him back to his ship. In his mental reconstruction of the facts to relate to the young Frenchwoman, he could not rid his mind of the one thought which, to say the least, he found extremely troubling. The kick to his shin, which had virtually put him out of action in the course of the scuffle, had been dealt him by no other than Larry. He would almost swear to that, despite the fact that in all the confusion, even for a phlegmatic Englishman, it would have been quite in order to have made an error of judgement.

When he tapped at the door of Cabin 42, one or two doors were ajar as the cabin cleaners were already about their chores. Trevor tapped lightly, then, because there was no reply, he rapped louder with his knuckles. Perhaps she had dozed off, in which case it would be a pity to disturb her, but the situation was such that he could not delay. The third time, as well as knocking, he called out:

"Madame Solange."

A black steward suddenly emerged from a small side passage.

"Good morning, sir. The cabin is empty. I've just finished cleaning it."

"Nonsense," Trevor snapped, losing his temper. "The woman who has this cabin had a very high temperature. I saw her myself only a short time ago."

He instantly regretted what he had just blurted out, as he saw a thin and cunning smile spread across the black steward's face.

"I can assure you she's left her cabin, sir. I saw her myself," the steward said.

"And when was this?"

"An hour ago. It couldn't have been more than that."

Trevor turned away and shut himself in his cabin. He poured himself a noggin of whisky to calm his nerves and try to make some sense of that most ill-fated morning. And he ended up by thinking that the whole thing would be laughable were it not for the fact that he was the person in the middle of the whole fine mess: a father who could not be found, a son who had vanished, and an invalid who apparently had undergone a sudden miraculous cure.

We have come to the second interruption in our story. Which version of this gripping tale you will now choose to take up, will depend on your answers to the next three questions below and on page 129. Bit by bit, with your answers to the previous set of questions and the other two tests still to follow, you are gradually building up your own character Identikit.

Take a good look at these very different pairs of eyes. Which do you think could be the eyes of Madame Solange Ranier? Mark down, or remember, which pair you have chosen.

Which of these two verses appeals to you most, irrespective of whom they are by, or what comes before or after? Mark down, or remember, your choice for later use.

Continuing with our sexuality test. Opposite is photograph I and overleaf photo II. Having made your choice, match it up with the previous photograph you chose, E or F, and then turn to page 181 to read the psychological meaning behind your combined choice.

A well-brought-up child (5)

As he rang the bell of the Haitian consul's residence, Trevor could not help wondering what, if any, positive outcome could result from such a move. On the other hand, this resort to the second address which Madame Solange Ranier had provided him with in the event of some emergency, still seemed to him the only right thing to do, after having made so many wrong moves. So when the door finally opened, he felt a sense of relief.

But the door had opened on its own, or rather it had yielded to some pressure that was stronger than Trevor's finger. It had obviously not been properly closed in the first place, but had simply been pushed to. Trevor did not feel particularly surprised that in a residence of that style it was customary to leave the front door ajar. He was quite used to travelling around the world, and what is more, he was a British subject, so far away from England that he tended to regard as picturesque and therefore acceptable things that would have appeared somewhat odd at home.

Once inside the empty hallway, Trevor stood immobile for a second or two, just long enough for him to spy another half-open door, through which he could glimpse the interior of a drawing-room. By now, used to what he considered to be rather strange local customs, Trevor stepped forward, pushed the door wide open and advanced a few steps into the drawing-room.

But the young Englishman was soon to regret that he had ever ventured into a strange house with doors left ajar, because what he saw certainly had nothing to do with peculiar local traditions. In fact, lying on the floor in the far corner of the room lay the body of a middle-aged man.

Trevor cleared his throat, partly to bolster up his courage, but more as an incentive to the prone figure to adopt a slightly less dramatic pose; nothing on that score, no appreciable movement occurred. He now saw that a white envelope had been placed on the dead body's chest. He went over, knelt down and almost despite himself, took up the envelope, as if therein might be found the solution to all the disasters that had befallen him already that morning. Seeing that the envelope was not sealed down, and that inside was a sheet of paper, Trevor drew it out and read what was written thereon:

"I am Adam Benson, Larry's father, the boy you should have handed over to me this morning. If something should happen to me you can contact . . ."

At this point the words petered out, as if some unforeseen and traumatic event – death, in all probability – had checked the hand while engaged in the act of writing.

Trevor had no time for further thought as, from somewhere behind him, a piercing scream shattered the silence of the room. His whole body reacted violently; it was as if all his internal organs had decided to fly off somewhere of their own accord. Terrified of what might meet his gaze, he turned slowly round, to find himself staring into the contorted visage of Madame Solange.

"Madame Solange . . .?" Trevor could only stutter.

The woman gave vent to another piercing scream, and then muttered something to herself in French. Trevor regretted that he had not learnt that altogether pleasant language at school. He addressed her, almost in a whisper.

"Madame Solange, what in God's name is this all about?"

Summoned back to reality, the woman turned her terror-stricken gaze on him.

"You've killed Adam Benson," she moaned in a voice hardly above a whisper. "Why, Trevor? Why?"

Suddenly Trevor realized the full implication of the situation in which he now found himself. He asked:

"How can you say such a thing, Madame Solange? I found this man dead when I came into this room."

"What about Larry? What have you done with Larry?"

At this juncture, Trevor sensed that his explanations about all that had happened would not make much sense under the circumstances, so he made no reply.

Madame Solange walked over to a telephone.

"I trust you don't think I am to be implicated as your accomplice in this double crime?" she uttered darkly. "I must call the police at once."

Trevor started up in alarm; at that particular moment a foreign policeman was the last person he wanted to see.

"Madame Solange," he said, trying to make his words sound as convincing as possible, "I have done nothing. Benson was dead before I came in here. I don't know where Larry is, but that is not my fault."

"Fine," Madame Solange said, visibly trying hard not to swoon. "If you've nothing to hide, you won't mind if I call the police, will you?"

"Bringing in the police won't get us anywhere."

"You want to make me an accomplice after the fact?"

"You are supposed to be my friend. You know very well why you find me here."

"No, I don't. I haven't got a clue why you're here. You should have been at Mr. Benson's house. With Larry."

Mention of the young brat made Trevor loose all control of himself. Gripping Madame Solange by the upper arms, he shook her fiercely, shouting:

"All of you are trying to drive me crazy!"

"No! No!" the Frenchwoman shouted in her turn, trying to wriggle free. "Spare me, at least, murderer!"

At that moment the whole room started to shake violently, and there was a dull underground rumble. Everything not attached to the walls toppled on to the floor.

"An earthquake!" Madame Solange screamed, and while Trevor was trying to keep his balance in the dreadful swaying motion, the woman fled from the house. After a moment's hesitation Trevor set off after her, but lost her.

Trevor tried to keep his head; he knew what course of action he should take. He ran all the way to the harbour, and up the gangway on to the "Haiti" which, despite its size, was rolling at its moorings, as it tossed about on the boiling sea. He made straight for his cabin.

And there, sitting on the bed, with a cruel smile playing about his lips, was Larry, while gripped in his hands, as if he wanted to crush it, was the silver frame in which, despite all that had happened, Trevor still kept a picture of Hatty, his ex-fiancée.

A well-brought-up child (6)

As he rang the bell of the Haitian consul's residence, Trevor could not help wondering what, if any, positive outcome could result from such a move. On the other hand, this resort to the second address, which Madame Solange Ranier had provided him with in the event of some emergency, still seemed the right thing to do, considering the failure of his earlier attempt to hand Larry over to his father. So when the door was opened by a footman in livery, he felt a sense of relief: perhaps the solution to all the tangled muddle lay on the other side of this door.

The footman ushered the Englishman into a drawing-room, at the far end of which, standing at a window bathed in sunlight, was Madame Solange. Trevor felt a certain tremor of dismay run through him.

"What are you doing here?" he asked.

"I'll tell you later," the woman replied, looking terribly agitated. "Tell me about Larry. Have you taken him to Mr. Benson?"

At that moment Trevor wished he was back on the "Haiti," anywhere in fact but here.

"No, I didn't manage to find Mr. Benson," he replied, feeling almost a sense of shame saying it. "And right now I have no idea where Larry is either."

"What do you mean, you 'have no idea where he is?' "

"Please don't distress youself, Madame Solange. I know everything looks pretty much against me. Believe me, it's really not my fault. And sooner or later I'll find him again, even if I have to jump ship to look for him."

"Poor little Larry," said Madame Solange and suddenly her knees seemed to give way beneath her, as if they felt like fainting of their own accord. Trevor dashed forward to hold her and found himself clasping her in his arms, as she continued gently sobbing. And try as he might he could not fathom if he had drawn her close to him, or if it had been she who had clung to him. The fact was that the two of them found themselves in each other's arms and they both let the situation take its course. The middle-aged man who had suddenly appeared in the drawing-room could not but mistake them for lovers.

"Solange!" he greeted her, and the woman broke away from Trevor with a stifled groan.

"Solange!" the man repeated with a break in his voice, "even here, before my very eyes, you play me false."

Trevor tried to intervene.

"Sir, I don't know who you are, but I can assure you that you have got the wrong impression. Contrary to how it may appear, this lady and I were not embracing."

The man seemed to ignore the words of the Englishman, and continued to concentrate his gaze on the woman, as if he and she were the sole occupants of the room.

"I love you, Solange. I've always loved you. Why do you make me suffer? There was a time when you too ..."

Trevor turned his full gaze on Madame Solange.

"What have you got to say? Tell him the truth."

"As if that would serve any purpose. I know him too well. More's the pity. He would never believe me."

"You might at least tell me who he is?" cried Trevor with a hint of belligerency in his voice.

"I'm Adam Benson. Larry's father."

"Larry's father?" Trevor repeated, dumbfounded.

"It's true," Madame Solange added in a listless tone.

"A stranger was meant to hand Larry over to me this morning," Benson went on. "But nothing happened. I'm worried sick about my son."

Trevor sensed that this was not the right moment to get involved in talking about Larry, so he skirted the subject.

"What is the relationship between you two, if you don't mind me asking?"

The woman did not answer, and walked towards the other end of the drawing-room. Benson instead turned to Trevor, stared him hard in the eyes, and said:

"I'll tell you what kind of a relationship there is between us, if you're so interested. We've been together for more than five years, I and this woman here. Our relationship has been one long succession of her whims and infidelities."

"That's not true," the woman spoke up from the other side of the room. "There was a time when I was in love with you ... when I really loved you. But you soon put an end to that, with your violence and your absurd jealousy."

"Yes. You're right. Our relationship has been going on too long. But I know how to end it once and for all."

With these words, Benson produced from his jacket pocket a small pistol and placed the barrel to his temple. Madame Solange had barely moved a step towards him, while Trevor remained as if rooted to the floor, before the shot rang out, and Benson slumped lifeless to the floor. Trevor turned to Madame Solange, whose hands were raised to her mouth to stifle a scream.

"Now they'll put all the blame on us," she said.

For a moment Trevor could not bring himself to approach her, or kneel down to inspect the body. And in that fraction of time Madame Solange ran headlong from the drawing-room.

"Madame Solange," Trevor shouted after her, as he set off in pursuit, since he had no desire at all to stay alone in that room. But the woman had already got well beyond the house, and in a trice she was lost amid the traffic.

Almost as if he were walking in his sleep, Trevor went back into the consul's house which suddenly, appropriately enough, has assumed the silence of the grave, and went into the drawing-room, where Benson's body still lay sprawled on the floor. The Englishman was thinking what to do next, when, all of a sudden, he felt the whole house shake violently, accompanied by a dull underground rumble. Everything started to dance in front of his eyes, and Trevor realized he was in the middle of an earthquake. As he ran from the house, the thought struck him that the earthquake had to some extent got him out of the jam he was in. He ran all the way to the harbour and up the gangway on to the "Haiti" which, despite its size, was heaving at its moorings, as it tossed about on the boiling sea. He made for his cabin.

And there, sitting on the bed, with a cruel smile playing about his lips, was Larry, while gripped in his hands, as if he wanted to crush it, was the silver frame in which Trevor still kept a picture of Hatty, his ex-fiancée.

We have arrived at our third break in the story, and once again your answers to the three questions posed below and overleaf will determine which version of the story you will continue with. We are now more than halfway through our physchological "do-it-yourself" investigation to reveal the personality traits of the four basic "moments" in a lifetime – your lifetime – childhood, adolescence, adulthood and old age.

It would appear that in primitive times, as illustrated by the drawing above, the forebears of Trevor Landen and Adam Benson were neighbours. One of the two, to be precise the one on the right in the drawing, invented writing, while the other, on the left, invented the system for lighting fires. With which of the two do you identify most closely? In a word, if you yourself had lived at the dawn of mankind, what would you have rather invented: fire (A) or writing (B)? Note down or remember, your choice.

It seems that among the men with Christopher Columbus when he set foot on American soil during his first expedition, were two ancestors of Solange Ranier and Elsie Fammer. Of the two, one – on the left of the picture – appears to have been a banker who went along to check out the New World's potential. The other, center, appears to have been a draughtsman and an artist; he was given the task by the Spanish court to commit to paper whatever he saw that was unusual and exotic. With which person do you identify most closely? In a word, if you had gone with Columbus on that voyage of discovery would you rather have been: a banker (A) or a draughtsman (B)? Note down, or remember the choice you make.

It is very probable, that among the grandchildren of Trevor Landen and Adam Benson, there would be a couple of astronauts as depicted in the two drawings. The astronaut on the right travels alone in space, in search of new cosmic mysteries. The astronaut below is sampling, with a certain relish, an unusual food, from some strange "thing" discovered on an unexplored planet. With which astronaut do you identify more closely? Note down, or remember the choice you make.

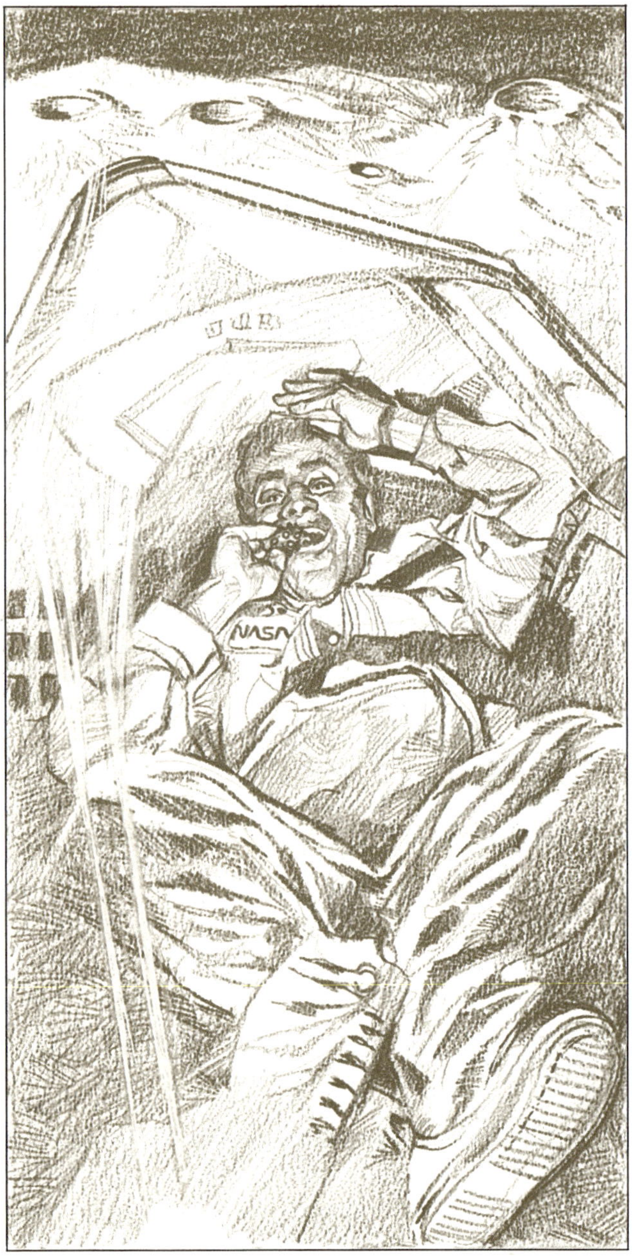

The version you read next
Add up the numbers of As and Bs you have chosen in the three tests, 7, 8 and 9.
If you have chosen 3 As, continue with version 7 on page 135.
If you chosen 3 Bs, continue with version 8 on page 137.
If you have chosen 2 As + 1 B or 2 Bs + 1 A, continue with version 9 on page 139.
You will need to remember how many As and Bs you have chosen in these three tests as they will be discussed for their psychological significance in the next chapter.

A well-brought-up child (7)

Trevor looked hard at Larry, as if he saw in him the root cause of all his troubles; but Larry did not seem to be unduly bothered. He kept on smiling, with the same insolent look on his face, as in a slow, calculated tone he said:

"Second Officer, you're in a mess. I followed you around all morning but you didn't notice me. I saw everything. You murdered my father."

Trevor twitched nervously, since he realized at once that Larry was quite capable of thinking the worst, and that he could not offer any proof to the contrary. Nevertheless, he made an effort to keep a grip on himself.

"If you did follow me, and if you did see everything, then you know very well that it isn't true. I did not murder your father."

Very calmly, Larry then laid the picture of Hatty on the bedside table. He had turned suddenly serious.

"I might even believe you. But if I say that you killed my father, and if I add that I also saw you do it, how can you prove that it wasn't you, when they find the body?"

The child was nothing short of a devil, and Trevor realized that for the moment at least, Larry definitely had the upper hand. His first priority, he reasoned, was to try to gain some idea of how the boy's mind worked.

"Will you tell them it was I who killed your father?"

"Of course I will. I shall tell the police first."

"Where will that get you?"

The boy did not answer. He got off the bed and went to look inside a large half-open wardrobe trunk where Trevor kept all his things – clothes and other goods and chattels. Trevor let him carry on, mastering a gust of anger which became more and more uncontrollable as the minutes passed.

"Second Officer, you asked me where it would get me if I tell on you. So let me ask you something: where will it get me if I don't tell on you?"

Trevor could only look at him, speechless. The little monster was a blackmailer to boot, even if, for the time being, it was not clear how far he might go. Nevertheless, as of now, it was better to play the game his way, for, everything considered, there were not really many alternatives.

"What do you think I could give you in exchange for your silence?" Trevor asked, trying hard to sound as naive as possible.

"'The 'Haiti'," came the reply.

"I'm sorry, would you say that again?"

"I want the ship."

Trevor had tried hard to think of the worst that could happen, because by now he was accustomed to Larry's devilish fantasies, but his request for the ship went far beyond his wildest imagination. He decided nonetheless to play along with Larry's little game, if only for the fact that no other alternative existed.

"The ship doesn't belong to me. How can you think I could hand it over to you?"

"It's very simple. You'll have to find a way of stopping it sailing tonight."

"How on earth do you think I can do that?"

"You're the technician. You can sabotage the engines. Or say that an epidemic of cholera has broken out on board. It's up to you. The important thing is that you keep the ship at her moorings, at least for tonight."

"Why do you want the ship to stay in port tonight?"

"Because something is going to happen tonight."

"What?"

"I don't mind telling you. You know, I really rather like you. Tonight some friends of mine will come on board, under cover of darkness, without being invited."

"What then?"

"They'll take over the ship. By hook or by crook."

"And once they've taken it over?"

"They'll steam around for a bit, once they've got rid of the passengers. Ships are used in wars, you know. Or didn't you know?"

"Wars? What are you talking about?"

"You know too much already. And I'm getting bored. I'll give you five minutes to think it over. If you agree to sabotage the ship, I won't tell anyone that you murdered my father. If you refuse to cooperate, I'll go and tell the police. I know their telephone number. I can get them on this phone."

Trevor felt himself well and truly cornered. He did not have much room left to maneuver, even though he knew full well that he had not murdered Larry's father. On the other hand, he realized that appearances were all against him and that he could not rely even on Madame Solange to help him out. Perhaps in time he would manage to prove his innocence, but at what price? For the time being, nobody would be able to prevent him from going to prison.

Trevor paced to and fro in his cabin for those eternal five minutes granted to him by Larry to make up his mind. Larry stared at him in silence, looking very serious, having taken up a position in the corner close to the telephone.

Eventually Trevor stood before the boy with a wide smile on his face and spoke in a tone of voice that expressed relief:

"Young Larry. You're the most nauseous little boy I've ever come across. Since knowing you, I've had a complete change of mind about the methods of King Herod. I'm delighted to tell you that you've picked on the wrong man to advance your little scheme. I shall go to the ship's captain and give myself up. I shall say I killed your father and they can arrest me. Once they've done that, they'll start their investigations and I shall be able to prove my innocence. You can tell your pals that they'll never be able to get their hands on the 'Haiti.'"

Without waiting for the boy's reaction, Trevor strode to the door, which he opened with the most dignified of gestures, and walked off, unhurried, through the maze of the ship's passages.

The ship's captain, having listened to Trevor's confession, was, naturally enough, shocked to the roots of his being.

"Second Officer, I don't understand a word of what you've told me. But I must inform the police at once. Or maybe the mental hospital. I'm not quite sure which. In the meantime I shall have to lock you up in the brig."

"At your service, sir," Trevor said with finality, as if a great weight had been removed from his mind. Whistling as he went, he let himself be taken off to the dank, warm place that is known in naval parlance as the "brig."

It was a different Trevor who, several hours later, bored and lonely in his prison cell, began to feel the dark clouds of gloomy despair closing around him, having, by now, lost all hope that he would ever be able to prove his innocence.

After a further passage of time, which seemed interminable, he heard the familiar noises which meant that the ship was about to set sail, and he was amazed that the local police, who would certainly have been alerted by the captain, had not come to take him away. For a moment he hoped that the captain, who was a stickler for protocol, had decided to take him – under arrest of course – to London, but he thought again when he heard the clatter of footsteps approaching. When he heard the key turning in the lock, he got to his feet and tried to assume the attitude which, he thought was fitting for an innocent person who was being wrongfully accused. But he had not time to assume the role of martyr, not even for a brief moment, because his cell was suddenly invaded, not by the representatives of the law he had been expecting, but by four people who were certainly known to him, and whom, in the circumstances, he had not expected to see.

The four people in question were Madame Solange, Mr. Benson, in the guise of a latter-day Lazarus, the inevitable Larry, and – most shattering surprise of all – his ex-fiancée, Hatty Glamps.

Trevor was too dumbfounded even to attempt to speak. So it was Hatty, his erstwhile fiancée, who first broke the silence.

"Dearest Trevor, it's all over. It was I who set up this little show, because I wanted to prove, that the day we were attacked by those four louts, what you showed was true British self-control, and not the cowardice of a faintheart from one of those countries on the Continent. I could not get you out of my mind, but on the other hand I did not want to spend the rest of my life married to a coward. Then I had the idea of putting you to a test, this test, and, as I had hoped, you've passed it with flying colours. You are not endowed with a great deal of courage, but you have plenty of self-control. Now I'm ready to marry you."

Trevor could barely summon the will to ask:

"Who are these people then?" pointing to the others.

Hatty seemed to be thoroughly enjoying herself.

"This is Mr. Benson, a lawyer whom I chose for the part in London, because of his sense of humour. He died a splendid death. This is his wife, who really is French, and who really is called Solange Ranier. And this incomparable young lad is Larry, Mr. Benson's son by his first wife. They all played their parts with the help of a little local colour. I certainly won't forget the whole thing that easily."

Trevor emitted the word "brilliant," which was intended to sound sarcastic, but was taken literally by Hatty, the true daughter of a Methodist minister.

"Truly brilliant," she said. "Especially young Larry, who's always top at school when it comes to acting in plays. He really is a well-brought-up child. And that slight earthquake also gave us an unexpected helping hand."

Trevor leant against something for support, because he really felt faint. But Hatty refused to allow him even that luxury.

"Trevor, dear, this is not the moment to feel fainthearted or lose your self-control. You must keep it all for our wedding night."

The prison cell resounded with a chorus of politely controlled giggles. And while he wiped the sweat from his brow, Trevor noticed that Larry, that well-brought-up little boy, was also laughing mischievously.

A well-brought-up child (8)

Trevor looked hard at Larry, as if he saw in him the root cause of all his troubles, but Larry did not seem to be unduly bothered. He kept on smiling, with the same insolent look on his face, as in a slow, calculated tone, he said:

"Second Officer, you're in a mess. I followed you around all morning and you didn't notice me. I saw everything. You murdered my father."

Trevor twitched nervously, since he realized at once that Larry was quite capable of thinking the worst, and that he could not offer any proof to the contrary. Nevertheless he made an effort to keep a grip on himself.

"If you did follow me, and if you did see everything, then you know very well that it isn't true. I did not murder your father."

Very calmly, Larry then laid the picture of Hatty on the bedside table. He had turned suddenly serious.

"I might even believe you. But if I say that you killed my father, and if I add that I also saw you do it, how can you prove that it wasn't you, when they find the body?"

The child was nothing short of a devil, and Trevor realized that for the moment at least, Larry definitely had the upper hand. His first priority, he reasoned, was to try to gain some idea of how the boy's mind worked.

"Will you tell them it was I who killed your father?"

"Of course I will. I shall tell the police first."

"Where will that get you?"

The boy did not answer. He got off the bed and went to look inside a large, half-open wardrobe trunk where Trevor kept all his things – clothes and other goods and chattels. Trevor let him carry on, mastering a gust of anger which became more and more uncontrollable as the minutes passed.

"Second Officer, you asked me where it would get me if I tell on you. So let me ask you something: where will it get me if I don't tell on you?"

Trevor could only look at him, speechless. The little monster was a blackmailer to boot, even if, for the time being, it was not clear how far he might go. Nevertheless, as of now, it was better to play the game his way, for, everything considered, there were not really many alternatives.

"What do you think I could give you in exchange for your silence?" Trevor asked, trying hard to sound as naive as possible.

"The 'Haiti,'" came the reply.

"I'm sorry, would you say that again?"

"I want the ship."

Trevor had tried to think of the worst that could happen, because by now he was accustomed to Larry's devilish fantasies, but his request for the ship went far beyond his wildest imagination. He decided nonetheless to play along with Larry's little scheme, if only for the fact that no other alternative existed.

"The ship doesn't belong to me. How can you think I could hand it over to you?"

"It's very simple. You'll have to find a way of stopping it sailing tonight."

"How on earth do you think I can do that?"

"You're the technician. You can sabotage the engines. Or say that an epidemic of cholera has broken out on board. It's up to you. The important thing is that you keep the ship at her moorings, at least for tonight."

"Why do you want the ship to stay in port tonight?"

"Because something is going to happen tonight."

"What?"

"I don't mind telling you. You know, I really rather like you. Tonight some friends of mine will come on board, under cover of darkness, without being invited."

"What then?"

"They'll take over the ship. By hook or by crook."

"And once they've taken it over?"

"They'll steam around for a bit, once they've got rid of the passengers. Ships are used in wars, you know. Or didn't you know?"

"Wars? What are you talking about?"

"You know too much already. And I'm getting bored. I'll give you five minutes to think it over. If you agree to sabotage the ship, I won't tell anyone that you murdered my father. If you refuse to cooperate, I'll go and tell the police. I know their telephone number. I can get them on this phone."

Trevor felt himself well and truly cornered. He did not have much room left to maneuver, even though he knew full well that he had not murdered Larry's father. On the other hand he realized that appearances were all against him and that he could not rely even on Madame Solange to help him out. Perhaps in time he would manage to prove his innocence, but at what price? For the time being, nobody would be able to prevent him from going to prison.

Trevor paced to and fro in his cabin for those eternal five minutes granted to him by Larry to make up his mind, while Larry stared at him in silence, looking very serious, having taken up a position in the corner close to the telephone.

When the five minutes were up, Trevor walked over to Larry moving his legs stiffly and slowly, because he felt that there was a great weight on his shoulders.

"Okay, Larry," he said, "you win. I'll make sure the ship doesn't sail tonight. You can let your pals know. But you should also know that it wasn't me who killed your father."

"That's a matter for your conscience. We're only interested in the ship – and nothing else."

"I'd better be on my way then, to see what I can do to make you happy."

Larry got to his feet and tapped Trevor lightly on the arm.

"You mean, we'd better be on our way. From now on I'm not letting you out of my sight for a minute. You'll have to put up with me until my friends arrive."

"Young Larry," Trevor said with finality. "I can promise you that having to spend all my time with you, makes this the worst day of my life."

Larry opened the door, effecting a comic bow as the second officer led the way out.

It was almost midnight when Trevor, in pursuance of Larry's crazy plan, went on to the deck of the "Haiti," followed by the boy, silent as a shadow.

"Keep down," he barked gruffly at Larry. "If they find us we'll both be for the high jump."

"You, not me. I'm too young. They can't send me to prison."

"Okay, as you say. What should I do now? The ship isn't sailing anywhere tonight. You can see that for yourself."

"Yes. Being with you all day I've learnt a lot of things. Including how to put something as huge as a transatlantic liner out of action. And it didn't take all that much either."

"I asked you what I should do now."

"Did you bring the electric torch I told you?"

"Yes."

"Good. Make three long signals, then two short ones, then two long ones followed by three short ones, and end up with one very long one. Over in that direction, towards the quay. If that doesn't work, try again."

"I didn't quite get what you said. Three long ones followed by two short ones, then three long ..."

"No. Two long ones. I'll tell you exactly what to do. I'll look at my watch and tell you when. Okay?"

"Yessir!"

"Right ... off you go. Long. Long. Long. Short. Short. Long. Long. Short. Short. Short. And a good long one to end up."

Trevor had scarcely finished signalling when he saw four vague shadows emerging from the darkness and advancing towards the ship.

"Okay. Now make yourself scarce," Larry said to him hurriedly.

"Where to?"

"Wherever you like. If it were me, I'd go back to your cabin. Big things are going to happen on board tonight. Go on, beat it."

Trevor obeyed mechanically and, feeling like a programmed robot, retreated to his cabin. There he flung himself down on his bed, fully dressed, in wait for whatever was about to happen – and he did not have too long to wait either. In fact after a few minutes, he heard footsteps approaching his cabin, and saw the door being pushed slowly open. He gathered all his available strength together and got to his feet since a second officer in the British Navy, merchant or otherwise, must at all times, come what may, hang on to his dignity, and keep a stiff upper lip. For a split second he thought he was seeing a group of revolutionaries enter his cabin, who would kill him on the spot if he did not reveal himself. Instead he saw four people, the very last he would have expected in the circumstances to see.

The four people in question were Madame Solange, Mr. Benson, in the guise of a latter-day Lazarus, the inevitable Larry and – most shattering surprise of all – his ex-fiancée, Hatty Glamps.

Trevor was too dumbfounded even to attempt to speak. So it was Hatty, his erstwhile fiancée, who first broke the silence.

"Dearest Trevor, it's all over. It was I who set up this little show, because I wanted to prove that the day we were attacked by those four louts, what you showed was true British self-control, and not the cowardice of a faintheart from one of those countries on the Continent. I could not get you out of my mind, but on the other hand I did not want to spend the rest of my life married to a coward. Then I had the

idea of putting you to a test, this test, and, as I had hoped you would, you've passed it with flying colours. You are not endowed with a great deal of courage, but you have plenty of self-control. Now I'm ready to marry you."

Trevor could barely summon the will to ask:

"Who are these people then?" pointing to the others.

Hatty seemed to be thoroughly enjoying herself.

"This is Mr. Benson, a lawyer whom I chose for the part in London, because of his sense of humour. He died a splendid death. This is his wife, who really is French, and who really is called Solange Ranier. And this incomparable young lad is Larry, Mr. Benson's son by his first wife. They all played their parts with the help of a little local colour. I certainly won't forget the whole thing that easily."

Trevor emitted the word "brilliant," which was intended to sound sarcastic, but was taken literally by Hatty, true daughter of a Methodist minister.

"Truly brilliant," she said. "Especially young Larry, who's always top at school when it comes to acting in plays. He really is a well-brought-up child. And that slight earthquake also gave us an unexpected helping hand."

Trevor leant against something for support, because he really felt faint. But Hatty would have none of it.

"Trevor, dear, this is not the moment to feel fainthearted or lose your self-control. You must keep it all for our wedding night."

The cabin resounded with a chorus of politely controlled giggles. And while he wiped the sweat from his brow, Trevor noticed that Larry, that well-brought-up little boy, was also laughing mischievously.

A well-brought-up child (9)

Trevor looked hard at Larry, as if he saw in him the root cause of all his troubles, but Larry did not seem to be unduly bothered. He kept on smiling, with the same insolent look on his face, as in a slow, calculated tone, he said:

"Second officer, you're in a mess. I followed you around all morning but you didn't notice me. I saw everything. You murdered my father."

Trevor twitched nervously since he realized at once that Larry was quite capable of thinking the worst, and that he could not offer any proof to the contrary. Nevertheless, he made an effort to keep a grip on himself.

"If you did follow me, and if you did see everything, then you know very well that it isn't true. I did not murder your father."

Very calmly Larry then laid the picture of Hatty on the bedside table. He had turned suddenly serious.

"I might even believe you. But if I say that you killed my father, and if I add that I also saw you do it, how can you prove that it wasn't you, when they find the body?"

The child was nothing short of a devil, and Trevor realized that for the moment at least, Larry definitely had the upper hand. His first priority, he reasoned, was to try to gain some idea of how the boy's mind worked.

"Will you tell them that it was I who killed your father?"

"Of course I will. I shall tell the police first".

"Where will that get you?"

The boy did not answer. He got off the bed and went to look inside a large, half-open wardrobe trunk where Trevor kept all his things – clothes and other goods and chattels. Trevor let him carry on, mastering a gust of anger which became more and more uncontrollable as the minutes passed.

"Second Officer, you asked me where it would get me if I tell on you. So let me ask you something: where will it get me if I don't tell on you?"

Trevor could only look at him, speechless. The little monster was a blackmailer to boot, even if, for the time being, it was not clear how far he might go. Nevertheless, as of now, it was better to play the game his way, for everything considered, there were not really many alternatives.

"What do you think I could give you in exchange for your silence?" Trevor asked, trying hard to sound as naive as possible.

"The 'Haiti,'" came the reply.

"I'm sorry, would you say that again?"

"I want the ship."

Trevor had tried hard to think of the worst that could happen, because by now he was accustomed to Larry's devilish fantasies, but his request for the ship went far beyond his wildest imagination. He decided nonetheless to play along with Larry's little scheme, if only for the fact that no other alternative existed.

"The ship doesn't belong to me. How can you think I could hand it over to you?"

"It's very simple. You'll have to find a way of stopping it sailing tonight."

"How on earth do you think I can do that?"

"You're the technician. You can sabotage the engines. Or say that an epidemic of cholera has broken out on board. It's up to you. The important thing is that you keep the ship at her moorings at least for tonight."

"Why do you want the ship to stay in port tonight?"

"Because something is going to happen tonight."

"What?"

"I don't mind telling you. You know, I really rather like you. Tonight some friends of mine will come on board, under cover of darkness, without being invited."

"What then?"

"They'll take over the ship. By hook or by crook."

"And once they've taken it over?"

"They'll steam around for a bit, once they've got rid of the passengers. Ships are used in wars, you know. Or didn't you know?"

"Wars? What are you talking about?"

"You know too much already. And I'm getting bored. I'll give you five minutes to think it over. If you agree to sabotage the ship, I won't tell anyone that you murdered my father. If you refuse to cooperate, I'll go and tell the police. I know their telephone number. I can get them on this phone."

Trevor felt himself well and truly cornered. He did not have much room left to maneuver, even though he knew full well that he had not murdered Larry's father. On the other hand, he realized that appearances were all against him, and that he could not even rely on Madame Solange to help him out. Perhaps in time he would manage to prove his innocence, but at what price? For the time being, nobody would be able to prevent him from going to prison.

Trevor paced to and fro in his cabin for those eternal five minutes granted him by Larry to make up his mind, while Larry stared at him in silence, looking very serious, having seated himself in the corner close to the telephone.

When the five minutes were up, Larry got to his feet, and, arms akimbo, stood facing Trevor, who asked in a cocksure tone of voice:

"Well, what have you decided?"

Trevor stared at him for a moment without saying a word. Then he walked threateningly over to the boy, and prodding at his chest with his finger, said:

"You slimy little toad. You're the nastiest piece of work I've ever come across. I feel like tearing your tongue out, just to stop you talking. I could also cut off your hands, to stop you writing anything down. And to blot out your evil little eyes, I'd pull them out too. But I don't like the idea of getting my hands that dirty. I also had the idea of kicking the living daylights out of you until you were no more than a lump of pulp, but I actually cleaned my shoes this very morning, and I don't much fancy having to clean little bits of you off them. On the other hand I don't like the idea of you calling the police and spilling the beans. So, I'll put up with you until your mother gets back. Or rather, until Madame Solange Ranier gets back, although I'm none too sure where she fits into your life. In the meantime, you'd better not try using that telephone, because my patience has got its limits and I might just give up the idea of keeping my hands – and my shoes – clean."

Having said his piece, Trevor sat down on the bed with a triumphant look on his face. He was sure that the boy would not have the courage to square up to him after those dire threats.

So he was more than slightly taken aback when he saw Larry quite calmly taking from his trouser pocket a crumpled slip of paper with some numbers written on it. And he was even more nonplussed when he saw the infernal child go over to the telephone and start dialling a number, reading from the slip of paper as he did so.

"Who are you calling?" he found himself asking.

"The police, who else?" came the reply, with not a glimmer of childish fear in the words.

It was then that Trevor launched into the emergency plan which, in the last resort, he had always had in mind. If the tactic of frightening the bestial child did not work, then the only thing for it was to take to his heels. So Trevor made a swift dash for the door, flung it open, and ran off through the maze of passages, through which he could find his way blindfold, but Larry could not. To throw off his pursuer, he took a circuitous route. After a while he stopped to listen. There was not a sound to be heard. He could not be sure if Larry had decided not come after him, or if he had not even bothered to leave the cabin.

He directed his steps towards the ship's gangway, which had been lowered onto the quay again, following the earthquake tremor, and would stay in position until the "Haiti" set sail again. He nonchalantly passed by the sailor standing on guard at the top of the gangway, who saluted Trevor as usual as he was used to the ship's officers breaking the rules now and then. Trevor stepped ashore and after a quick look in every direction, he disappeared into the gloom of the quayside buildings. Maybe he really had managed to make good his escape. He had no real plan as to what he would do once he had got away, but the important thing, here and now, was to get well away from the whole nightmarish situation.

He had taken no more than a dozen steps when he felt himself grabbed by several pairs of arms, and in that same moment he smelt the unmistakable smell of chloroform as a wad of cotton wool was placed over his nose and mouth. He remembered nothing more until he reawoke and found himself back in his cabin. The scene that met his eyes was enough to dispel the residual effects of the anaesthetic, and bring him back to full consciousness. Around his bed, looking vaguely amused, were four people, the last Trevor would ever have expected to see in the circumstances.

The four in question were Madame Solange, Mr. Benson, in the guise of a latter-day Lazarus, the inevitable Larry, and – most shattering surprise of all – his ex-fiancée, Hatty Glamps.

Trevor was too dumbfounded even to attempt to speak. So it was Hatty, his erstwhile fiancée, who first broke the silence.

"Dearest Trevor, it's all over. It was I who set up this little show, because I wanted to prove that, the day we were attacked by those four louts, what you showed was true British self-control, and not the cowardice of a faintheart from one of those countries on the Continent. I could not get you out of my mind, but on the other hand I did not want to spend the rest of my life married to a coward. Then I had the idea of putting you to a test, this test, and, as I had hoped you would, you've passed it with flying colours. You are not endowed with a great deal of courage, but you have plenty of self-control. Now I'm ready to marry you."

Trevor could barely summon the will to ask:

"Who are these people then?" pointing to the others.

Hatty seemed to be thoroughly enjoying herself.

"This is Mr. Benson, a lawyer whom I chose for the part in London, because of his sense of humour. He died a splendid death. This is his wife, who really is French, and who really is called Solange Ranier. And this incomparable young lad is Larry, Mr. Benson's son by his first wife. They all played their parts with the help of a little local colour. I certainly won't forget the whole thing that easily."

Trevor emitted the word "brilliant," which was intenteded to sound sarcastic, but was taken literally by Hatty, true daughter of a Methodist minister.

"Truly brilliant," she said. "Especially young Larry, who's always top at school when it comes to acting in plays. He really is a well-brought-up child. And that slight earthquake also gave us an unexpected helping hand."

Trevor leant against something for support, because he really felt faint. But Hatty would have none of it.

"Trevor, dear, this is not the moment to feel fainthearted or lose your self-control. You must keep it all for our wedding night."

The cabin resounded with a chorus of politely controlled giggles. And while he wiped the sweat from his brow, Trevor noticed that Larry, that well-brought-up little boy, was also laughing mischievously.

We have now come to the fourth and final break in our story. Depending on the answers you give to the three last questions (below and overleaf), you have now chosen your own personal dénouement to this multi-plot tale. What your total choices mean in psychological terms, is explained in pages 146–147.

In which of the two scenes pictured here, would you prefer to find yourself at this very moment – your companion perhaps one of the characters in the story? Jot down, or remember – A or B.

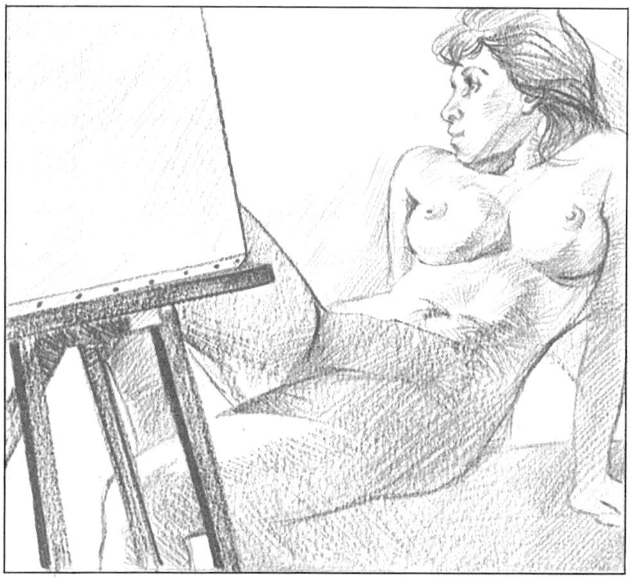

Imagine for a moment that you are a painter and you have been invited to paint a full-length portrait of Elsie Fammer, the pretty, young, English waitress. It should be added that Elsie is prepared to sit for you in any pose you suggest, nude or otherwise. How would you depict her: draped (A) in an ancient Greek garment or peplus, or wearing nothing (B)?

When Second Officer Trevor Landen is in London, he can spend hours watching the ebb and flow of life in the city streets and parks. It could be that among his musings, as he gazes at what is probably the most diverse mass of humanity of any city in the world, he imagines there must be many who are more foolish or more unhappy than others. Which type, do you think predominates? If you think there are more who are unhappy, mark your choice. A. If you think the foolish carry the day, mark your choice B.

Now read your final version of the story
Add up the numbers of As and Bs you have chosen in the final three tests 10, 11 and 12.
If you have chosen 3 As, continue with version 10 on page 143.
If you have chosen 2 As + 1 B, or 2 Bs + 1 A, continue with version 11 on page 144.
If you have chosen 3 Bs, continue with version 12 on page 145.
Finally, remember how many As and Bs you have chosen in these three tests. For the psychological significance of your choices, see page 147.

A well-bought-up child (10)

Hatty and Trevor's wedding took place on board the "Haiti" soon after the ship set sail from her port of call in the Azores, while she steamed towards London. For the occasion the captain wore his neatest uniform and kept a grip on the ceremony with a certain degree of edginess, not least because it was the very first time in his entire naval career that he had had to assume such a delicate duty. Witnesses for the bridegroom were Madame Solange Ranier, and for the bride, Mr. Adam Benson, the beautiful Frenchwoman's husband. Larry, Benson's son by his first wife, played the part of pageboy, cooing that Hatty had bought a white wedding gown while she was in London with a very long train to it, and it was Larry's job to hold the end of the train, which he did with impressive dignity, even though he found it hard to conceal a certain feeling of disappointment. Clearly, he was ill-used to playing such minor roles.

All the passengers on board clearly regarded themselves as invited, and after the couple had uttered their fateful "I do's," an atmosphere of unrestrained jollity took over on the liner out there on the high seas. Many of the passengers found themselves subjected to long-forgotten, or even suppressed, stirrings of the libido, possibly because the idea of two newlyweds on board brought a certain sexual excitement to the fore. Bored couples felt kindled by each other once more, even if the flame was a passing one; others found themselves prey to certain sentimental longings that brooked no moralizing on their part.

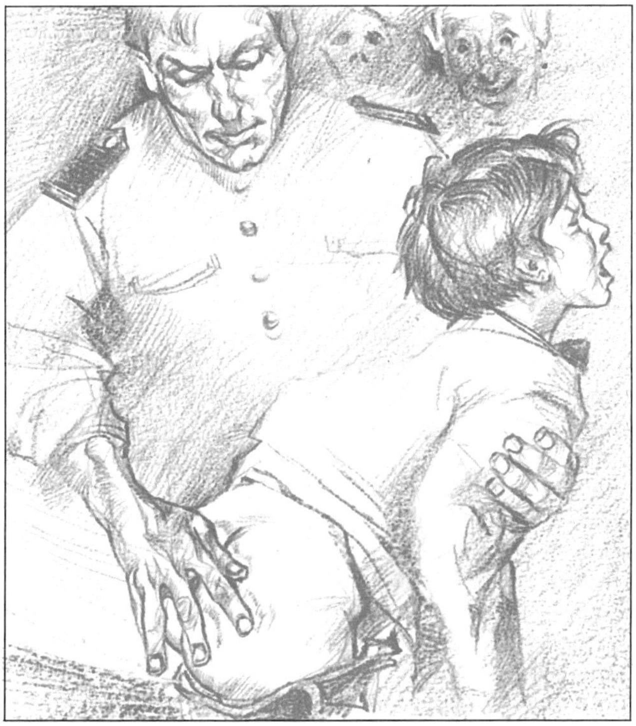

That evening there was a grand ball on board following a sumptuous dinner, punctuated by the pop of many a champagne cork. The newlyweds were several times called on to dance, and as midnight drew near Trevor leapt on to the platform where the band was playing, to address the gathering.

"Dear friends," he said, "and I know I speak for my beloved Hatty too, may I thank you all for sharing in our happiness. I know that, for the moment, I can count on your understanding." At this, a unanimous "Yes" went up, accompanied by thunderous applause.

"When we go ashore in London we shall all go our separate ways. We cannot avoid that, and I myself shall resign from the Merchant Navy. So we shall all take up our lives again where we left off. So now I'm going to ask you for a collective gift," and here again people shouted and clapped.

"And I know that not one of you will dare deny a source of satisfaction which I've been nurturing since yesterday morning." Here a chorus of insistent "No's" went up. "Well, my friends, I want young Larry, the boy who has made such a contribution to our wedding, to jump up on to this platform beside me, and take down his trousers."

To begin with, there was a murmur of stunned surprise from the revellers, but soon, not least because of all the champagne everyone had drunk, the murmur turned into enthusiastic clappings of agreement. Even Madame Solange and Mr. Benson, Larry's father, gave their agreement with expressions of amused surprise. Only Larry himself scowled and turned slightly pale, but he could not get out of it as he was grabbed by many pairs of hands and pushed towards the bandstand alongside Trevor.

"And now, dear Larry," Trevor said with a smile, patting the boy's head, "would you rather take your trousers down yourself, or shall I lend a hand?"

In unison, no doubt inflamed by the excitement of anticipation, the onlookers all shouted, "Yourself." Larry scowled even more darkly and slowly pulled down his trousers.

"Don't forget your pants too, laddie," Trevor insisted with an impish smile. And everybody crowding around the platform let out yells of approval, while Larry carried out this last order with the last scrap of dignity he could muster. Who knows why the sight of his posterior regions, all naked, trigged off a round of applause that bordered on the sadistic. When Trevor managed to restore some semblance of order, a seat was already in place beside the boy. The second officer beckoned Larry to bend forward over the chair, then he turned to the band.

"A gallop, please."

The band started up with gusto and Trevor got the onlookers clapping in time with the beat of the music. And to the same beat he started smacking the naked posterior of the well-brought-up child, the slaps resounding above the hubbub of the swaying crowd.

The clapping of the onlookers soon turned into a standing ovation, and some of the less carried away passengers found themselves thinking that happiness does not always show itself with a lightness of touch.

A well-brought-up child (11)

The departure of a transatlantic liner like the "Haiti" is usually preceded by a certain amount of confusion, a situation Trevor made the most of, to steal ashore with a large package under his arm. Without as much as a goodbye, he left on board the Bensons and their odious appendage, Larry. Even more to the point, he was walking out on the scheming Hatty, whose mind, by now, was focused on just one thing – the ship's arrival in London, and the happy nuptials that would follow.

Trevor sought out a semi-deserted warehouse on the quayside, no longer used for any discernible purpose, and waited for the liner to pull away with the usual ceremonial flurry. When at last he saw that the liner had left the outer breakwater, gradually growing smaller as it sailed towards the horizon, he opened the package and took out some civilian clothes. Making sure that nobody was about, he took off his second officer's uniform and slipped on a well-cut sports jacket and trousers. He bundled up his uniform, stuffed a heavy stone inside it, and then went to toss the whole lot into the dirty waters of the harbour. As the last bubbles drifted away on the oily surface, with the package already on the bottom, he turned about and, with a light step, walked towards the center of the town.

It was the decision he had come to which made him feel so light and unburdened, as if, for the very first time in his whole life, he suddenly found himself without any obligations – duties, timetables, deadlines – anything, in a word, which turned life into a rut.

Until just a few hours earlier, he was probably destined to being an officer in the Merchant Navy for the rest of his life, not altogether the most humdrum of occupations, he had to admit, when one considered it was the British Merchant Navy. Now, after this decision which, so far had, proved to be plain sailing, he suddenly found himself as free as a bird to roam the highways and byways of an island paradise, in which he would find all the happiness he could wish for, despite the experiences he had heretofore encountered.

As he walked through the center of the town, he bought himself a pipe, something he had always wanted, but had always gone without for a variety of reasons, all of which were logical enough, and to do with other people. In another shop he made an on-the-spot decision to buy an Alsatian puppy, something which people had invariably discouraged him from doing in the past. With the pipe in his mouth and the warm puppy in his arms, he went to the restaurant where he had met Elsie Fammer, and having inveigled the pretty waitress to come outside into the road, where they were out of earshot, he addressed her:

"I am quite different from the man you met before. Right now, I'm free. I've got a few savings, and I really want to enjoy myself. May I share all these possibilities with the prettiest English girl I've met on any voyage I've ever made?"

Elsie, obviously an expert in British psychology, did not bat an eyelid on hearing the proposition – if anything, in fact, she behaved as if she had been expecting it.

"I finish my shift at midnight. If you come and pick me up we can go back to my place."

"May I remind you that my name is Trevor."

"And mine's Elsie."

"So let's be on Christian name terms?"

"Fine. See you at midnight."

"Which is your favourite champagne?"

"Dom Perignon '79."

Trevor pressed his lips to the girl's mouth and a feeling of the uttermost tenderness consumed his whole being; the aroma of her flesh was that of a new born babe. It was some time before they interrupted their embrace, when Trevor gazing lovingly into the girl's eyes, asked:

"Elsie, tell me truthfully. Were you one of Hatty Glamps's extras too?"

"I don't understand." the girl answered, and Trevor never gave it another thought.

Their night together was one long paean of joy, because time, for lovers, never abides by the normal rules, its passing dictated by a rhythm all its own.

A well-brought-up child (12)

The "Haiti's" passage across the Atlantic was drawing to a close. In the misty dawn, in that greyness in which the sky and the sea almost merge, one could already make out the English coast.

Trevor was on the first-class deck, but not on the call of duty. He had not slept a wink all night. He had been visited in his cabin by Hatty, keen for some matrimonial action before their wedding which was to take place in London at the end of the month. Then, later, when Hatty had returned to her own cabin, Trevor's thoughts all seemed to gather at once in a confused jumble inside his head, making it impossible for him to drop off to sleep again. Now here he was on deck, gazing at that typically British dawn, which certainly did not bring out the most sanguine of thoughts. There was no point in hiding it, not even from himself: he was not happy.

Plunged in his solitary thoughts, he did not notice a pale shadow which had slipped close beside him and was now staring hard at him. He jumped when he heard his rank being called from a few feet away from him:

"Second Officer."

There beside him stood Madame Solange, looking every bit as miserable as he himself.

"Madame Solange. What are you doing up so early?"

"I couldn't sleep a wink all night."

"Nor could I."

"It was the thought of going back to London. It's almost unbearable."

"I feel the same."

"We seem to have a lot of things in common, Trevor."

"Perhaps more than we realize, Solange."

"As soon as we land I want to run away. I don't know where to."

"I feel like doing the same. Except that I don't want to run away on my own."

"With whom then?"

"With you, Solange."

She shivered slightly and wrapped her dressing-gown close about her. Then, in a scarcely audible voice, she said:

"Poor Trevor."

Trevor thought that perhaps he had gone too far, and had said something that had displeased her.

"I'm sorry," he said, turning to look out to sea.

Solange leant on the railing beside him.

"I'm whimsical, stubborn, even touchy sometimes. I become too attached, to the point where I seem to be clinging. But above all else I need a great deal of tenderness. Up until now I haven't found it – ever."

"I'm a phlegmatic type, a creature of habit, sometimes even a bit dull. And I tend to fall in love too easily, but I feel there is a lot of tenderness inside me, which, up until now, I've always kept in check – just as I've kept people who said they loved me at arm's length."

"Trevor!" breathed Solange, as she turned to face him.

"Solange!" Trevor whispered, as he took her in his arms.

In a short while they had formulated their ideas, and had even managed to work out a plan – a perfect one, they believed, down to the last detail. They both went to their respective cabins, and after a while met once more on deck, wearing their best clothes, each holding a suitcase containing just the bare essentials of clothing. In their respective cabins, Hatty, Mr. Benson and Larry were still fast asleep; no one had thought about rousing them, not even their steward, who, for a small tip, had pretended to forget all about them. In the meantime the liner had reached the port of London and was being maneuvered alongside her mooring.

Solange pressed herself closer to Trevor, saying:

"I must tell you a secret that I would have kept to myself forever if things hadn't turned out the way they have."

"If it's about your past, I'd rather not know."

"It's about you, I'd say."

"Me?"

"Yes. I'll tell you because you don't have any qualms about leaving Hatty behind."

"What's Hatty got to do with it?"

"She's been having an affair with my husband for quite a while now."

"And you knew about it?"

"Of course. What's more, she wasn't the first and she certainly won't be the last of Mr. Benson's lovers."

"And even though she was your rival, you helped Hatty to organize that whole charade against me?"

"I thought by marrying you she might leave my husband alone."

"Do you still love him then?"

"By no means. But when Adam has a lover, he gets very short-tempered. He gets his revenge on me by betraying me. In between affairs he's more or less bearable. Because he doesn't bother me."

"And why would Hatty marry me if she was in love with your husband?"

"I don't know the answer to that. Human beings are never as simple as that – although it would make things easier if they were sometimes."

Instead of frowning or scowling, Trevor's face lit up with a smile of satisfaction.

"Do you think Hatty and your husband will get together, now that we've walked out on them?"

"It seems more than likely. Shipwrecked survivors tend to grab hold of the first lifebelt that comes their way."

"Well, I'm glad."

"What do you mean?"

"Hatty will get the punishment she deserves for having been unfaithful to me even before we were married."

"Are you talking about the sort of life she'll have with my husband?"

"I'm talking about Larry. She'll have to put up with Benson and the odious little monster. And I can assure you, she'll pay dearly for her misdemeanours."

Together, Solange and Trevor burst out laughing; their nightmare was over, a new life awaited them. Then, with the gangway already lowered onto the quay, they hurried down it and were soon swallowed up in the London throng. Hand-in-hand, they walked away, each lost in his or her own romantic daydreams.

Psychological explanations of the twelve tests

The course of our story has been interrupted four times to allow you to take part in four series of tests, each consisting of three questions. Your responses to these character-revealing questions, put to you at each story-break stage, have indicated a psychological preference, on your part, for one particular story-continuation, as opposed to others, so that it could be said that you have constructed for yourself, as it were, a made-to-measure story.
Moreover, it so happens that the twelve test questions (divided into four groups of three), introduced in the breaks in the story, also correspond to the four divisions of our existence.We refer of course to childhood, adolescence, adulthood and old age. By engaging in these twelve tests, you will have increased your awareness of the personality traits which mark these four basic "moments" in your own lifetime.
Character traits marking childhood, adolescence, adulthood and old age, as shown by your answers to the twleve tests, are given below. These assessments retain their validity even if the reader may have already passed a particular "moment" in his or her life, or may even have not yet reached it.

Let us start with **childhood**, which was the subject of tests 1, 2 and 3 on pages 118 and 119.

▮ If you chose 3 As, you have a detached attitude as far as your childhood is concerned. There was a time when your childhood experience was very lively, but now it has no effect on your character. The impressions – pleasant and unpleasant alike – which you experienced then have left no trace on your present attitudes and behaviour.

▮ If you chose 2 As + 1 B, you have a detached attitude towards your childhood, which does not have a great deal of influence on your current attitudes and behaviour. But a few impressions, positive or negative, still persist.

▯ If you chose 3 Bs, your childhood still has an influence on many of your attitudes. Certain specific impressions, either positive or negative, which you experienced back in those days, still remain in your mnd and definitely influence certain aspects of your behaviour. You probably lived through your childhood years as in some kind of dream, invariably reacting rather slowly to whatever befell you. But now the influence of these experiences lingers on like an indelible stamp.

▯ If you chose 2 Bs + 1 A, you are still very affected by your childhood, even though one part of your character has shaken itself completely free of it. Perhaps your childhood still has claims on you in a sentimental way, but it has little or no influence when it comes to attitudes where reason prevails.

Adolescence was the subject of tests 4, 5 and 6 on pages 126 and 129.

△ If you chose 3 As, your adolescence is marked by a desire to dominate and stand out. Where this period is concerned you are active and do not necessarily try to avoid life's problems. But you also harbour a certain taste for violence, which sometimes makes you seem brusque and unscrupulous.

△ If you chose 2 As + 1 B, during your adolescence you had a keen desire to dominate and stand out from the crowd, and as a result you feel prepared to tackle reality with plenty of determination. But you also sense a limit to this natural aggressiveness in you, which is why you would not be prepared to resort to any form of violence, even for the sake of affirming your personality.

▲ If you chose 3 Bs, your adolescence tends to reject the hidden hazards of existence and to flee from quite a lot of responsibilities. Reality scares you somewhat, especially when it reveals its pitiless face – as a result you decide not to confront it head-on. Nor do you even justify the violent or aggressive attitudes assumed by other people; rather, you fight hard for non-violence and mutual understanding.

▲ If you chose 2 Bs + 1 A, you are/were opposed to all forms of violence and aggression during your adolescence. You are happiest confronting reality with a certain degree of caution, without being dishonest in any way. But there lingers on in you the conviction that you cannot always refuse to fight. So every so often you persuade yourself that a little bit of self-assertion, self-will, even a modicum of aggression are not out of place, albeit controlled by reason and taste.

Adulthood was the subject of tests 7, 8 and 9 on pages 133 and 134.

□ If you chose 3 As, this means that when you reach maturity and adulthood you do your damndest to come to terms with reality, without bothering to investigate much further. Everything must revolve around your egocentricity, which drives you to take more than you give. By now you feel that you have reached the peak of your potential and you consider that the time is ripe to make the most of whatever you have been able to construct in life. For you, adulthood is a time for reaping, and for enjoying fully the crop you harvest.

□ If you chose 2 As + 1B, you regard adulthood and maturity as the time to enjoy the fruits of past endeavours. In this period reality for you is a fruit from which one should squeeze the most pleasurable juices possible. But despite this basically egoistic attitude, you do not feel prepared to accept everything blindly. You still retain a little curiosity, on the basis of which you believe that it is pertinent to take a deeper look at certain problems and certain aspects of life.

■ If you chose 3 Bs, your adulthood is aimed mainly at comprehending, and going deeper into things. Mature experience offers you the ability to thoroughly examine, if not dissect, many aspects of reality, and you have no intention of frittering away any inner wealth. For you, living – and living your own adult life above all – means essentially comprehending.

■ If you chose 2 Bs + 1 A, you have a predominant tendency to understand and grasp reality and to probe deeper into its various aspects, especially in your years of adulthood. But you also show a determination to enjoy the fruits of your past endeavours and efforts. You want to carry on along the road of awareness and consciousness, but at the same time you remember now and then, to enjoy what you had earlier sometimes overlooked.

Old age was the subject of tests 10, 11 and 12 on pages 141 and 142.

♦ If you chose 3 As, you live your old age by closing yourself off in a somewhat disgruntled form of conservatism. For you there is little worth appreciating in this period of your life, because the best things are locked in the past. You are very frightened by the idea of physical and mental degeneration, and disabilities, but you do not make much effort to stave these off. Grumbling about, or extolling the past only makes you sceptical, embittered and unhappy. In life, there is never absolute stasis, things are always in motion, though we can also help with the odd nudge, at the same time making sure to keep in step.

♦ If you chose 2 As + 1 B, you tend to hang on to whatever you have and regret what is no longer there, but you still do not lack a certain dynamism. At these moments you are ready to tackle any new situation, and take a positive pleasure in doing so.

◇ If you chose 3 Bs, for you old age has merely a statistical connotation, because, psychologically speaking, you are young at heart, still imbued with a certain existential dynamism. Basically, you still feel very much alive, keen to enjoy many aspects of life, while retaining that ironical sense of detachment which is the hallmark of true experience.

◇ If you chose 2 Bs + 1 A, you live an active old age which is full of stimuli, because you refuse to live in the past. In fact you feel quite ready for any number of new, even unexpected, experiences. However there is still a part of you that houses feelings of distrust or negation, negative elements in your character of which you must beware.

A summing up

By now you are in the position of being able to combine the four answers you have given, to correspond with the four main periods of life, ranging from childhood to old age, and by comparing them, you can put together a composite picture of your own psychological being.

The overall result will certainly not be a horoscope or anything of the sort. It will mean that in relation to the different situations that mark our passage through life, your character will force you to assume one set of attitudes as opposed to another.

The attitudes we assume in the face of situations presented to us in our lifetime, influence our personality to a large extent. In fact there are two fundamental issues in our psychological life: interpersonal relations: our attitudes towards other people; and our reactions to external reality, the way we adapt to various situations.

With regard to other people, and life's various situations, we react basically in three ways: either we lag behind, or we keep up, or we forge ahead. If each and every situation or personal interaction can be compared to a point in space and time, our attitudes will be behind, alongside, or in front of this existential point.

Let us consider interpersonal relations. In relation to another person there are basically three attitudes: behind, alongside, or in front. "Behind" means dependence on another, letting someone else do the leading, or it may mean being powerless to stand up to another's will, or it could express itself in direct passive dislike. This type of psychological contact involves a whole series of rancour and recrimination.

"Alongside" means respect for one's own and the other person's dignity, maturity and awareness. In a negative sense it may mean a certain habituation, a somewhat vaguely defined psychological sluggishness and an excess of reasoning. "Ahead" means a sharing or involvement in our own hopes and the hopes of the other person, courageous leadership and making full use of one's imagination. In a negative sense it may mean adventurousness, overbearing behaviour towards other people and a lack of rationality.

If on the other hand, we think not of people, but of our attitudes towards external situations, we can also see that the notion of behind, alongside or ahead is again valid.

If we stay "behind" situations, we find ourselves piling up frustrations, inferiority complexes, unmotivated longing and everything that operates in the realms of distrust and regret. If we are placed alongside or even within situations, we are capable of confronting reality with courage and determination, and this in turn makes us active, positive achievers. But we run the risk of losing sight of broader perspectives, we attach ourselves to details and thus tend to overlook the whole, and as a result we end up imposing on ourselves narrow limits which lead to dissatisfaction in the long-term as if there were no past behind us, and no future ahead. If on the other hand, we forge ahead of situations, we can be capricious, imaginative (fanciful), and idealistic, but we run the risk of ending up being over-ambitious and neglecting possible realities by concentrating on an improbable tomorrow.

Fixed positions with regard to behind, alongside and ahead, with reference to both interpersonal relations and situations, will invariably lead us astray if used without discretion. If, however, we manage to vary the possibilities – ring the changes in a moderate way – we are on the way to playing the cards that make up our character in the best and most satisfactory combinations.

It is quite true that we all find ourselves in any situation in life, by dint of our own character; but character should never be taken to be something predestined and immutable. It is not true that one's character is formed as a result of genetic forces and environmental conditioning, so that it is impossible to evade the "destiny" imposed on us. If we can never escape from our character, changes of a substantial nature can nevertheless come about, in both an ameliorative and a pejorative sense. The destiny of an individual is not written in any star, nor is it some ordained reverberation of a nebulous hereafter. It is simply the most tangible fruit of the personality, as moulded via the stimuli of the world about us.

Given that our character is not static, we should always be alert to any kind of change and new feature, which can lead to enrichment or change, nor should we reject past experience, because it represents for us an irreplaceable source of inspiration.

We should always be aware of the plastic potential of our personality, which is not constituted to remain static at a certain stage in its development, but tends continuously towards expansion and dynamism. It is enough to think how greatly we can be changed, fundamentally and for the better, by love, or freedom, or a gratifying job, and how deeply we change, for the worse, by some wrongly interpreted success, or wealth accumulated for its own sake, or the abuse of power.

All that takes place round us is capable of bringing about quite important changes to our character. For this reason we should live side by side with reality, either to alter it, or to conserve certain aspects of it, without closing ourselves away in some numbing form of existence which is a prelude to inactivity.

Behind, alongside and ahead must become for us three constant points of reference when it comes to handling others and external reality because our personality does not exist on its own, it continually interacts with people and with a multiform reality.

If, as we hope, our test-games have come to mean something for you, we trust it is in a heightened sense of movement, an expansion of personality, and most important of all, joy of living and communicating with one's fellow men.

Find out your psychological type

In the foreword we mentioned that at the end of the tests there would be – at least for readers who have borne with us thus far – an opportunity to find out more about their own individual psychological type.
Here, then, we present 32 psychological types, with a general outline of their principal characteristics. Of course, as well as offering a challenge to the compiler of such a list, any psychological classification must, of necessity, be a kind of Procrustean bed, in which it is always possible to add or remove something.
In drawing up this classification we have taken into account five psychological characteristics obviously with their opposites:

1 Our attitude to ourselves, such as emotivity or rationality.

2 The ability to be self-sufficient and hence independent of conditioning and, contrarywise, dependence on something or someone.

3 Our attitude towards external reality – extroversion or introversion.

4 Behaviour in relation to other people, in other words, blatant egocentricity of the instinctive variety, or a form of egoism tempered by a respect for other people.

5 The ability to confront situations realistically, or on the other hand the need to have ideals as a guide for general patterns of behaviour.
In our view these are the fundamental elements of a character, but they do not necessarily exclude others which, to differing degrees, go to make up the entire personality. But the more elements one adds, so the possibility of various combinations increases with the speed of geometric progression, so much so that, if we were to take other traits of human character into consideration, we would have ended up with an entirely different kind of book.
Thus the rider, that the strict format of these 32 types corresponds to actual fact only in a summary manner, that is, synthetically which leaves plenty of room for more complicated compilations, rather like the different shades of a primary colour.
To find the psychological type which sums up the whole gamut of choices you have made in the various tests, you must add together the geometric signs to be found alongside most of these choices, bearing in mind that one and the same sign is either black or white, and thus corresponds to a psychological characteristic which has two contrasting sides.
In the final calculation, it is necessary to remove from one and the same sign that which has been chosen less – either black or white – in practical terms, by referring the results of your choices to the table on page 12. You must then take into account only the white sign or the black sign, whichever of the two turns out to be the more numerous in the final reckoning.
At the end of your calculation, by getting rid of either the black or the white of each sign, you will have five different geometric signs (circle, triangle, square, rectangle, and rhomb) in different combinations of black and white, or perhaps all black and all white.
At this point, you must consult the index (overleaf) where you will find all the possible combinations of the five signs, and alongside the combination which concerns you, you can read the page number which refers you to your own psychological type.

Index of combinations

1 The uneasy achiever

An individual with an extrovert, sanguine character, who is directly involved in the life about him, interested above all in the positive aspects of living, a doer rather than a thinker. He is an individual who carries himself confidently, but to describe him as an all-out egoist would not be quite true: he is an admirer of culture, even capable of altruistic gestures, admittedly when these do not interfere with his own wheelings and dealings. He is of sufficient strength of mind, however, to feel that he can, to a large extent succeed on his own: it would not occur to him to feel he had to rely on the support of others.

Nonetheless, he prefers to move in an environment he knows; he tends to be suspicious of progress and novelty for its own sake. While conforming to social moves, however, even if he may outwardly profess adherence to a religious faith, within himself he feels no particular call towards the afterlife or any form of mysticism.

Being basically an emotional person, he feels confident in his feelings, and in fact at times lets himself be carried away by his instincts. He thus reaches levels of impulsiveness which make him appear irresponsible in certain situations.

He does not really abide by any principles, which leaves him open to the charge of being an opportunist, especially when it concerns his own interests. This opportunism tends to be especially manifest on occasions when he fears he may not be able to impose his personality on others.

There are so many contradictions in him that he could be defined as an individual who enjoys lightning successes but is just as swiftly disheartened. While he sets out to confront reality with a great deal of confidence and in a mood of high optimism, it needs only one problem or obstacle too many to sow doubts in his mind as to his own qualities.

Despite the fact that he has an essentially optimistic view of life, he is quite often the prey to doubting moods, even experiencing moments of bitter regret whenever logic cannot allay his doubts. It is understandable therefore that the unfathomable, the irrational, and the mysterious affect him more than most, as factors beyond his ability to control.

This man of contradictory character also reveals an embryonic form of authoritarianism, often exercized against those who appear to him as illogical and irrational. Given enough rein, this authoritarianism could become a downright weakness.

2 The submissive idealist

A more or less egoistic individual who nonetheless does not have the capacity to face up to reality, and consequently encloses himself in an inner world in which he becomes the yardstick for everything around him. Nor is he capable of developing on his own any independent attitudes, and so he becomes reliant on things or people, for some form of support for his basic insecurity. He nevertheless tends to idealize reality, because his egoistic instincts are not directed towards material well-being, but to inner fulfilment.

Though abstract and often naive, this idealism has a refining influence on his egoism, not least because, in social matters, he is a perfervid propagandist of all ideas to do with progress, where the rights of the group must be respected to a greater or lesser extent.

As far as irrational attitudes or beliefs are concerned, he accepts them, although ready to argue over their formal aspects. He is also often conditioned by past experiences, in particular those of his childhood.

This is not an emotional type of individual exposed to the winds of all manner of feelings; he tends rather to be cold, assuming wherever possible reasoned attitudes and appearing well-balanced and unswerving. This reflective capacity also enables this basically shy and immature person to achieve a kind of serenity. In a word, here is a responsible type of person, the fascination of whose character lies precisely in his contradictions, which often assume aspects of a well-balanced humanity.

3 The live-for-the-moment egoist

An extrovert who lives for the moment. What matters for him is not so much the overall result, as the esteem that comes from winning, or at least being up there among the leaders.

In reality he is not wholly self-sufficient; he is always in need of something or someone to lean upon. A success achieved in solitude would be inconceivable in his case, nor would it have the slightest interest for him – from the plaudits of the crowd comes the adrenalin that sparks him off.

He is open in his human relationships and appears to be very sociable, but for these involvements he pays too great a price because he ends up not being able to do without them.

In social terms, he is a conformist, preferring to side with the majority and operate in proven situations. While accepting current ideas without making any attempt at evaluating them, he does not allow himself to be carried away by idealism. In situations which he finds stimulating, he may even grow bold and reckless, but the initial impetus will not be sustained for long, unless some sign of outward support is forthcoming.

He displays a certain degree of immaturity, in particular because the past, and especially his childhood, still have a hold on him, and can sometimes lead to complexes. In such circumstances a basic sense of insecurity comes to the surface.

He must continually square up to his own emotional nature, which makes him impulsive in many situations, even to the point of downright irresponsibility. His sentimental nature is easily aroused, but those close to him should take into account the fact that he can be fickle. His egoism tends to be held in check by respect for others, but even if from time to time a degree of altruism can be detected, it is more of a cerebral attitude, a rational reaction to the situation.

He is endowed with a basic shrewdness which should not be under-estimated, well able to calculate his own interests. He is particularly conscious of an innate streak of aggression. The mollifying effect of culture helps him to hold this in check.

Basically, it is circumstances which force him to assume one attitude rather than another, given that he has a particularly receptive personality. When things turn out well for him, he experiences a resurge of optimism, if they go badly, he subsides into a state of pessimism. In any event he would rather blame everything on external circumstances than on himself.

4 The rigorous idealist

An individual who exudes strength of character since the foundations of his personality are self-sufficiency and a reasoning intelligence, a formidable combination. This self-sufficiency is accompanied by an intelligence unaffected by any form of conditioning, so he is able to express himself totally. He is mature, confident, and at times authoritarian, especially when he is afraid that he may not be able to go it alone.

His lack of emotivity makes him logical and rational, given to a high opinion of himself. In this respect too he is stable and balanced since his sense of security is buttressed by a deeply reflective nature.

Decisive and determined as he is, his introvert character also causes him to see himself as the measure of all things around him. What counts for him is personal experience, and as a result he is not particularly sociable, somewhat reserved, even shy, and he does not put himself out to any great extent for others. He is unreservedly an egoist, and thus tends to satisfy his own needs even at the expense of others; these needs are above all of an idealistic nature and so tend towards the abstract.

Though egoistic, he has genuine and instinctive attitudes, maybe sometimes unpolished, but he inevitably recognizes his responsibilities since he has enough culture and good taste not to be oblivious to the unjust or the gratuitous. He has no propensities towards mysticism, superstition or any credulous beliefs; he does not allow himself to be conditioned by the past – his childhood experiences, positive or negative, play no conscious role in his mental makeup.

As an egoist, and more particularly as a logical and self-sufficient one, he has a very keen sense of what he wants, and knows how to come by it. But these needs are far from unrefined: they are rich in idealism, revealing a thirst for knowledge and concern for problems of human existence. An individual of this type belongs on the whole to the category of dominating intellectual, in other words, someone who tends to be a point of reference.

The contradictions in a character of this type emerge in relation to his reactions to external realities which cannot be modified by individual action; he may emerge from such encounters in a mood of deep gloom, or on the other hand, his logic will see him through. These contradictions are the inevitable price to be paid for a kind of solitude filled with noble and ideal aspirations, but encased in an authoritarian egoism that is sometimes too rigorous.

5 Egoist in disguise

We are talking here about a natural achiever who faces up to reality with casual confidence, and makes use of both his own strength and the weakness of those close to him. He is a realist par excellence, in that he does not let himself be carried away by false appearances; he pursues success as the primary objective of his existence. He often appears aggressive, even authoritarian, an attitude that is justified by the fact that he feels himself a giant in a world of pygmies.

His self-confidence is only matched by his self-esteem. But he can be foolhardy to the point of recklessness. Logic rules his actions, to the point that he tries to analyze the reasons behind every situation, which again indicates the particularly reflective type he is. Of course a personality as dominating as this cannot function without a degree of shrewdness, even duplicity. His opportunism is often in evidence, because like all who are attached to success, he never acts before calculating every move. In this respect, he is cold, untrusting, because he well knows the limitations and weaknesses of those with whom he is closely involved. He is not prodigal in placing his confidence in others, at times even apt to shy away from human contact, altogether all the more strange for his being extrovert.

Basically, he is an egoist in disguise, who realizes that one cannot set oneself at the center of the universe and not attract the odd bolt from the blue. Even here, his egoism remains rational, controlled, measured. As a rule culture and good taste teach him that at times it is a good idea to open oneself to other people, that altruism is an intelligent or shrewd way of approaching reality without overlooking any aspect of it. He is convinced that aggressivness, in its purely raw state, harms above all the person who uses it. On the contrary, respect for others is also a tactic which enables him to operate with a maximum of consensus.

He is never afraid of taking up a challenge no matter what, so he always appears active and efficient. Given that he is aware of his own possibilities, he is essentially an optimist, who is unhurried in his decisions, and does not allow himself to be affected by the past. Childhood experiences do not create bogeymen complexes for him, because like all realists and extroverts he is principally concerned with the present. In social terms, he is conformist, not being enamoured of adventures or battles undertaken in the name of abstract ideals. He likes to be on the side of the majority, but only up to a point, as any dalliance with mystical, superstitious or credulous beliefs, leaves him cold. He only believes what his senses tell him, eschewing improbability or irrationality in whatever form.

He is mature, intelligent and responsible. His weak points may lie in an excess of self-confidence and too great a reliance on falsity, which can ever confuse his relationship with himself. In fact, it is precisely the feelings of others which he understands least, and manipulates with the greatest difficulty. The world of the emotions is something alien to him, which if he is ever lured into, can really lead him astray.

6 The emotional egoist

The type of idealist who achieves inner satisfaction from knowing about things and investigating problems rather than success in its practical guise: any dealings with external reality are simply not for him; he prefers to take his guiding truths from culture or alternatively from his own reflective experiences. Hence his unrealistic and non-active attitudes, judged by the conventional meaning of these terms.

Keeping his distance from reality, he ends up by locking himself away in his inner world, from which he excludes others, and in which he himself is the center or the measure of everything. He is proud of this inner climate of culture and reflection, which he finds impossible to find in the world outside. It is a form of pride that contains a great deal of coherence as well as dogmatism, because he does not enjoy discussing his principles with others. As a result he appears to be unsociable, reserved, even shy, if not outright timorous.

In reality, behind this pride, enclosed within itself, is a hidden streak of instinctive egoism, bent on satisfying its own ideal needs at the expense of others. It shows at times in the subject's rather crude impulses to impose his own views, when he seems to renounce the very ideals he claims to pursue in his sophisticated solitude.

An individual who is religious, at least in a formal sense, even superstitious; he accepts certain commonly held beliefs, is attached to the past and his own childhood experiences, to the point of creating complexes for himself. He readily falls in with majority opinion, proof of his need to find other forms of support and consensus outside of himself. Besides, by temperament he is very emotional, and therefore prey to feelings and instincts which as a rule will lead him from the path of his own ideal objectives. He can be impulsive, fickle, even irresponsible, because of his inner tensions which find outward release in a great deal of emotional energy.

7 Realist at any price

We are dealing with an individual who must of necessity face up to reality, because he recognizes that he cannot count himself alone, and whenever he shuts himself off in his own inner world, he feels for the most part, basically insecure. Given that he is essentially a type that holds material success in high esteem, he cannot but gravitate towards others; hence he is open and sociable. In reality, he needs to lean on something or someone, because he lacks self-assurance and this turning towards reality, sometimes even with vestiges of altruism, is a somewhat ambiguous form of depending on ideas or attitudes which are not original.

He cannot do without the world that is everywhere about him because it is the only world which can give him the success to which he aspires, but at the same time the world conditions him and strips him of his liberty as well as his capacity to fend for himself. One certain thing, however, is that once this double-sided game of taking and letting oneself be taken has got under way, his attitudes will be lucid and coherent. In fact this is a very logical individual, even though he has to proceed slowly in his reasoning processes, while his intelligence is never truly independent.

This is the fundamental reason why the idea and the attitudes of the majority offer him the highest degree of security, and why he accepts, without dispute, whatever comes to him from outside, on condition that he does not have to invest too much of himself.

As a general rule he tends to be conservative, uninterested in progress or new ideas. From the majority he accepts his models of conduct, especially moral ideas, religious attitudes, superstitions and run-of-the-mill beliefs. He is in no sense unrefined, in fact he admires culture and good taste, even if these enriching factors are for him basically utilitarian.

His involvement with reality is linked with a considerable capacity for adaptation; in situations which he finds stimulating, above all where he feels that he has some kind of support behind him, he can reveal qualities of unsuspected daring. Although a go-getter, he gives pride of place to reflection. In his relations with others, especially when he knows that he is not acting on his own, he is fairly responsible.

Because he brings consistency and an extrovert exuberance to the attainment of his functional goals, he tends to be opportunistic, and can become underhand and calculating whenever he considers his own interests are at stake. When he fastens on to something that implies certainty, he can be stable and well-balanced. But every time he feels unprotected, and has to tackle reality on his own, his initial optimism tends to desert him and a feeling of insecurity gets the better of him.

In essence, this individual has the wherewithal to establish healthy relations with his fellow human beings, and also achieve success because he is on the whole clear-sighted and realistic; capable of moderating his own egoism by drawing on his cultural heritage; and he puts his trust unfailingly in logic, careful to avoid falling too often into the snare of the emotions.

But he does have a possible weak spot – an immaturity that calls into question his self-sufficiency. A contributing factor is an excessive attachment to the past, especially childhood.

8 The solitary idealist

An individual who is interested above all in the quest for knowledge; the practical issues of life – well-being, success – do not interest him in the least: the proper study of mankind is the be-all and end-all of his existence. Precisely because his discoveries are a priori rather than a posteriori – theoretical, and not derived from experience, he gives the impression of being somewhat abstract, even naive, especially when he puts his trust in imagination and fantasy. Once, however, he has found the ideals he seeks and made his choices, he is resolute to the point of being dogmatic. His strength as an idealist resides in his self-sufficiency, in other words in those qualities of independent intelligence which enable him to express himself both freely and fully.

He is not merely a passive exploiter of ideals. He is above all an activator, if not an original promoter. In this respect, he is authoritarian, since he is not easily persuaded to accept the ideas of others or to change his own. He is confident and mature, to the point where he does not let himself be carried away by mystical ideas, superstitions or suchlike beliefs. He is not attached to the past, or to his childhood because such memories do not affect him, and certainly do not create any particular complexes for him.

He looks to the future, never to the past, so he is a progressive type of person, mainly because he is all the time driven to producing new ideals, or at least improving those already existing. But he is not interested in any confrontation of his own ideals with reality. Not only is he not concerned with personal well-being or success, he rejects reality in its most positive and tangible aspects. As an abstract thinker, he is ever putting his own ideas to the test, as he tries to discover the motivations that drive mankind.

Sociable he is not. Introverted and very reserved, he has no great desire to become actively involved in affairs, preferring his own company and thoughts. In all this there is a pronounced streak of pessimism, which at times expresses itself as disillusioned cynicism, as happens with all those who delve into the major themes of existence in a state of solitude.

This fundamental pessimism is further aggravated by the subject's emotivity, which makes constant demands on his feelings and instincts, rendering him tense, volatile and sometimes unhappy. Impulsive, he is also insecure and must continually confront the fact that his idealism and introversion are at times at the mercy of uncontrollable, emotional attitudes. He masks this insecurity by a strong, raw egoism.

When he feels deeply about any of his ideals, he is prepared to ride roughshod over others. He does so with an instinctive ingenuousness, without the least cunning; the result, however, is to increase his egocentricity, so he becomes even more isolated.

9 The persuasive idealist

A basically idealistic individual who looks for the real values of his own existence in the quest for knowledge. He subordinates practical concerns to the need to enrich himself culturally, and to the possibility of expressing himself in an artistic or scientific setting.

It follows that he is intelligent and knows how to use his innate good taste to tackle any manner of situation. Although an idealist, he is not too given to abstraction, nor does he take refuge in an inner world of his own. He strives to confront his ideals with day-to-day reality, but in such a way as to impose his own, inner needs, in order to derive from them the greatest possible advantage, which in a temperament such as his, is mainly in terms of opinion or esteem.

His brand of optimism is slightly naive and at worst muddleheaded, but at least it leads to positive ends. In his constant confrontation with reality, this individual, who has powerful mental and cultural weapons, never lacks initiative, is always alert, sometimes even bold. Although of a sociable nature, he nevertheless continually questions the ideas and attitudes of the majority. He is by nature, progressive and nonconformist, always infused by the desire to understand things more fully and explore new experiences. He refuses to take his opinions and beliefs from others. He feels free of any kind of conditioning by the past, especially where it concerns his childhood. In fact his ideal home is in the future, not in the past. His fundamental attitude is one not of regret, but of hope.

The desire to reconcile idealism with the demands of reality serves to moderate his egoism, even to the point of achieving truly impressive altruistic results. His culture and essentially ethical ideas tend to facilitate the achievement of collective targets, in which however, he is not above promoting his own inner interests. He is an egoist who is tempered by his own idealism, and who aims at both material and spiritual progress, even though he does not like to have to depend on others.

His quota of self-sufficiency is of such a high degree as to make him appear a born leader or a true spiritual guide who can persuade others to follow him. In this respect he may at times become authoritarian because he is also dogmatic and not easy to shift from his personal convictions, nor is he readily prepared to give credit to anyone. Rather, he has a degree of trust in collective ideals, within which it is possible for him to retain his own independent judgement.

In his quest to reconcile reality with ideals, he meets with obstacles which sometimes seem insurmountable. In fact he has a very high degree of emotivity which sometimes leads him to forget the lessons of culture and experience. In addition, this capacity to be fired by emotion and feeling stirs up the fires of his idealism, and consequently he is at times driven to impulsive gestures. Also uncertainty sometimes shows when he has to change one set of ideas for another for whatever reason.

10 The eclectic egoist

A character full of contradictions who lives in a state of great uncertainty, and consumed with many inner problems. He is at once realistic and egoistic, in the sense that he is principally interested in practical wellbeing and success. As a result, he tends instinctively to satisfy his own existential needs, with little concern for those of others. He is accustomed to measuring his successes objectively, but he does not have the necessary courage to confront reality with the open-mindedness or freedom from prejudice which are vital to bring certain premises to fruition. He tends to close himself off in his inner world, where he can exhibit himself as the measure of all things.

Naturally, in such attitudes there is not much realism and a great deal of ambition. As one concerned with his own interests first and foremost, he is positive, efficient and even aggressive, but being introvert, he is reserved, shy, sometimes even ultra-cautious.

Another fundamental contradiction which marks this individual is the clash between his capacity for logical thinking and his need to make himself dependent on something or someone. He is not endowed with the independent intelligence that is capable of self-sufficient creativity, and as a consequence he latches on to the ideas of others, and often becomes a slave to them. In other words, he is an effective achiever, when it comes to other peoples' ideas.

As an antidote to all his contradictions, this individual resorts to shrewdness, in him a direct product of his egoism. He will often conduct himself in the most opportunistic way, because he has no ideal commitments to defend, and so everything seems possible and acceptable. This practical sense of opportunism can persuade him to accept the ideas and the attitudes of the majority, especially when they seem to support and bolster his own interests.

He is therefore conformist in his attitudes, conservative in his acceptance of social ideas, mores, and, at least in a formal sense, religious, with a leaning to credulous, even superstitious beliefs. He displays an inordinate attachment to the past and to his own childhood experiences.

11 The conforming altruist

An open, sociable individual who strives to operate within the terms of reality, with the avowed aim of achieving success, and earning the esteem and goodwill of one and all. To achieve these results, however, he needs something or someone to serve as a prop to his insecurity. He holds in the highest regard culture and knowledge in general, as a continuing source of enrichment of his own idealism. In this rather fatiguing search, he often comes across ideas, maybe somewhat abstract, and which he adopts as his own, in the hope that they will stand him in good stead in moments of uncertainty and disappointment. In the event, the result, in many instances, may be bungled with contradictory attitudes, which at times make him appear trusting, at others naive. And the vaguer his ideals become, the closer he clings to them with a tenacity bordering on dogmatism. In this way it is possible to explain some of his attachments to religious ideals, or even to forms of fanaticism and superstition, which involve him at least on an emotional level.

Sometimes he will admit to progressive aspirations with a view to a more secure future for himself, but sentimentally he is very attached to the past, in particular his childhood.

All these complex, and at times contradictory, aspects of his personality mark him as an emotional person, who often puts his trust in feelings and instincts which cannot always be governed by reason. As far as his emotivity is concerned, he is also impulsive, even reckless. Each new situation finds him tense and nervous, as to what the outcome will be.

Basically he is immature, despite all his ideals and culture. He also lacks the necessary respect that is the feedbed for creativity. His natural aggressiveness also turns out to be masked, because he measures it against the fear he has of others. Culture and ethics combine to convince him that egoism does not always pay, hence an inclination to an altruism that almost invariably turns out to be cerebral, with no real inner conviction.

In a word, he is an idealist who readily becomes a slave to what he idealizes. And he is also an emotional person who instinctively interprets what he fails to grasp by logic alone.

12 The solitary leader

An individual who sees his personal well-being and success in life as the paramount objectives of his existence. He is an egoist who tends to make others pay the price of his successes. He is, in brief, an egocentric who positively revels in his realistic approach to life. He is efficient, forceful, aggressive even, but never to the point that he fails to overlook these qualities in others.

He is not a particular advocate of culture, which he tends to regard as coming a bad second to practicality. He loathes refined attitudes and is not exactly in a class of his own when it comes to good taste – in fact at times he can be downright coarse. As far as social mores are concerned, he takes the ideas of the majority as he finds them and uses them in a conformist, conventional way, being not the least bit interested either in discussing or in developing them.

To this quest for success, he brings an independent intelligence which has no need of props, spiritual or otherwise. He is capable of giving complete expression to all his possibilities and potential, having a sanguine temperament befitting a mature and confident individual. He has undisputed gifts of leadership, always carrying himself with an air of authority.

Neither the past nor his childhood have any hold on him. He might be compared to a marcher who unburdens himself of every possible item so that he can step out more confidently. In this, as he sees it, quest for an ordered life, carried out with intelligent self-sufficiency, he uses logic and rationality as his lodestars. Given that reason holds such sway over him, he always appears well-balanced, stable and confident. At times he can be cold, operating with a shrewdness that serves opportunistic ends. And in one who aspires to practical achievements, these are usually qualities that count.

Endowed with a reflective nature and a good deal of common sense, he is well equipped to ride out the defeats which must inevitably come his way. As a rule, he acts in a relaxed way, appearing serene, calm, happy even. This logical and self-sufficient course towards success is mostly a solitary one. In fact he is an introvert who avoids contact with others. He is a leader destined to conquer alone, a situation that inevitably breeds pessimism, not to say an embittered cynicism.

We are now at the penultimate stage of our sexuality test: photograph G opposite and photograph H overleaf. Note down, or remember, which photograph of the two you prefer: G or H.

13 The idealistic achiever

Here is an idealist who tempers his ideals with realistic attitudes, logic being the mainspring of his approach to existence. For the most part, his patterns of behaviour tend to be stabilized. Even in his emotional life he always appears to have the situation well in hand.

He has a cultural background, or at least the inclination to come by one, which enables him to see things in depth and to act with rationality. His intellectual maturity is free of any conditioning by the past. His particular strength is the ability, both instinctive and rational, to adjudge any situation in its proper proportions. Consequently he is capable of tackling most situations with a strong likelihood of success. Admittedly, this capacity for clear-sighted thinking may sometimes point to a character which is somewhat rigid, even coldly calculating; it is nonetheless part and parcel of his basic mode of behaviour.

He can be seen as an idealist with the smell of success in his nostrils because he knows how to control events and consequently ensure the implementation of his own ideas. Also a contributory factor, perhaps, is a generally low-key emotional response to the vicissitudes of life generally.

He is indisputably progressive in spirit because his ideas are orientated to the future, improving a present which demands continuous readjustment.

He is an abiding devotee of culture in all its forms; his intelligence has constantly to feed off culture – and he sees intelligence as the very foundation of his independence. This predilection for culture serves to reinforce an already innate logical rigour, as well as a pronounced capacity for reflection.

With such a well-balanced combination of realism and idealism, it can only be that his basic attitude is one of optimism. He is highly conscious of his own individuality and well aware of the disruptive force of ideals when they are used with measured intelligence. His is not a world of anxiety neuroses: he is the epitome of relaxed calm.

Because he so passionately wants to see the realization of his dreams, his conduct may at times appear somewhat disorderly, even rash – the lot, it seems, of most extrovert idealists who find themselves nursing so many projects and trying to realize them all. Alas, we are none of us perfect.

14 The insecure egoist

We are in the presence of a natural egoist who instinctively goes for the main chance, irrespective of how he gets it. In this quest to satisfy his own interests, he operates with a vivid sense of realism, the tangible product of which is an efficient, not to say aggressive nature.

As a general rule, he is conformist, opting for the tried and proven rather than the role of the pioneer. He is hampered, however, by a feeling of inadequacy, unless he can count on outside support. He certainly does not see this coming from any form of culture, which could, if he only knew it, help him to achieve greater self-sufficiency.

The fact that he has to depend on something or someone in his egoistic quest for success, means he is immature and insecure, to the point where he will latch on to ideas and attitudes which are far from realistic, thus contradicting his predilection for the here and now. A strongly-felt emotional nature can drive him to impulsive, even irresponsible actions.

Faced with such contradictions of character, he retires within himself, into a cocoon of introverted solitude, which provides a false sense of security. In reality, he becomes unsociable, reserved in his relations with others, even positively timid. This introverted attitude gradually leads to a diminution of activity, and eventually to regrets over possibilities missed. It is at these moments that culture might have come to his rescue.

15 The down-to-earth idealist

Fundamentally idealistic, this individual pursues the path of knowledge and inner enrichment, to the exclusion of success for its own sake. He has a love of culture in general, because it continuously renovates and enriches his own ideas. However, once these ideas have taken possession, he remains bound to them with a tenacity which actually harms his mental independence. He is basically insecure, lacking that vital confidence, without which one has to look for moral support elsewhere.

The past, for example, plays a significant role in moulding his character, his childhood experiences especially, having conditioned him – positively or negatively, as the case may be. Of necessity, as an extrovert, he has to concern himself with day-to-day reality, even if his behaviour is not motivated by the pursuit of success for its own sake, but by the need for esteem and moral recognition. His ideals do not prevent him from keeping his feet firmly on the ground, and in effect he tries to translate into reality what he imagines and feels in an ideal way.

For these reasons he appears to be open and sociable, not shut off in an inner world of abstractions. When moved idealistically he can attain the highest flights of altruism. Although he tends to be insecure and immature, this is not his attitude whenever he regards himself as committed to something for ideal reasons. As someone who as a rule tends to naivety and muddleheadedness when it comes to practical things, he can appear intransigent and dogmatic whenever it is a matter of defending a position about which he feels convinced idealistically.

Whenever his ideals square with reality, he cuts an impressive figure of logical rationality, all the more meritorious for it being, sometimes, a hard won battle. Few things come easily to him, but for all that, his idealism – the idealism of an extrovert – brings serenity of spirit because, when confidence fails him, he finds solace in the ideal motivations to which he is so steadfastly committed. His finest hour is when his ideals match up with the remorseless demands of reality. In the long run he manages to temper his egoism with his culture and regard for others' needs.

efficient, not to say, opportunistic in the short-term, when his shrewdness and initiative needed to derive the maximum personal benefit from every situation, are at their maximum.

Suspicion dominates in his dealings with others, though when it comes to practical matters, he adopts the ideas and attitudes of the majority. Conservative and conformist that he is, he places his trust in the proven rather than the untried.

Yet, emotional and introverted though he is, he still strives to assert his independence both emotionally and realistically. In this respect, he is helped to some degree by his egoism and intelligence, though not always successfully as the emotive and unsociable sides of his character sometimes get in the way.

He can be said to be self-confident, mature, even authoritarian at times. Generally, he is untrammelled by memories of the past: superstitious or irrational beliefs leave him cold.

16 The uneasy egocentric

An individual who is very much of the call of his emotions, in other words, he is a person whose reaction to outside stimuli is governed by the emotional tensions which are stirred up inside him, his emotional nature is complex, in that he approaches and withdraws from external stimuli in a manner which can only he described as exaggerated. Temperamentally he is always tense and volatile, and has his moments of insecurity, even of unhappiness, when his emotive nature is deeply stirred.

His reaction to this emotional onslaught by the outside world, is to retire into himself so that personal experience is all that matters. Consequently his capacity for sociability suffers. He grows reserved to the point of shyness. Because he is afraid of being forcefully involved in reality, he tends not to be particularly active; in fact, an innate pessimism is the reality he must face up to. With such a character, at once defensive and enigmatic – others cannot make head or tail of him – he is at heart an egoist, who instinctively sees everything only from his own point of view and material needs. In this respect, however, he is true to himself because he acts in accordance with his nature, though with a certain coarseness, the result of his disparagement of culture and refined or sophisticated attitudes.

Basic to all his desires is his own self-interest, though even here his objectives are limited because he cannot conceive of things on the grand scale, and because he attaches so much value to practical things, he does a great injustice to himself. He is positive,

17 The "hampered" go-getter

An introverted individual who makes his own inner world the primary reason for whatever he feels and does. Given that he is not very good at adapting to outward reality, he sets himself up as the bench mark for everything, a basic attitude to which he manages to bring a distinctive form of decisiveness. He is basically self-sufficient, and while recognizing the conventional ideas of the majority he accepts only those which are useful to him, revealing himself as conservative in his thinking. On the other hand he rejects the illogical and the irrational, nor does he consent to being conditioned by memories of the past, or the echoes of childhood experiences.

He is not a solitary, abstract thinker in any sense; in fact he has a conspicuous awareness of the here and now, an attitude which bodes well for his eventual success. To achieve this success, however, he is not prepared to over-exert himself; he sees it as the inevitable reward of his own individual qualities.

This individual's character contains a great many contradictions, even though they may be quite skilfully concealed. He combines a sense of the concrete and the realistic with a certain detachment from the broader aspects of reality itself. In his character there is a centripetal tendency, which tends to attract everything in towards him, whereas he lacks almost entirely any centrifugal tendency towards the world outside.

A strong sense of self-control and an innate balance befitting a cultured, refined person are in contrast to the emotive side of his character, which makes him tense, sensitive to moods, impulsive, and sometimes even irresponsible. Therefore he faces a major task in resolving this dichotomy between his two "selves" as it were.

Although sure of himself, and in addition authoritarian in terms of being self-sufficient with regard to other people, he is nevertheless weak in as much as he is a little afraid of his own egoism.

Those who intend to make themselves the yardstick for things, with a conspicuous store of self-sufficiency, and who aspire to realizing themselves with a healthy ration of realism, cannot permit themselves the luxury of emotional and sentimental weaknesses, to which they may become slaves. In reestablishing a difficult balance between such contradictory tendencies he is helped by his own form of polished egoistic moderation, which in some cases can aspire to altruism.

It is precisely this, as it were "hampered" aggressiveness, which enables him to keep the awkward factors in his own character in a state of balance.

18 The enigmatic egocentric

A very complicated individual, a mass of intricacies and contradictions, he is extrovert, and thus equipped with a healthy ration of realism, ready and willing to face up to whatever life has in store for him. He is essentially a go-getter, open-minded and amiable, a natural optimist, with a tendency at times to over-reach himself.

In facing up to reality, he can rely on two basic character traits – an innate stability and a powerful egoism. From this stability he derives his propensity for logical thinking, his constancy of behaviour, and acute sense of responsibility. His egoism, which serves to heighten his instincts, sometimes leads him to adopt a raw, unsubtle approach to matters which could do with more adroit handling. We are therefore dealing with an individual who is sure of himself, constant in his attitudes; someone who is capable of combining both reflection and a sense of responsibility. For this reason he acts in a relaxed way and appears to other people to be cool, calm and collected – in short a well-integrated individual.

Culture, he feels, is something he can do without because it can divert his attention from the practical aims he has set for himself. But if he is in possession of two character traits which help him in pursuit of these aims, there are two others which act as restraining factors, namely, idealism, and the need to have the support of something or someone behind him. His idealism makes demands on him for a deeper understanding of life, in other words, he comes up against culture, about which he now has two minds. Furthermore, idealism makes him – for all his tendency towards the real – a somewhat abstract individual, because he puts too much trust in ideas. Though it brings a certain coherency to his existence, his idealism may also render him dogmatic and rather inflexible.

The progressive mind of the true idealist inevitably makes him cope with his innate conservatism – part and parcel of the dependent person who prefers to follow the ideas of the majority. He is also very dependent on past experiences, in particular those of his childhood, which are sometimes relived positively, and at others negatively. His not very indepedent brand of intelligence and his feeling of dependence makes him immature and insecure.

In short, this character is so complex and contradictory that he often seems to be as much of an enigma to himself as he is to others.

19 The shrewd emotionalist

An individual who tends to shut himself in his inner self, who is not capable of adapting to reality because on the one hand he is centered in on himself, and on the other, he has little confidence in his own independent potential. He always feels the need to lean on something or someone, and ends up by being snared in ideas or situations which impose limits on his already limited independence. Those who need to rely on other things or other people show that, however unwittingly, they have little self-esteem.

This fear of facing up to reality also derives in this type from the fact that he is emotional, his behavioural patterns for the most part dependent on his instincts. In this respect he often appears tense and anxious, as if he were constantly looking for a safe point of reference. His intelligence forces him into continual computations and adaptations, which place a burden on his decision-making abilities.

A further sign of his insecurity is the attitude which he usually assumes in relation to the past, to his own childhood, and to the opinions of the majority. The past, and his childhood, both affect him considerably, and at times create rather obscure complexes. As for the ideas of the majority, he accepts these without dissent on the whole, because they offer him security and stability. Things that are new frighten him, whereas anything that is proven and shared gets his vote every time.

He is therefore a conformist, not only in the social sphere, but also with regard to irrational phenomena: he can be superstitious, on the whole he is reluctant to engage in any form of existential thinking.

His innate pessimism makes him at times melancholy, as when, for example, he realizes that he is over-dependent, or when his emotions get the better of him. Against these anxiety-producing insecurities, culture offers certain palliatives: his good taste preserves him from what could be mistaken attitudes; his altruism is undoubtedly of help here too: his is a controlled and measured egoism, in that it takes into account the needs of others.

If an individual of this type had to face up to reality, his only weapons being his introversion, dependent nature, and his emotivity, he would surely come off second-best. What saves him in this instance is a hard core of shrewdness, which to others may make him appear distrustful, even phoney, whereas in actual fact he is using the one weapon available to him to come to terms with the realities of life.

20 The egocentric idealist

An essentially idealistic character, who is interested not so much in individual success as in the acquisition of knowledge and illumination generally. His ideals derive more from culture than from personal experience, and tend to be realistic rather than abstract. He is in fact an extrovert, who enjoys measuring his potentialities against reality, and this makes him forthcoming in his human relations: socializing comes naturally to him. In new situations, especially those stimulated by his ideals, he can show great boldness, perhaps to the point of over-enthusiasm. He is active, even if he trusts to inspiration and fantasy, which makes him appear at times as somewhat naive, not to say, muddleheaded. His ideas are orientated towards progress, as he is attracted by the dynamics of the new, and he feels stimulated by new experiences. By operating within reality to achieve his own ideals, he is capable of expressing himself clearly and with an independent intelligence because he has no tendency to depend on others. In this respect he can appear dogmatic and even authoritarian, because he is not easily dissuaded once his mind is made up.

He is confident and mature, seemingly immune to conditioning by the past or his childhood. He scorns superstitions and all credulous beliefs as they are invariably inimical to culture and progress. Logic and rationality further strengthen his self-sufficiency, which may take on a sheen of pride. As a reflective and responsible person, he has all the potential of being able to achieve his ideals and become a fulfilled individual.

With attitudes at once extrovert and positive, there has to be a certain element of egoism, in the exercise of which, scruples tend to go by the board especially when he is convinced that the ideal he sets out to achieve is valid (which often is the case) then he pursues his objective instinctively.

This egoism does not appear exaggerated, in fact it seems natural and genuine in a character such as his, but to some extent it contradicts that ideal refinement with which all his intentions start.

21 The shy realist

The type of individual we are concerned with here is essentially an introvert; he tends to see himself as the center of everything, a state of affairs partly explained by a superabundance of self-esteem, and partly because he does not have a great deal of aggression in him – at least not enough to enable him to confront reality with a sufficient degree of conviction. Closed in though he is, he is not one for abstract thinking; his sights are well and truly aimed at material success, even though his ability to make himself felt in situations which are outside his control, is not much in evidence. He is rather like a general who wants to win the war without ever having to show up on the battlefield.

So there is in this individual a fundamental contradiction between the desire to impose himself on reality and his need for reserve. He is not particularly sociable, in fact he is more often reserved, but his natural shyness sometimes breaks forth, by way of contrast, into a kind of aggressivity. As one whose interests lie in practical achievements, he is positive in his approach and efficient as one would expect with his innate qualities of logic and reason. Culture too plays its part in this attitude of calm objectivity: it has taught him to value courteous and reflective behaviour. He lays much stress on spiritual enrichment because he is not capable of remaining enclosed within himself for too long without having at least some moral input and justification.

Even his particular brand of egoism is that of a courteous person, and may sometimes attain to a degree of altruism, in as much as this individual needs to attach himself to others. His realistic intelligence and his capacity for logic, however, open the way to a streak of opportunism, always present in one who measures himself against himself.

In his dealings with society, he is conformist, highly suspicious of what smacks of adventure, and of ideas not proven by experience. But where majority beliefs are concerned, he rejects those he finds illogical or offensive to human credence. Similarly, his self-sufficiency is such as to offset any conditioning by past or childhood experiences.

Despite his self-esteem and the self-evident aura of invincibility, he too has his moments of pessimism, but these are never so intense, as to cause undue distress. Like any intelligent person, who is mature and self-assured, he cannot escape his moments of pessimism. The danger is, this could develop into a form of cynicism without his being aware of it.

He knows himself and reality too well, to build up illusions. In fact moderation is perhaps his most obvious merit, despite certain contradictions and excesses of egoism. His character is poised within a series of intelligent counterweights, which, in better moments, enable him to function like a well programmed mechanism.

22 The errant idealist

An idealist concerned with getting to know the nature of things, his method of thought is realistic rather than abstract. He is extrovert, and thus open to others, sociable, and enterprising. There is the possibility, however, that his character is such that he has to rely to a great extent on others; at such times he can reveal himself as over-trusting – naive, in other words. Indeed, being extrovert and idealistic, he puts a great deal of trust in others.

He can also be a highly emotive person, instinctive and sentimental, tense, volatile, a combination of character traits not calculated to reinforce his sense of security. Consequently, he can appear fickle, even self-disparaging. At such times he can be very unhappy.

A countervailing agent, to a large extent, is his egoism, a genuine and natural part of his character, but if he could, he would always have others pay for the satisfaction of his aspirations. When his egoism gets the upper hand, he can appear a very different individual from the idealist who set out with such high hopes.

23 The calculating introvert

An introverted individual who thinks of himself as the center of the universe and who tries as much as possible to keep reality at bay. He needs, however, the help of something or someone before he acts; his aims are blatantly materialistic, hence he conducts his affairs with logic and realism, free of any illusions.

Once he has become reliant on something or someone capable of safeguarding his particular need for reserve and remoteness from the outside world, he operates with great efficiency. He is well-balanced, stable, responsible, secure – as long as he does not have to act independently. He tends rather to be someone who carries out orders to perfection rather than one who is creative, but he retains his self-esteem, mostly because of the realistic streak in his character. He is therefore relaxed and calm, despite the fact that there is in him the basic pessimism of most individuals who are closed in and reserved.

This fact of being turned in on himself, and yet achieve practical results, enables him to adopt this detached attitude, which is slightly ironical, sometimes even cynical, and which is peculiar to egoists of his type, who are basically reflective. He can be cold and calculating, to the point of opportunism, while the restraining influence of culture tends to curb a natural egoism.

His attitudes are essentially those of the conforming majority, at whose service he may even put himself. He in no way questions mystical-cum-religious types of behaviour, or superstitions, or beliefs. He accepts them for what they are, possible stepping stones to his own advancement. Basically, be puts his trust in the proven rather than the unproven. He is receptive to experiences from the past and his childhood.

His constant need to understand and investigate brings out certain altruistic attitudes which, however, are of a cerebral kind, calculated rather than felt.

24 The extrovert idealist

An idealist whose basic interests are the problems of existence – he is not interested in practical success as such. Naturally, he sets great store by culture and science in general, at the risk of appearing abstract because his experiences are more bound up with the spirit than with outside reality. He is saved, however, from any excess of abstractness by another basic factor of his character – his extroversion. In fact as an extrovert, he tends to measure his own ideals against reality as part of a contest of achievement.

His involvement in actual situations invariably comes about in order to seek out the realization of his own ideas, and for him, as a result, success is not something practical, but merely a matter of opinion or esteem. Given that he is also an egoist, the realization of his lofty objectives takes little note of what it may cost to others. At this point he forgets about his culture and spiritually refined attitudes, and acts with a ruggedness that might bring blushes to the cheeks of the most committed of entrepreneurs.

To find a proper place for his own ideals in the real world, he commits himself wholeheartedly both in his workaday and social life. In seeking to put his ideals into practice, he has the advantage of an extrovert optimism, which sometimes, however, leads him to take chances that a more considered judgement might advise against. He can also be trustful to the point of naivety.

He is progressive in his ideas, and seems to be influenced neither by religious nor any superstitions or credulous beliefs; and here again, neither the past nor his childhood appear to have left any decisive reverberations on his behaviour. That part of his character which contradicts so many ideal certainties and poses questions about his self-sufficiency is motivated by strong emotive tendencies, which at times cause him to react in an exaggerated way, so much so that he can be carried away by his emotions.

25 The complete intellectual

An idealist who is not so much interested in material success as in knowledge and research into the more taxing problems of our human existence. It goes without saying that culture, with its enriching intellectual experiences, is a prerequisite to any such undertaking.

Neglecting reality in favour of ideals, this individual tends to retire within himself, where he resides, as it were, in an ivory tower, oblivious to everything except himself. Once his choices are made and invariably oriented towards spiritual enrichment, he does not need anyone's help. His aim is to give complete expression to what has matured within himself; somewhat grandiose, artistic, scientific or humanitarian ideals. This self-sufficiency does not cancel out a streak of altruism because he tends to share with others his own ideals, and to draw them into some kind of common purpose.

He is a progressive in that he refuses to go along with the preconceived ideas of the majority. He is intrigued by the grand themes of existence, especially those which hinge on progress – man's progress. As a result, anything that is new earns his passionate attention, at least as material for in-depth examination. He is especially antagonistic to majority-held beliefs that defy credulity or reason. He is, however, not without a certain intellectual arrogance. In short, he is an intellectual to his fingertips. Those who act on the basis of their more irrational instincts, earn his total scorn. It is therefore inevitable that he should appear to be slightly abstract in his ideas, and, in his culture, bookish.

In the formation of his ideals, he emerges as mature, sure of himself, to the point of being authoritarian; he is rarely prepared to give in over his ideals. On the other hand, in the actual utilization of these ideals, he can be confused, over-trusting, naive, as is the case with those who choose inner isolation to the exclusion of mundane reality.

He could be more active were it not for a certain pessimism in his makeup. His real weakness, however, may reside in his high level of emotivity, which he sees at times as endangering his ideal propositions.

26 The dependent egocentric

An egocentric individual, whose instincts, irrespective of the consequences for others, have all to do with his own aggrandizement. It is true that he makes no bones about it, even if getting his own way can at times bring out an innate uncouthness. As for culture, it only gets in the way of his real objectives.

He is a natural extrovert, always ready to face, and put to his own ends, whatever fate may bring. He is a born socializer, ever optimistic, but with a propensity to foolhardiness when his feelings get the better of him. Despite his apparent sociability, however, deep down he really distrusts others, whom he will use rather than befriend. This shows his dependence on others for the achievement of his own ends.

He is a pragmatist who pays heed to substance, not form; he is also an opportunist in that he takes advantage of every possibility to advance his own interests.

He is conformist by instinct, in that he prefers to operate within situations and ideas which have already been tested and tried, and which are not likely to blow up in his face. In all, he operates with logic and rationality; his self-confidence is such, that he appears a contented and well-adjusted individual.

27 The insecure intellectual

An individual who prefers to ponder the realities of his inner, private world rather than the mundanities of everyday existence. Here, in a word, is the quintessential intellectual, sure in himself in his idealistic questings, yet less secure in other respects.

Culture of course rules his life, the corollary of which must be a certain air of abstraction. Introverted, he is also something of a compulsive altruist, in that he has need of others, even if, at heart, he remains closed and reserved. His cultural background gives him that measure of civility and common sense which are his most appreciated outward characteristics. His introversion and dependence can be further complicated by a strong emotional nature, which is another basic feature of his character. He is always tense in his emotions, forthright in his feelings, and instinctively impulsive, a combination of factors which does not help towards an ordered existence, in fact the very reverse.

The customary pessimism of the solitary is not unknown to him, nor is a consequent propensity to the arcane, in the shape of superstitious attitudes or beliefs. The past and his childhood experiences can also have an effect on his character.

This type of individual should not expect an easy life because of his emotive and intense character.

28 The all-out egocentric

A born egoist who knows only too well how to play the part because he is endowed with all the vital ingredients: extroversion, realism, self-sufficiency and stability. He is in effect an egocentric who tends, instinctively, towards the satisfaction of his own needs, and often none too scrupulous how he achieves them.

He is in no way given to intellectual attitudinizing, as this would be the very antithesis of his belief that culture generally only weakens the resolve to do battle with reality. Such an outlook only serves to reinforce the already rigid nature of his egocentricity.

It could be said that he accepts life as it comes, making the best of every situation, with no ifs or buts about it. He is naturally gregarious. With a character such as his, opportunism is almost a fact of life. Efficient and thrusting that he is, however, he is in no sense an innovator; not for him the adventurous or idealistic; he prefers to operate in the familiar ambient of the tried and proven.

On his chosen ground, however, he is calculating and shrewd, with a self-sufficiency which others find is his most striking characteristic.

29 The forceful idealist

An introverted individual who shows the door to reality since he maintains that for him the only valid experiences are those matured within himself. He voluntarily lets material success pass him by. In so doing he comes by a set of ideals which constitute his real driving force and with which he manages to find full self-expression. In fact he is basically self-sufficient, which makes him free from all sorts of external conditioning. He relies purely on his own ideals, which as a rule he manages to realize completely, not least because he is prepared to defend them to the death. Despite this streak of obstinacy, his is a vestigial egoism. He shows great logical rigour in the pursuit of his ideals, and his reflective character also gives him a deep sense of responsibility.

He appears unaffected either by the past or childhood experiences; in fact what logic spurns, he will effectively mistrust.

He cannot always avoid reality and when he has to face up to concrete problems he may well find himself in difficulty. When this happens some of his character contradictions emerge, so that his logical reasoning may desert him. All in all, we are dealing with a closed, hard, at times pessimistic, none too sociable, altruistic character, who finds his true expression through his ideals.

30 The ambitious egocentric

For all his ambition, this individual has to strive against a highly emotive nature, and an endemic sense of insecurity, which are certainly hampering factors in his quest for self-realization.

No intellectual or culture vulture, he unashamedly goes after his own ends, with little care as to whom he may hurt in the process. He is an extrovert egoist, whose battles are fought, for good or ill, in the real world. He makes no claim to ideals one way or another, his whole attention being rooted in the here and now.

He is optimistic by nature, socially gregarious up to a point, and a confirmed opportunist. Optimism, however, flies out of the window when he falls prey to his emotions, as happens when success is slow in coming.

He is conformist by nature – not for him the lure of far horizons – content to keep to the well-trodden paths of majority thinking.

Sensitive as he is to his emotions, he does not manage to steer a set course, as the result of which, his self-confidence is undermined by irrational and impulsive attitudes, the bugbear of his continual battle with himself.

31 The no-fight idealist

An individual who is closed in on himself, lacking any basic self-confidence, and desperately in need of someone or something to lean on. The most potent means of satisfying this latter requirement are his ideals, for it is here, inside himself, that he operates with logic and a self-assuredness that are in direct contrast to his reaction to external phenomena. Another factor which militates against his coming to terms with outside reality is his innate reserve and shyness.

Because he does not have a developed sense of reality, his manner of behaviour reflects his dependence on personal experience, which is invariably limited, and unreservedly abstract. He is not noticeably active, as would be one who lives for material success. A propensity to pessimism must of necessity also play its part in the lethargy which at times can stultify his best intentions.

Although he has a basic need of others, he is never at ease in his human contacts, which is not to say he cannot act altruistically when the need arises.

He is an individual who can never be relied upon to enter the lists against reality, but who can contribute a great deal if he is left unencumbered to carry on his intellectual quest.

32 The embattled egocentric

The embattled egoist who calls no truce with reality, but whose strong emotional nature means he has to fight with one hand tied behind his back. The very fact that he has to contend with such powerful emotive forces only serves to enhance his humanity in the eyes of others. Precisely because he does not believe that culture can have a civilizing effect on ideas or patterns of behaviour, he can be boorish and overbearing.

His extroversion begets optimism, and a gift for getting on with people, not to say a certain predilection for opportunism.

He is no adherent of the new and up-to-date, in fact exactly the opposite, as he bases his ideas and lifestyle on the social mores of the majority. Nonetheless, he is an individual with a mind of his own, so he appears confident, authoritarian even, especially when he seeks to impose his will on those around him.

What checks the upward climb of this individual, so lucid, and with such potential to achieve his aims, is an excessive sensitivity to emotion, which invalidates his freedom of choice when taking decisions, leaving him open to charges of impulsiveness, even foolhardiness. Sudden jolts like this can also undermine his natural self-confidence, to the point of causing him acute distress.

In essence, however, his humanity dominates, rescued, as it were, from the harsher consequences of a forceful nature, but the price that has to be paid is high in terms of personal feelings.

Appendix

Games for couples

To round off the selection of psychological games in the main body of this book, we have prepared, in the pages that follow, a few more designed for couples instead of individuals. Important aspects of personality are only revealed in our regular or occasional relationships with others, so the deeper and more intimate features of our character find truest expression in day-to-day contacts with the person who most closely shares our life. In the privacy of the home, traits of character emerge which perhaps have no relevance or application to our routine, professional and business activities. They find an outlet in a wide variety of interests, whether this be a love of pets, an enthusiasm for certain sports and hobbies or a preoccupation with intellectual pursuits.
The tests listed in this Appendix therefore relate to specific psychological features that apply to the individual vis-à-vis his or her partner. We suggest you tackle them together, not merely with a view to discovering something about yourselves as individuals but as a constant reminder that personal relationships are always changing and that we can all complement and enrich one another.

Couples test 1

Proverbs are short, incisive sayings based on normal everyday behaviour. So they can provide apt material for a test, seeing that each of us possesses more or less instinctive inner standards that guide our actions. Choosing one proverb in preference to another is thus a sign of closeness or distance from certain individual and collective criteria of behaviour.

The following test should, like the others contained in this Appendix, be played in pairs and you should not try to find out what trait of character is concerned until you have finished. Either of you can start by choosing one proverb that appeals to you and marking the number below. Then the other should do the same, choosing any proverb that has not so far been selected, marking the number similarly. Then continue in turn to the end, until you have each chosen ten proverbs.

When you have both chosen your proverbs as it were instinctively, without giving it too much thought, and without attempting to influence each other, look at the explanation at the end of the section.

[1] Better late than never

[2] What is new cannot be true

[3] A penny saved is a penny gained

[4] Variety is the spice of life

[5] The leopard cannot change his spots

[6] Actions speak louder than words

[7] A rolling stone gathers no moss

[8] All is not gold that glisters

[9] Measure twice, cut but once

[10] Nothing ventured, nothing gained

[11] He that counts all costs will never put plough in the earth

[12] Cut your coat according to your cloth

[13] Things done cannot be undone

[14] A bird in the hand is worth two in the bush

[15] First think and then speak

[16] Who lives by hope will die by hunger

[17] Strike while the iron is hot

[18] No rose without a thorn

[19] New meat begets a new appetite

[20] It's no use crying over spilt milk

Mark your respective choices here:

SHE — — — — — — — — — —

HE — — — — — — — — — —

(explanations of couples test 1 on page 177)

Couples test 2

You are each invited to answer these questions, choosing one or other reply instinctively, without trying to influence your partner. The character trait concerned will be discovered at the end.

	SHE	HE
1 What kind of laugh do you have?		
a free and instinctive	☐	☐
b infrequent and wary	☐	☐
2 What do you value most highly in this modern age?		
a sexual freedom	☐	☐
b technological progress	☐	☐
3 As a child did you prefer to get:		
a a kiss	☐	☐
b a present	☐	☐
4 A day without your partner is:		
a sad	☐	☐
b stimulating	☐	☐
5 What image does the word "liberty" call to mind?		
a a nest	☐	☐
b a ladder	☐	☐
6 Sexually, did your parents influence you:		
a positively	☐	☐
b negatively	☐	☐
7 Would you prefer to hear something extraordinary:		
a from your partner	☐	☐
b from a knowledgeable outsider	☐	☐
8 What is the chief feeling you get from a dip in the sea?		
a a feeling of health	☐	☐
b a feeling of freedom	☐	☐
9 Which of these two objects do you associate instinctively with the word "I?"		
a a ball of wool	☐	☐
b a blank sheet of paper	☐	☐
10 Where would you prefer to spend a weekend with your partner?		
a on a desert island	☐	☐
b in Paris	☐	☐
11 What gives you more pleasure?		
a submitting to your partner	☐	☐
b dominating your partner	☐	☐
12 If in company with your partner you hear a friend tell a dirty joke:		
a do you feel a bit embarrassed	☐	☐
b do you laugh out loud	☐	☐
13 Which smell stimulates you more?		
a the smell of rain	☐	☐
b the smell of print	☐	☐
14 Everything considered, what, predominantly, has love given you?		
a enjoyment	☐	☐
b suffering	☐	☐
15 Who are more self-centered when in love?		
a men	☐	☐
b women	☐	☐
16 What does crying mean to you?		
a something important	☐	☐
b something trivial	☐	☐

Each partner gets one mark for every "a" answer and no marks for every "b" answer. Insert scores below and then add up totals.

	1	2	3	4	5	6	7	8	9	10	11	12	13	14	15	16
SHE																
HE																

(explanations of couples test 2 on page 177)

Couples test 3

Answer the following questions, ten for each of you. Don't interfere with your partner's choice and don't press for reasons why he or she replied in that way. By now you should realize that in these tests answers need to be given instinctively and almost automatically.

For HER

1. If someone you have just met says "We both have the same character," does it please you? YES NO
2. Is it difficult for you to give up certain habits? YES NO
3. Do you think he is always consistent in his behaviour? YES NO
4. Are you curious to discover the contents of a closed box? YES NO
5. Under normal circumstances, do your periods of sleep more or less coincide? YES NO
6. On meeting a foreign woman for the first time, do you instinctively trust her? YES NO
7. As a rule, does an opinion contrary to yours annoy you? YES NO
8. Does it stimulate you to find you share common interests? YES NO
9. Have the other men in your life had different types of character? YES NO
10. Can you truly say of him that in some things "he has no peer?" YES NO

For HIM

1. When she chooses something to wear for you, do you at least show agreeable surprise? YES NO
2. Would you like to live in a world where everybody thought the same way? YES NO
3. Do you have a high regard for her ideas? YES NO
4. Are you pleased when someone says "You're not like anyone else?" YES NO
5. Would you ride tandem on a dangerous gradient, she in front, you behind? YES NO
6. Do you find it hard always to be true to yourself? YES NO
7. Are you irritated when she has the same ideas and attitudes as yourself? YES NO
8. Do you often disagree on how and where to hang a picture in your home? YES NO
9. When she suddenly admits you are right, do you feel fully reconciled? YES NO
10. Do you often say to her: "As you like. It's all the same to me?" YES NO

(explanations of couples test 3 on page 177)

We have now reached the final stage of our sexuality test. Having chosen between photograph I opposite and photograph II overleaf, match up your choice with your previous preference for photograph G and H, and then turn to page 181 to read the psychological meaning behind your combined choice.

Couples test 4

Each of you should answer the questions freely, putting a tick against "a" or "b."

	SHE	HE
1 Who do you consider more useful?		
- a dustman	a	a
- a private detective	b	b
2 Whom do you like more as a character?		
- Othello	b	b
- Hamlet	a	a
3 Your cat purrs at somebody you don't like:		
- you are glad it is being friendly	a	a
- you shoo it out of the room for being a nuisance	b	b
4 You drop some fruit from a plate while eating alone:		
- you pick it off the floor	b	b
- you throw it away	a	a
5 Someone complains of a headache:		
- you offer consolation	a	a
- you suggest a miraculous remedy	b	b
6 What hurts you more?		
- a slap from your partner	a	a
- an admiring look from your partner for someone of the opposite sex	b	b
7 Which would you prefer to invent?		
- an invisible camera	b	b
- a seawater motor	a	a
8 As a rule, do you feel happier:		
- alone together	b	b
- part of a crowd	a	a
9 If somebody wrongs you, do you prefer:		
- to have your revenge	b	b
- banish that person from your life	a	a
10 In your opinion, how are two persons of opposite sex, finding themselves alone, likely to react?		
- have a chat	a	a
- make love	b	b
11 You notice a branch of your apple tree bearing a lot of fruit is hanging over the fence into your neighbour's garden. What do you do?		
- lop off the protruding branch	b	b
- suggest to your neighbour that you both share the fruit	a	a
12 A new National Anthem is proposed:		
- you accept that it is more up to date	a	a
- you are rather annoyed	b	b
13 A younger person, whom you do not know, is appointed your superior:		
- you suspect favouritism	b	b
- you agree that a breath of fresh air was needed	a	a
14 Trust, according to you:		
- is a weakness	b	b
- is a virtue	a	a
15 When you are introduced to someone of the same sex, do you instinctively think that he or she:		
- may become a friend	a	a
- may become a rival	b	b
16 As a photograph of you or your partner, do you prefer:		
- a single one which has not come out very well	b	b
- a group one, which has come out very well	a	a
17 If you were, like Robinson Crusoe, shipwrecked on a desert island, with your partner, would you prefer:		
- to find a native of the opposite sex	a	a
- fend for yourselves	b	b
18 What does the word "doubt" immediately call to mind?		
- the notion of "finding out"	a	a
- the notion of "betrayal"	b	b
19 If a person of the opposite sex winks at you, what is your instinctive reaction?		
- a possible affair	b	b
- a friendly greeting	a	a

20 **You are a guest in a large unknown house; during the night you lose your way in a darkened corridor. What is your instinctive reaction?**
- to try to find your way alone b b
- call out for someone a a

21 **You are invited to play cards:**
- you announce that you are an expert card player a a
- you protest that you are no good at cards b b

22 **You attend an important meeting with a nasty pimple on your face:**
- you try to conceal it with your hand b b
- remark right away that you ate too many strawberries last night a a

23 **You receive an impromptu invitation from Queen Elizabeth II:**
- you telephone Buckingham Palace to find out what it's all about a a
- decide at once it can only be a mistake b b

24 **Your partner is dancing with someone else. Would you prefer to see them dance:**
- disco style b b
- a tango a a

25 **You are sitting in an armchair, when a mosquito zings in around your head:**
- you get up to find an insecticide a a
- remain seated, trying to swot it one way or another b b

26 **You are visiting one of Napoleon's bedrooms. What is the first thought that crosses your mind?**
- the Emperor's nocturnal escapades with women b b
- his nightly meditations on battle strategy a a

27 **Someone calls to you in the street:**
- you pay not the slightest attention a a
- you have to overcome a momentary feeling of fear b b

28 **You are on a boat, your suntan lotion falls into the water:**
- you at once dive in to recover it b b
- you grab a net to fish it out a a

29 **You are alone, gazing at the moon:**
- hoping your absent partner is also looking at it b b
- wishing you had a telescope so you could see the moon's craters a a

30 **If your partner had to make a trip somewhere without you, would you prefer it were:**
- the West Indies b b
- North Pole a a

Each of you should count up the number of answers with the letter "b" and enter the score below:

SHE		HE
	1	
	2	
	3	
	4	
	5	
	6	
	7	
	8	
	9	
	10	
	11	
	12	
	13	
	14	
	15	
	16	
	17	
	18	
	19	
	20	
	21	
	22	
	23	
	24	
	25	
	26	
	27	
	28	
	29	
	30	

(explanations of couples test 4 on page 178)

Couples test 5

As in all the tests in this Appendix , each of you should try to answer the following questions without giving them too much thought and without pressure from your partner. The character trait under investigation here will, as in the case of the other tests, be revealed only at the end, in the explanations.

	SHE	HE
1 As a child, who did you love more?		
a an elderly governess	☐	☐
b a schoolmistress	☐	☐
2 In which do you prefer to see your partner?		
a in evening dress	☐	☐
b dressing gown	☐	☐
3 Just for fun, you ask your partner what he or she would do if you proved unfaithful. What answer would you prefer to hear?		
a you will never see me again	☐	☐
b I'd like to know who my rival is	☐	☐
4 What image does the word "couple" immediately bring to mind?		
a two beautiful people making love	☐	☐
b two people working together	☐	☐
5 In fairy tales which characters do you like more?		
a handsome princes waking their beloved with a kiss	☐	☐
b workaday gnomes	☐	☐
6 When you are introduced to an attractive person of the opposite sex, what kind of handshake do you prefer?		
a strong	☐	☐
b soft	☐	☐
7 How do you feel about your partner's inevitable sense of possessiveness, however slight, towards you?		
a a touch of pride	☐	☐
b a sense of irritation	☐	☐
8 What do you look at first in an attractive person of the opposite sex?		
a mouth	☐	☐
b eyes	☐	☐
9 Shakespeare makes Hamlet say, "Frailty, thy name is woman:"		
a agree	☐	☐
b disagree	☐	☐
10 Would you prefer to see your partner stop and stare into the window of:		
a a drugstore	☐	☐
b a bookstore	☐	☐
11 You notice your partner is upset. Would you prefer the cause to be:		
a something definite you know about	☐	☐
b something you know nothing about	☐	☐
12 Which would you prefer your partner to get excited about:		
a a stock market share going up	☐	☐
b a beautiful sunset	☐	☐
13 Where presents are concerned, do you prefer:		
a to receive	☐	☐
b to give	☐	☐
14 In your view, which is more difficult to overcome?		
a a rock face	☐	☐
b a principle	☐	☐
15 What do you think was the first question the faithful Penelope asked Ulysses when he returned home after so long away?		
a how often were you unfaithful to me?	☐	☐
b what have you brought me from your travels?	☐	☐
16 Which, in your opinion, is more boring as a subject?		
a purity	☐	☐
b sin	☐	☐

(explanations of couples test 5 on page 178)

Couples test 6

This test consists of a series of quotations. Each of you should choose nine out of the eighteen quotations given here. Do not deliberate too much on your choice, selecting those verses that you like most, either because the image evoked in them triggers off particular memories in you or because of their melodious appeal.
These quotations aim to delve into your unconscious in order to throw light on a vital character trait that plays a very important role in human relationships.

1 I have everything I do not want
(Angiolieri)

2 My heart leaps up when I behold
a rainbow in the sky
(Wordsworth)

3 The greatest sorrow is
not knowing the cause
(Verlaine)

4 O nightingale, that on yon bloomy spray
Warbl'st at eve, when all the woods are still
(Milton)

5 Evil pursues me:
My feet enchained,
I flee
(Ferlinghetti)

6 You were not made that you might live
as brutes, but so as to follow virtue and knowledge
(Dante)

7 This is the truth the poet sings,
That a sorrow's crown of sorrow is remembering
happier things.
(Tennyson)

8 I play my zither tenderly
And sing sweet songs of love to my beloved
(Anacreon)

9 A lifetime of happiness! No man alive
could bear it: it would be hell on earth.
(Shaw)

10 O why cannot man's powers
be as infinite as his desire?
(D'Annunzio)

11 How sweet to drown in this ocean
(Leopardi)

12 Unborn tomorrow, and dead yesterday
Why fret about them if to-day be sweet!
(Fitzgerald)

13 Deep as love,
Deep as first love, and wild with all regret;
O Death in Life, the days that are no more
(Tennyson)

14 Let us build the future.
We have naught else
(Zerpass)

15 I knew it was love, and I felt it was glory
(Byron)

16 And when Love speaks, the voice of all the gods
Makes heaven drowsy with harmony.
(Shakespeare)

17 Where is there a better world?
Anywhere but here
(Griboedov)

18 Better by far you should forget and smile
Than that you should remember and be sad.
(Christina Rossetti)

(explanations of couples test 6 on page 179)

Explanations

Couples test 1

Proverbs 1, 4, 6, 7, 10, 11, 14, 17, 19 and 20 score 1 point. Proverbs 2, 3, 5, 8, 9, 12, 13, 15, 16 and 18 score no points.

If you have scored 10 points or many more points than your partner, you are the bolder and more enterprising of the two, less prone to fears and prejudices. You are more in touch with the times and tend to be a decisive leader. Even so, in personal relationships the leader is not invariably the guide. You often need your partner's advice to keep a rein on your enthusiasm, and in such circumstances the roles may be reversed or, better still, may complement each other.

If you have scored no points or far fewer points than your partner, you are the less enterprising of the two, using a great deal of prudence and not taking too many risks. You are not as much interested in current affairs and are content to play the role of adviser, taking a more practical attitude. Your partner may see the broad vistas ahead but you are needed to show the way.

If both of you have scored 5 points or thereabouts it means that you are in step with each other, using prudence or boldness according to circumstances and exchanging the roles of guide and adviser harmoniously.

Couples test 2

This test attempts to discover which of the two partners has more capacity for loving, which often has nothing to do with the situation in hand. In fact, each of us has a potentiality for loving that is not substantially altered either by time or place, although these may bring us pleasure or pain. Thus a person with a very passionate temperament may love with absolute dedication, whereas another person with more apathetic leanings will love with discernment and perhaps caution. This does not mean that the former loves more and the latter less, merely that the first person's emotional activity is less controlled and more totally involving. Clearly the partner who has scored more points also has a higher capacity for loving, while the one who has scored less is more wary in expressing his or her sentimental feelings.

Couples test 3

This game aims to find out whether you are attracted to a partner who has similar character traits and habits to yourself or whether you need someone who is the exact opposite of yourself.

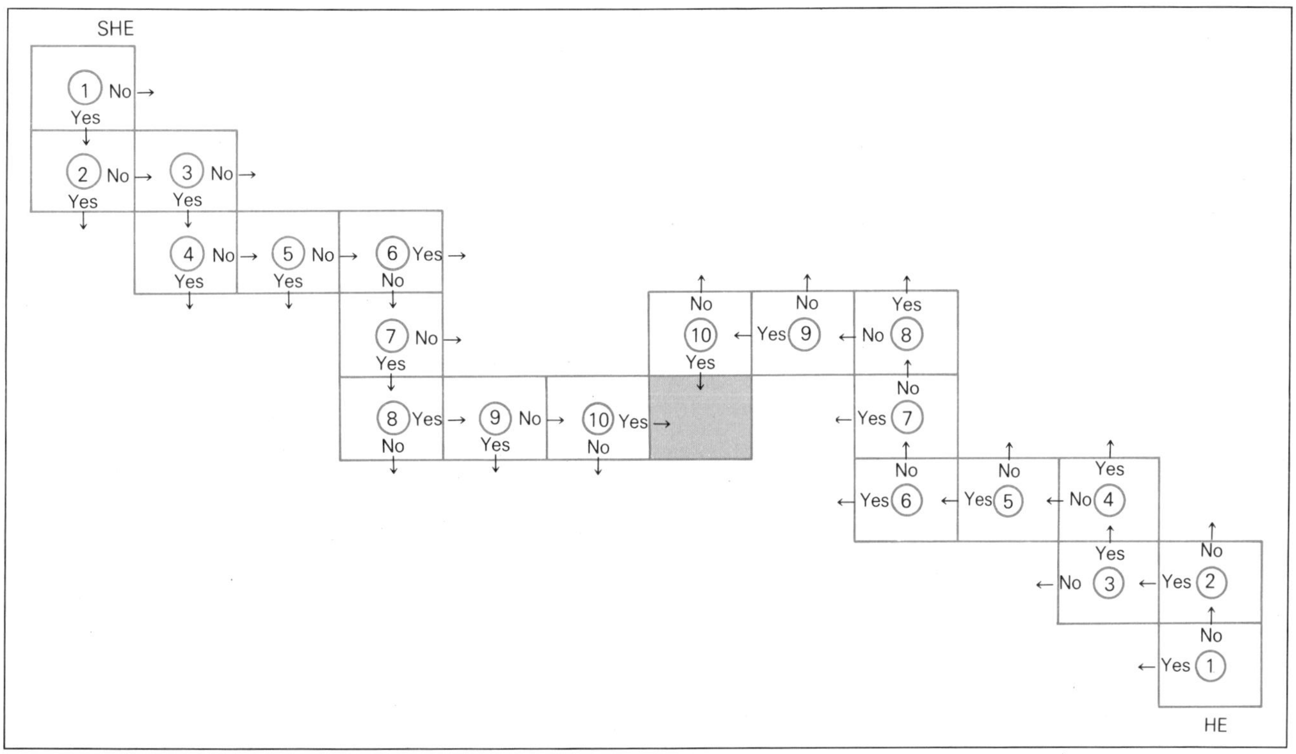

This has always been a much-discussed question, and of course it is difficult to determine what kind of partner suits each and every one of us. Not only is it difficult, it may well be pointless, since although a twin soul can offer understanding and, if need be, sympathy, and thus be a comforting presence, a partner with a diametrically opposed character can open up new horizons and perhaps be much more stimulating.

Whatever the outcome of the test – twin soul or partner with contrasting character – there is no need to worry about it. Happiness in love is hard to classify and the reasons for loving are not always easy to analyze. The main thing is that it happens.

Compare your answers by referring to the chart on page 177, following the instructions. In practice you should continue from box to box or not proceed further according to whether you have answered YES or NO.

At the end, although you have started from either end, you may or may not meet in the brown box.

If you have come together as a result of your ten replies, this means that you both want a similar partner. Your common ideal is thus a twin soul. namely a partner who always shares your ideas and never provides cause for serious arguments. You both wish to live with a complementary partner, virtually your own double. So, in love at any rate, you refuse to look at yourself in a mirror that might reveal hidden depths or distressing contradictions, and aim to avoid surprises, what is unknown or any adventures beyond your immediate reach. To walk hand in hand with your loved one, keeping perfect step and seeing the same things is your greatest joy. The danger, however, may be that you do not love your partner enough as an individual, but rather the image of yourself as reflected in him or her.

If you have not come together in the same final box, i.e. if one or both of you have got lost along the way, you are convinced that differences are stimulating and enriching, while similarities tend to be psychologically stultifying. Broadly speaking, you like taking risks, especially in personal relationships. An individual such as yourself, if forced to be solitary, feels trapped and therefore needs to expand and open out with the help of others, particularly the stimulus of the loved one. The psychological contrast with your partner helps to broaden your horizons, enabling you to develop fully as an individual.

Couples test 4

This test is all about jealousy, and it aims to find out which of the two partners is more jealous of the other.

If your "b" answers add up to between 0 and 5 points, you are not a jealous person, but tolerant and altruistic. Basically, you have few illusions about overwhelming or everlasting feelings and believe, as a rule, that it is better to play down rather than exaggerate emotions. Likewise you consider it better to be flexible than rigid where ideas are concerned. In your opinion, a touch of disenchantment or even cynicism does little harm when it comes to approaching and handling serious emotional issues.

If your "b" answers total from 6 to 12 points, you do not appear to be all that interested in hanging on to what belongs to you, either in terms of sentiments or material possessions. This attitude indicates a measure of instinctive coldness, stemming from a rational outlook, sometimes tinged with cynicism. You are sufficiently proud to believe in yourself and in your view logic and reason represent maximum security. The rest you regard as too uncertain and unpredictable to be worth bothering about.

If you scored 13 to 18 points with your "b" answers, you tend to be prone to doubts and indecisions. Sometimes you behave artlessly, sometimes with indifference and even cynicism. Jealousy for you is rather like a tide, which comes and goes, often without any justification. The result is that you are unwilling to enter into too many commitments. Deep down you do not trust others because you hardly trust yourself. Perhaps you are trying to protect your sensitivity without letting it become obvious. However, by hiding your feelings in this way you are preventing other people from getting to know you properly.

If your score of "b" replies added up to between 19 and 25 points, your jealous attitude would appear to relate primarily to emotions and ideas, and not so much to material possessions. Thus your jealousy stems more from the heart than from the head; it is more instinctive than rational. You are assuredly not an altruistic person and you are much subject to envy. It does not take much to break down that mechanism of self-defense that makes you so suspicious. You should try to rely more on the reasonable approach that you bring to practical matters and which might prevent your feelings running away with you.

If your score of "b" answers totalled from 26 to 30 points, you clearly have such an inborn sense of possession that you become over-attached to the people and things surrounding you. This attitude can cast a veil over your eyes and prevent you from seeing clearly on occasions. You are more concerned to keep than to renew, so that you risk being trapped in this yearning for possession, unable to form proper relationships with others. Remember that jealousy does most harm to oneself.

Couples test 5

This test is devised to determine which of the two partners is more drawn towards the spiritual aspects and which towards the material aspects of the loving relationship. In love, as in all psychological attitudes, two constrasting tendencies exist side by side, which balance in varying measure. One veers towards a mainly spiritual attachment, in which material things are not regarded as all that important, the other towards a mainly carnal conception of love, where the attitude is a more physical one. Both are reasonable attitudes provided one does not swamp the other entirely.

Give yourself one point for every "b" choice and no points for every "a" choice, then add them up.

If you have scored from 0 to 5, you put the emphasis on the more realistic aspects of your relationship. This does not mean you are preoccupied only with sensuality; but you bring to the partnership a measure of egotism which aims to comfort and thus ignores some of the more delicate and gracious spiritual implications which you regard as unimportant.

If you have scored from 6 to 10 points, your preferences are neither markedly spiritual nor notably material. You are open to opposing experiences and sometimes you may appear fickle inasmuch as you try to avoid absolute certainties.

If your score is between 11 and 16 points, you are basically aware of spiritual values, even in love. You offer and seek delicacy, inner grace, depth of feeling and absolute certainties. The risk is that you may lose yourself in the mists of idealism without making firm contact with reality.

Couples test 6

This test is about optimism and pessimism, trying to determine which of the two partners shows the one or the other attitude more clearly.

The more optimistic will have chosen excerpts 2, 4, 6, 8, 10, 12, 15, 16 and 18.

The more pessimistic will have chosen excerpts 1, 3, 5, 7, 9, 11, 13, 14 and 17.

The partner who has chosen a majority of optimistic excerpts, at least six, is more likely to have a positive outlook when confronted by new situations involving both parties. Such an attitude makes it more likely that this partner will find the necessary incentive to solve the problem in hand and will be more open to discussion with other people, although there is a possibility that he or she will yield too easily in some situations which perhaps call for more aggressiveness and even guile. The optimist likes looking ahead and forcing the pace a bit and the danger is that, faced with this degree of enthusiasm, the partner may get left far behind.

The partner who has chosen a majority of pessimistic excerpts, at least six, sees the negative side of things more frequently than his or her partner. Shy of others, because unable to find promising qualities in them, this partner is more likely to avoid surprises and look at things more realistically, more suspiciously and with fewer illusions. So the risk is that situations will develop faster than prudence would dictate, and that the other partner will already be far ahead. This does not mean, however, that in daily life one partner will necessarily be less active than the other. Outsiders will not find it easy to say which of the two is by nature more pessimistic because this type of person undoubtedly possesses clear intelligence and a reasonable measure of prudence.

If both partners have chosen more or less the same number of optimistic and pessimistic extracts, it means they are well balanced as a couple and complement each other. The fact that they both need one another is encouraging, since it is obviously unhealthy for either to become self-centered, and there should always be room for other people and scope for new situations. Furthermore, both partners individually should now be able to cope with reality.

The sexuality test explained

A sexuality test like the one set here for you with the help of sixteen photographs, deserves a brief introductory explanation. In fact sexuality is one of the most intriguing themes of all, but also one of the most complicated because it has to do with the individual seen in terms of his genetic heritage and his psychic relationships. Thus, in a person's sexual behaviour we find an interaction between genetic factors and environmental factors, which is why sexuality fulfils a fundamental function in human life. Its influence is not restricted to the individual, but extends to the much wider social sphere.

The culture of a group is influenced by its sexual customs, to the point where the society creates a form of sexuality just as sexuality creates a society. This need, which is both physical and mental, and individual and collective, constitutes a complex world which is not always that easy to interpret.

With the help of sixteen photographs, no matter how beautiful and charming, we certainly could not hope to undertake an exhaustive examination of sexuality, but on the other hand we might be able to shed light on certain aspects – if anything the most stimulating aspects – of it. So we have tried to concentrate on one or two aspects which have to do with the individual relationship with a partner, based on certain realistic tendencies or certain idealizing tendencies, just as we have focused the attention of the reader on other aspects which are concerned with the relationship with social reality based on either sexual liberty or sexual reservedness.

In order to present fairly uncomplicated psychological explanations, we have arranged the photographs in four groups of four (A or B + I or II, C or D + I or II, E or F + I or II, and G or H + I or II), and we have provided concise explanations for each of these groups. So the reader can examine four aspects of his own sexuality, and even if these examinations remain separate in the explanations, it will not be difficult to put them together. Had we done otherwise, the possible combinations would have been so great as to make the whole exercise immensely complicated.

Look then for the four combinations, which will have emerged from your choices and read the corresponding explanations, which are of course as valid for one sex as they are for the other.

A + I

Your sexuality is of the passionate type, at least in the sense that you live it in a very emotional way, without letting yourself be over-affected by reason. And at times this trust you put in your instincts results in your finding yourself in situations from which it is not always easy to find a way out. You give a great deal to the person you love, but personally you pay a high price to keep a relationship going. Remember, that sexuality is not just instinct: it is also a search, a going-deeper and – why not? – a form of logic. The main thing is to live it like a moment of joy, not one of tension.

A + II

You are very passionate, but you manage to exercise your sexuality with calm. You start full of ardour but you somehow manage to find a natural limit to your passion. You are like a rushing river which eventually flows gently into a vast sea of tranquillity. Sometimes, however, you find yourself slightly ill at ease because certain basic contradictions come to the surface in your attitudes, to which, however, you do not always manage to reconcile yourself.

B + I

Your sexuality is essentially cerebral, in the sense that you mistrust instincts even in this field and you prefer to remain within the confines of logic. But this rational control of your instincts takes a great deal of effort, to a point where you become prone to bouts of neurosis. In all probability, your logic is unsatisfactory when it comes to sexuality, and it would do you no harm to have a little more faith in your instincts, which should never be blindly written off. We often mistrust our instincts because of too strict an upbringing or because of some moral attitude which tends to inhibit our naturalness.

B + II

You enjoy using logic where sexuality is concerned too, and this control over your instincts is gratifying for you, at least in the sense that it affords you peace and quiet. Your passionate energy turns out to be rather contained, but this does not make you feel frustrated or less of a person. One could sum up this position by saying that "the contented person enjoys himself." It is nevertheless certain that there is no strict yardstick for sexuality. Each of us is responsible for the amount of sex we find most gratifying.

C + I

Your sexuality is definitely extroverted. For this reason, you like taking the initiative, not least because you think that the natural joys of life are not a right which one passively waits for, but the fruit of a quest. In your judgement, modesty in this area tends to lower the level of things, and as a result you prefer to appear enterprising, sometimes even presumptuous. In addition, sex for you is also yet another existential reason to justify your love of freedom. Behind or alongside your sexuality, you also allow room for an enjoyment in upturning old habits and knocking down dusty idols.

C + II

Sexually, you impose no limits on your sense of enterprise and you enjoy acting with complete liberty, even at times with a dash of effrontery. But you prefer your choices to remain on an individual level. It does not suit you to rock boats or take a swing at conformity in the name of sexual freedom, which in your opinion should be restricted to interpersonal relationships, and not intrude into other sectors of life. In a word you are in favour of sexual freedom, but only within a one-to-one relationship. Where institutions and customs are concerned you prefer sexuality to be controlled.

D + I
You prefer to exercise your sexuality in a very reserved way. But you tend to live the moment of sexuality as something of a social tonic, which connotes an appreciation of freedom and the creation of new values. For you, in other words, the sexual relationship must, to begin with, stay within the couple, only eventually for it to spill over as a regenerative force into society.

D + II
You live your sexuality in a very reserved and closed way, without ever allowing it to overflow into your social life. You think that this modesty in terms of passion is also valid in the collective context, because you are basically opposed to innovation, changes, and aspects of life of the most vaguely revolutionary kind. Sex for you is a special moment, which must have a moderate influence on your persona and not involve your dealings with the rest of the world. But remember, that despite your cautious attitudes, sexuality can play a fundamental and constructive role in society, too.

E + I
Your sexuality is based essentially on egoism. This means that you use it to afford yourself the maximum amount of pleasure without any other existential involvements, to the point where your partner often becomes an object for you. Above all else, you are very fond of yourself, and this self-admiration is fairly harmful to a personal relationship. In practice, you take a lot and do not give much. But the game may not always go your way because, in love too, a respect for the rights of others is fundamental. Without a modicum of altruism, sexuality is just another form of dishonesty.

E + II
In your sexuality you set a great deal of egoism in motion, but you are not capable of dominating your partner. So, if on the one hand you take a lot, on the other you are not always very good at asking. This unfilled gap causes you a great deal of dissatisfaction, because you would like to be led by someone who could satisfy all your needs in every way. On the other hand one cannot ask too much of a partner who often feels treated like an object. Sexual egoism like yours, which nevertheless binds you to your partner in an attitude of dependence, contains many contradictions.

F + I
You have a slightly contradictory sexuality, because you are instinctively inclined to give a great deal, but you are also very fond of yourself and this causes incomprehension between you and your partner. Essentially, you prefer giving rather than receiving, and you would like your partner to be a kind of travelling companion, with whom to share all the sensations produced by a good relationship between two people. But you tend to stop too often to admire yourself, and thus your goal recedes further into the distance. In sex, every attitude which tends to exclude one's partner always hampers satisfaction.

F + II
You live your sexuality mainly as a relationship of dependence, within which there is plenty of mutual trust. But you tend to be a little disarmed by an excess of abandon and altruism. Being altruistic is fine where sexuality is concerned, but it is not quite so good to let yourself rely too much on your partner. Sexuality must also be lived with dignity, and without concessions or weaknesses, which are always to the detriment of a serene relationship.

G + I
Your sexuality is based above all on sensual satisfaction. For this reason the physical aspect of your relationship is the most gratifying for you. In fact when you act in this way you are always apparently satisfied, whereas if you let yourself become enmeshed in sentiment, you end up having no clear ideas left, and feeling dissatisfied. In your view, sexuality is quite simply fruit which you must know how to savour without wasting the tiniest part. You have plenty of vitality and this earns you your just deserts. But you do not pay much attention at all to your partner.

G + II
Sexuality for you is above all a physical fact, but it often leaves you ungratified. Probably a relationship based largely on satisfying the senses does not adequately satisfy some of your emotional demands which, to all appearances, or at the outset, you presume to pay little attention to. The physical part of your sexuality may be enough in itself, on condition that you do not require your sexuality to give you deeper satisfaction of a spiritual kind. What is more, a form of sexuality with no emotional values is, to say the least, a little fragile.

H + I
Your sexuality is idealized, assigning minor importance to the physical aspects of your relationship, while it exalts the sentimental aspects. However, this spirituality, which you constantly look for in relation to your partner, turns out to be gratifying for you and as a result there is no point in your trying to load it with more realistic values. Sexuality contains a little of everything and you manage to derive from it just the values which make you the most satisfied.

H + II
Your sexuality would readily make do without certain physical aspects of your relationship, whereas it tends to place greater value on sentimental and spiritual values. But in most cases this does not satisfy you. So by idealizing your sexuality, you see it pale before your very eyes like some untouchable specter.

You have probably built yourself preconceptions where sexuality is concerned either because your upbringing was too strict or because certain values, in which you believe, seem hard to reconcile with it. But sexuality is not something accidental which one can accept or reject to order, as a result of the thrust of certain ideas. It is so bound up with our personality that if we banish it on the one hand, we find it looming up again on the other. All in all, it is better to live it serenely, and try to get to know it fully, in an unbiased way.

Select Bibliography

Bernard, J. Leopold, *Test Yourself I.Q.*, Corgi 1965
Berloquin, P. *One hundred Games of Logic*, Scribner 1977
Bettelheim, B. *The Uses of Enchantment: meaning and importance of fairy tales*, Thames and Hudson 1976
Blum, G.S. *Psychological Theories of Personality*, McGraw Hill 1953
Cronbach, *Essentials of Psychology Testing*, Harper and Row 1979
Eysenck, H.J. *The Measurement of Intelligence* Medical and Technical Publishers 1973
Eysenck, H.J. *Know your own I.Q.* Penguin 1969
Parker, D. and J. *How do you know who you are?* Thames and Hudson 1980
Schofield, H. *Assessment and Testing* Allen & Unwin 1972
Semeonoff, B. *Personality Assessment* Penguin 1966, 2nd ed. 1970
Sullivan, N. *Use your intelligence* Fontana 1978
Tyler, L.E. *Tests and Measurements* 2nd ed. Prentice Hall 1971, 3rd ed. 1979
Wilson, G. and Grylls, D. *Know your child's I.Q.* Severn House 1977